BEYOND GAME NINE STEPS TOWARD CREATING BETTER VIDEOGAMES

RICHARD BARTLE, CHRIS BATEMAN, NOAH FALSTEIN,
MICHELLE HINN, KATHERINE ISBISTER, NICOLE LAZZARO,
SHERI GRAINER RAY, AND JOSEPH SAULTER

EDITED BY CHRIS BATEMAN

Charles River Media
A part of Course Technology, Cengage Learning

COURSE TECHNOLOGY
CENGAGE Learning™

Australia, Brazil, Japan, Korea, Mexico, Singapore, Spain, United Kingdom, United States

COURSE TECHNOLOGY
CENGAGE Learning™

Beyond Game Design: Nine Steps Toward Creating Better Videogames

Richard Bartle, Chris Bateman,
Noah Falstein, Michelle Hinn,
Katherine Isbister, Nicole Lazzaro,
Sheri Grainer Ray, and Joseph Saulter

Edited by Chris Bateman

Publisher and General Manager,
Course Technology PTR:
Stacy L. Hiquet

Associate Director of Marketing:
Sarah Panella

Content Project Manager:
Jessica McNavich

Marketing Manager: Jordan Casey

Acquisitions Editor: Emi Smith

Project/Copy Editor: Kezia Endsley

PTR Editorial Services Coordinator:
Erin Johnson

Interior Layout: Jill Flores

Cover Designer: Mike Tanamachi

Indexer: Katherine Stimson

Proofreader: Jenny Davidson

For product information and technology assistance, contact us at
Cengage Learning Customer & Sales Support, 1-800-354-9706

For permission to use material from this text or product,
submit all requests online at **cengage.com/permissions**
Further permissions questions can be emailed to
permissionrequest@cengage.com

Velcro brand hook-and-loop fasteners are a registered trademark of Velcro USA Inc. Barbie is a registered trademark of Mattel Inc. All references to the Myers-Briggs Type Indicator test or MBTI should be understood as references to trademarks of the Myers-Briggs Type Indicator Trust, owned by Consulting Psychologists Press. All references to the four Interaction Styles (In Charge, Get Things Going, Chart the Course, and Behind the Scenes) should be understood as trademarks of Linda Berens/Telos Publications.

All brand names and product names mentioned in this book are trademarks or service marks of their respective companies. Any omission or misuse (of any kind) of service marks or trademarks should not be regarded as intent to infringe on the property of others. The publisher recognizes and respects all marks used by companies, manufacturers, and developers as a means to distinguish their products.

Library of Congress Control Number: 2008933311

ISBN-13: 978-1-58450-671-3

ISBN-10: 1-58450-671-7

Course Technology
25 Thomson Place
Boston, MA 02210
USA

Cengage Learning is a leading provider of customized learning solutions with office locations around the globe, including Singapore, the United Kingdom, Australia, Mexico, Brazil, and Japan. Locate your local office at: **international. cengage.com/region**

Cengage Learning products are represented in Canada by Nelson Education, Ltd.

For your lifelong learning solutions, visit **courseptr.com**

Visit our corporate website at **cengage.com**

Printed in the United States of America
1 2 3 4 5 6 7 12 11 10 09

ACKNOWLEDGMENTS

The authors would like to extend their grateful thanks to Marvin Andronicus, Hal Barwood, Ashley Beitel, Chris Bennett, Eric Bethke, Jane Booth, Darryl Brock, Chip Bruce, Al Chang, Kevin Clark, Ben Cowley, Peter Crowther, Lydia and Barry Dobyns, Lura Dolas, Corvus Elrod, Judith Savina Falstein, Bill Fulton, Lee Gilmore, Russ Glaser, Brian "Psychochild" Green, Joe Greenstein, Joe Hewitt, the members of International Game Developers Association's (IGDA) Game Accessibility Special Interest Group (especially Mark Barlet, Kasey Bryant, Kevin Bierre, Barrie Ellis, Eelke Folmer, Giannis Georgalis, Reid Kimball, Richard Van Tol, Stephanie Walker, and Thomas Westin), Kevin Jones, Kevin Keeker, Shiela Kim, Raph Koster, Jeremy Liew, Becca Lowenhaupt, Ron Meiners, Steve Meretzky, Jerry Michalski, Rand Miller, Cliff Nass, Patricia Pizer, Jeff Pobst, Kent Quirk, Ben Rattray, Brian Robbins, Noah Schaffer, Charlene Saulter, Christopher Schoenherr, Michael Sellers, Jenny Singleton, Ann Smulka, Michael Steele, Mark Terrano, Gordon Walton, Richard A. Watson, Elisabeth Watson, Roderick Woodruff, Will Wright, and Adria Smiley.

The editors would also like to offer grateful thanks to Moby Games (http://mobygames.com/) for their invaluable record of videogame details, the Wikipedia (http://wikipedia.org/) for similar information, and the Killer List of Videogames (http://klov.com/), for their comprehensive list of arcade games, which were used extensively in referencing videogame titles in this book.

Finally, the authors would like to offer eternal thanks to game developers everywhere without whom a book like this would be utterly meaningless.

ABOUT THE EDITORS AND AUTHORS

ABOUT THE EDITOR

Chris Bateman is Managing Director of International Hobo, a specialist company in the field of market-oriented game design and narrative, and a noted game designer, writer, and "semi-professional" philosopher. Games he has written and designed include *Ghost Master, Discworld Noir, Heretic Kingdoms: The Inquisition and Attack on Pearl Harbor*. In 2007, he received the IGDA's prestigious Most Valuable Player award for his contributions to the game development community. He is the co-author of *21st Century Game Design*, and editor of the award-nominated *Game Writing: Narrative Skills for Videogames*. International Hobo's website, where Chris and other industry veterans blog about videogames, can be found at ihobo.com.

ABOUT THE CHAPTER AUTHORS

Each of the authors of this book is renowned for his or her contribution to the field of videogame development, gameplay research, or audience diversity.

Dr. Richard A. Bartle is considered one of the foremost voices in virtual world development. He co-wrote the very first virtual world, MUD, in 1978 and thus has been at the forefront of the MMO industry from its inception. He divides his time equally between being an industry consultant and an academic (Professor of Computer Game Design at the University of Essex, UK). His 2003 book, *Designing Virtual Worlds*, is the standard text on the subject, and he is an influential writer on all aspects of virtual world design and development.

Noah Falstein is the President of The Inspiracy (www.theinspiracy. com), a consulting firm specializing in game design and production. Designing and managing entertainment and educational software since 1980 for companies such as Williams Electronics, LucasArts Entertainment, The 3DO Company, and Dreamworks Interactive, Falstein has worked on everything from toys to CD-ROM games to edutainment to location-based entertainment. Some of his better-known titles include *Sinistar*, *PHM Pegasus*, *Indiana Jones and the Fate of Atlantis*, and *Hungry Red Planet*. Falstein is currently a leader in the emerging serious games field, having designed corporate training simulations and health-based games.

Michelle Hinn is the chair of the IGDA's Game Accessibility Special Interest Group, an advocacy group for creating mainstream games accessible to gamers with disabilities. Hinn's experience includes work at Microsoft Game Studios, where she piloted usability tests for Xbox multiplayer games and ran playtests for Xbox games such as *Halo: Combat Evolved, Oddworld: Munch's Oddysee, Fusion Frenzy, and Amped: Freestyle Snowboarding*. In 2006, she was named one of *Next Generation* magazine's "100 Most Influential Women in Gaming" for her work in game accessibility, and won a prestigious Most Valuable Player award from the IGDA. For more information about game accessibility, please contact IGDA SIG via email at accessibility@igda.org or visit the website at http://www.igda.org/accessibility.

Katherine Isbister is Director (and founder) of the Games Research Lab at Rensselaer (RPI). Before joining RPI's faculty, she developed and taught a course at Stanford on the Design of Characters for Games. She received her Ph.D. from Stanford, with a focus on using ideas from social psychology to design better, more effective interactive characters. Katherine's book—*Better Game Characters by Design: A Psychological Approach*—was nominated for a Frontline Award. She has published in a wide variety of venues, and given invited talks at research and academic venues, including Sony research labs in Japan, Banff Centre in Canada, IBM, Electronic Arts, the Royal Institute of Technology in Stockholm, and others. In 1999, Isbister was chosen as one of MIT Technology Review's Young Innovators, for her work on trans-cultural interface agents. More information about her work is available at www.friendlymedia.org.

Nicole Lazzaro is the leading expert of emotions in videogames. Founder and President of XEODesign, Inc., Nicole is an award-winning interface designer and an authority on emotion and the player experience. A frequent speaker at industry events, she writes extensively on games and why people play them. She has spent more than 16 years designing successful experiences for all levels of players and users, from novice to expert, in many game genres. She integrates her adventures living and travelling abroad into creating culture-crossing experiences. Her work on the emotional and cultural content of play has improved the player experiences for more than 40 million people and helped expand the game industry's emotional palette beyond the stereotypical range of anger, frustration, and fear.

Sheri Graner Ray has been in the game industry since 1990 and has worked for many of the largest companies in the field, including Electronic Arts, Origin Systems, Sony Online Entertainment, and Cartoon Network, and she has worked on such licenses as *Star Wars Galaxies*, *Ultima*, and *Nancy Drew*. She is author of the book, *Gender Inclusive Game Design—Expanding the Market*, and is the game industry's leading expert on gender and computer games. In 2005, she was awarded the IGDA's Game Developer's Choice award for her work in gender and games and she is currently serving as the chair of Women In Games International; an organization she co-founded. Although she has worked as everything from a writer/designer to head of her own studio, her first love is game design and she describes herself as a "hardcore gamer." She currently lives in Austin, Texas with her husband, Tim, their four dogs and two cats.

Joseph Saulter is the leading voice in game diversity issues. Featured in *EBONY* magazine's *Who's Who in the Technology Boom*, he is the author of *Introduction to Game Design and Development*, Chairman of the Game Design and Development Department at American InterContinental University in Atlanta, and CEO of Entertainment Arts Research—one of the first African-American 3D Video Game Development Companies in the U.S. Entertainment Arts Research is currently working on a number of major new game titles, including a futuristic urban stealth third-person title and *The Seventh Day*, a highly anticipated Christian-themed gospel 3D videogame. As well as his accomplishments in the games industry, he is also an award-winning musician and musical director, having worked on major broadways shows such as *Hair* and *Jesus Christ Superstar*, as well as winning the Drama Desk Award for his role in the Broadway Musical *I Love My Wife*.

ABOUT THE SUB-EDITORS

The book has also benefited from the skills and patience of two talented sub-editors.

Neil Bundy has worked on many of the International Hobo game projects (including *Ghost Master, Heretic Kingdoms: The Inquisition, Air Conflicts, Attack on Pearl Harbor,* and *Play with Fire*) as a game design assistant, game tester, usability and playability consultant, and general troubleshooter.

Richard Boon has written dialogue scripts for a dozen games while working for International Hobo. He also dabbles in game design, is the co-author of the book *21st Century Game Design*, and has taught videogame history, design, and theory as program leader for Salford University's Computer and Video Game course.

CONTENTS

PREFACE

"Beyond Game Design!" Yes, it's an extravagant title for a book that purports to be *about* game design, and I suspect you will not be in the least bit surprised to learn that marketing had a hand in selecting this name. The original title for this book was *Play Styles: The Diversity of Videogame Players*, but the publisher felt that this sounded too much like a high-brow coffee table book, and so, leveraging my years of experience appealing to marketing departments, I put on my hyperbole cap and came up with *Beyond Game Design: Nine Steps Toward Creating Better Videogames*. Now, all that remains is for me to justify this title. Challenge accepted!

What lies *beyond* game design, in the sense of imagining different domains of knowledge as a landscape?

Well, on the one hand psychology has an increasingly large border with modern game design, and Part I of this volume, the first four steps, all reflect this crossover between fields. There are psychologists working in the field of videogames like Katherine Isbister, who wrote Step 2 of this book, who are exploring all aspects of the psychology of play, bringing into the field of game design a studious knowledge of human interaction that can benefit anyone involved in making games. There is also a rich intellectual history on the subject of play, such as the pioneering work of Johan Huizinga and Roger Caillois, whose "patterns of play" form the basis for what I talk about in Step 3.

Another aspect of this border between game design and psychology is player modeling—the increasingly relevant process of finding tractable methods to describe the diverse ways players approach games. Richard Bartle, who wrote Step 4 of this book, practically invented this field with his 1996 "four suits" paper, which established the framework of what is now referred to as the *Bartle Types* model. This was the first attempt to recognize that players could not be treated as a single archetype, and it led in turn to later models such as the Four Fun Keys, developed by Nicole Lazzaro, who wrote Step 1 in this book. The Four Fun Keys have revolutionized our understanding of videogame play by building upon the work of Paul Ekman on emotions and connecting it with gameplay in a masterly fashion. Understanding this model is the first step towards making better videogames for everyone.

I have been fascinated by psychological modeling ever since I first discovered the Myers-Briggs instrument and other similar systems such as Temperament Theory and "Big Five". This is a badly understood part of the world of psychology, often because of an unspoken attachment to what I might, with my philosopher's hat on, call "Plato's error"—the idea that everything can be expressed as a manifestation of an ideal type. Yet none of these models is involved in identifying true "types"—personality is much more complicated than that—they involve modeling observable behaviors and grouping them into broadly measurable traits. In Step 4, Richard explains at some length why thinking about player type theories in idealized terms will always get designers into trouble.

Studying instruments such as those I mentioned here reveals the many different ways that people can be psychologically different from one another, and this can significantly impact videogame design. As I set out in Step 8, different players have developed different skills to varying degrees—a puzzle that might be easy for one player to solve could stump another entirely, and a reactions-based challenge that most gamer hobbyists would find tame could prove impossible for a player with less well-developed reflexes.

This is just one of many ways that the diversity of videogame players can be revealed. In Step 5, Sheri Graner Ray, the author of the popular book *Gender-Inclusive Game Design*, outlines how gender can have a significant bearing on how we make videogames. In Step 6, Joseph Saulter expresses his frustration at the way the videogame industry does little to set up mechanisms to tap into the creative potential of different cultural backgrounds, especially when compared to the music industry (about which he has considerable experience). In Step 7, Michelle Hinn describes the numerous accessibility problems that can block players with unique physiological constraints from enjoying the videogame medium.

All of the perspectives in Part II of this book focus on the opportunities for including the complete diversity of videogame players in the audience for games. This highlights another epistemological "region" which overlaps game design: ethics. This is a complex subject, and far too abstract to get into in a mere preface, especially since we live in an age of ethical diversity such that there is no guarantee that any two people will share the same premise for moral thinking. But there is no ethical framework that would not impart some kind of obligation for the people behind a creative medium to offer their unique experiences to all-comers— whether this is justified by a rights-focused approach (such as the categorical imperative of Immanuel Kant, with its idea of "the ethical as the universal") or an outcomes-focused approach (such as Jeremy Bentham and John Stuart Mill's utilitarianism, with its focus on "the greatest happiness for the greatest number of people").

But really, one doesn't need to get into moral philosophy to justify the need for the videogames industry to widen its idea of who comprises the audience for games. There is a firm financial motive here that even the most nihilistic capitalist would be foolish to overlook. One only has to look at the tremendous success that Nintendo is currently enjoying as a result of having tapped into the true mass market for videogames with its Wii and DS games consoles to appreciate that *we are all losing money when we narrow our understanding of what videogames can be.* Nintendo has reached a significantly large market of both female and elderly players, which conventional wisdom insisted were just not interested in videogames. This was a gross misconception—we were just making the *wrong kinds* of games to appeal to these audiences!

The gamer hobbyists, those "hardcore" gamers who have been the lifeblood of the videogames industry since its inception, will continue to be an important part of its cash flow, probably forever more, so when I talk about embracing the diversity of videogame players, I am not asking that our most loyal players be relegated to obscurity. As long as the gamer hobbyists want to play the kind of games they want to play, there will be developers willing to make those games, and publishers willing to fund them.

But the unspoken tragedy of the videogames industry is that as a result of the narrow focus of game design up until relatively recently, we have employed whole generations of development staff who believe that the kind of experiences that most thrilled and rewarded them— generally games of hard challenges and exciting thrills—were the only kind of games worth making. But as I hope to have demonstrated conclusively in Step 3, in which I tie my admiration for Roger Caillois' 1958 book *Les Jeux et Les Hommes* to recent neurobiological research, play is infinitely more diverse than any of us have previously considered.

We have barely begun to tap the creative potential of videogames. Getting out of our collective tunnel vision with respect to both player diversity and our conceptions of what a videogame *is* or *must be* would truly represent a step away from the old practices of game design. It would be to go beyond game design in another sense—to step out of the blinkered perspective of the games industry's past, and into an incredible future where the possibilities of what can be achieved in virtual worlds and other kinds of game are truly limitless.

—Chris Bateman

Editor

UNDERSTAND

In the first part of this book, you will learn ways to move beyond conventional game design rhetoric by exploring psychology of play and player modeling from some of the leading figures of this field.

In Step One, Nicole Lazzaro explains the key emotions of play in the context of her "Four Fun Keys" model.

In Step Two, Katherine Isbister explains social play and the many ways it can enhance the experience of any game—even a single-player game.

In Step Three, Chris Bateman describes Roger Caillois' "patterns of play" and connects these to neuro-biological mechanisms.

Finally, in Step Four, Richard Bartle—the pioneer of player modeling—explains the limits of a theoretical approach.

UNDERSTAND EMOTIONS

by Nicole Lazzaro

Why are videogames fun? What do we even mean when we say "fun"? If you talk to a dozen different players, you will get a dozen different answers. Making sense of the way people respond to the play of a videogame requires some comprehension of player experiences, and one of the best tools for exploring this is Nicole Lazzaro's "Four Fun Keys" model of player emotions. In this first step, you will learn about the key emotions of play— what they are, how they relate to one another, and what you can do to evoke them in your players.

PLAYER EXPERIENCES

"Games are a series of interesting choices." —Sid Meier

The first step to better game design is to understand how to design emotion from gameplay. If games are made of interesting choices, game designers need to know what makes choices interesting to players. This question lies at the heart of all game design, and answering it in new ways is essential for designing games that innovate by exploring new avenues of appeal.

Several factors create player interest. Games create *engagement* by how they shape attention and motivate action. To focus player attention, games simplify the world, enhance feedback, and suspend negative consequences—this maximizes the effect of emotions coming from player choices. In the simplest terms, *game mechanics engage the player by offering choices and providing feedback*. Looking at how games rivet player attention and motivate action unlocks many secrets you can use to create better gameplay.

What separates good game mechanics from the boring ones are how gripping they are, and how quickly and completely the choices absorb player attention. In other words, good games are measured by how well they create an emotional response in the player. Because the process of focusing attention and motivating action involves emotions, games that offer more than one type of engagement sustain player interest longer. The interplay between player actions, choices, and feedback from the game creates the series of internal sensations called *Player Experience* (PX). Strong PX creates engagement or grabs player attention and motivation to play. How games unlock this potential is the key to designing more engaging play.

Player Experiences Must Be Accessible and Fun

Effective gameplay requires ease of use so that players can access the inherent fun from play. For a game to be great, players must not only know what to do (know how to drive a car in a driving game, for instance), they also must easily discover opportunities for play (find entertaining things to do with the car in a driving game). Player experiences must create player emotions and engagement. As the practice of improving the quality of games matures, it becomes clearer that the goals and expectations people have for games are very different from their goals and expectations for other software. I often see games in development for which players know *how to play* but not *how to have fun*. There are two distinct challenges here. Making what to do too obvious removes all the challenge. Make the game world too open-ended, perhaps by offering too many choices, and players get lost in the decision-making process and fail to have fun. In games the "how to have fun" problem is often harder to solve than teaching players how to play. The practice of making games more fun must identify and balance those issues that relate to making choices, or *usability*, and those that relate to what makes those choices interesting, the *fun factor*. To differentiate usability issues from fun factor ones, I use the terms *user experience* (UX) and *player experience* (PX), which are defined as follows:

- **UX:** The experience of use; that is how accessible the game controls are and how easily players can accomplish what they expect.
- **PX:** The experience of play; that is, how well the game supports and provides the type of fun players want to have—players cannot simply push a button and feel that they won.

Put even more simply, for UX, researchers look at what prevents the ability to play. For PX, researchers look for what prevents players from having fun. To test games for accessibility and fun factors, the first step is to divide the features into these two buckets, and then apply different techniques to measure and improve the quality of each. Comparing user and player experiences reveals competing purposes, each striving to fulfill very different values, as depicted in the following table [Lazzaro04a].

UX Usability Goals: Productivity	PX Game Goals: Entertainment
Task completion	Entertainment
Eliminate errors	Fun to beat obstacles
External reward	Intrinsic reward
Outcome-based rewards	Process is its own reward
Intuitive	New things to learn
Reduce workload	Increase workload
Assumes technology needs to be humanized	Assumes humans enjoy being challenged

User experiences and player experiences require cooperation, much like the two wheels on a bicycle. One wheel connects to the drive chain to make the bike go (UX), and the other wheel steers and creates the fun (PX). The practice of improving software has only identified a few spokes (methods) on that rear UX wheel: heuristic evaluation, time on task, reducing error rates, satisfaction surveys, certain ethnography such as contextual inquiry, and so on. All of these improve interface design and the quality of the user experience, but none of these usability-related practices increases the fun factor or addresses specific emotions, aside from reducing player frustration to increase feelings of "satisfaction" without a precise definition of what this emotion is.

Taken to an extreme, a system that is 100% usable has few errors and requires little effort, but such a system risks boring people by making a task too routine. Also, it does nothing to increase a person's sense of accomplishment from a job well done, or from mastering a complex task. User experience design alone is not enough to improve all aspects of interactive experiences humans enjoy at work or at play. Player experience design's main focus is to enhance the emotions coming from play, and this is a comparatively young field. When I began work in this area, there were very few practices to improve a game's PX—in fact there was no term for the experiences that games create at all! [Lazzaro04b]

The Role of Emotion in Games

"The desire to experience or not experience an emotion motivates much of our behavior." —Paul Ekman

Emotions play a central role in all player experiences, not only because they add enjoyment, but also because emotions play an important role in decision making. While a good movie or book may make people laugh and cry, the neuroscience research of the past 10 years has revealed that emotions are not just for entertainment.

By definition, emotions are internal sensations that occur in relationship to pursuing a goal. Psychologists use this definition to separate emotions from other internal sensations such as hunger, pain, and sleepiness. Paradoxically, damage to the emotional system severely hampers a person's ability to make decisions! This vital link between emotion and pursuit of a goal makes emotions key to the design of engaging gameplay.

Because emotions relate directly to a person's goals, they are *always* involved in player experiences, regardless of whether the designer is aware of this. For instance, one of the top reasons people play games is to alleviate boredom. People play everything from *Bejeweled* (PopCap, 2001) to *Counter-Strike* (Le and Cliffe, 1999) to achieve a sense of calm, to "Zen out," or to feel more excited. They may also play to relieve unpleasant emotions, such as frustration—many players use a videogame to alleviate their work stress when they get home.

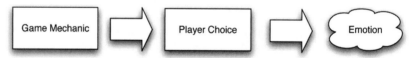

FIGURE 1.1 Game mechanics offer choices that in turn create emotions in the players.

Game designers cannot design emotions directly. Instead they design "the rules in the box" that offer player choices. Emotions emerge principally from the process of making choices an idea, which is expressed in Figure 1.1 (although of course, emotions can also happen as visceral responses to other aspects of a videogame, such as sound and animations). The tight coupling of motivation and emotions makes designing emotional responses a crucial tool for game designers.

Emotions and Engagement

The relationship between game mechanics and player emotions has several factors that can increase engagement. Often, poorly pairing a choice and the surrounding emotions decreases engagement. In exploring and tuning this relationship there are several factors to consider. Regardless of a game designer's intentions, emotions result from all gameplay, because the factors that create engagement are emotional responses.

Emotions play five distinct roles in increasing player engagement with a game [Lazzaro07], as illustrated in Figure 1.2.

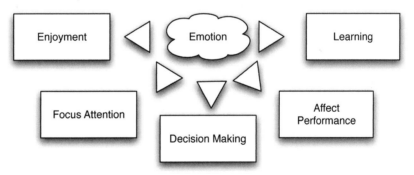

FIGURE 1.2 Even if designers are unaware of it, emotion plays a central role in games.

1. **Enjoyment:** Players enjoy the sensations that emotions create.
2. **Focus Attention:** Emotions affect the player's focus. For example, a boiling lava pit captures player's attention more than a city sidewalk.
3. **Decision Making:** Emotions aid in making decisions. People without emotional systems can logically compare the consequences of two options but cannot make the choice itself. For example, in *Tom Clancy's Splinter Cell* (Ubisoft Montreal, 2002), the choice between certain death and escape via a narrow window ledge is easier to make than selecting a door in an empty office corridor.
4. **Performance:** The negative emotions in *Battlefield 2: Modern Combat* (Digital Illusions, 2005) facilitate the type of repetitive behavior the game rewards—shoot the sniper and move on—whereas the positive

emotions from *Katamari Damacy* (Namco, 2004) inspire creativity and problem solving by helping the player figures out how to roll their little sticky balls from the floor up onto a table.

5. **Learning:** Finally, emotions reward and motivate learning, as all games teach.

Notice how the role of emotion in player engagement utilizes both positive and negative emotions—game designers need to be aware of the emotional carrot, and the emotional stick, not to mention other emotions that shape attention and facilitate different forms of action, ranging from the intellectual curiosity that drives players to figure out a clue in *Half-Life*, to the desire to help a friend learn to control the vehicles in *Mario Kart*.

It is ironic that the important role of emotions in human decision making and entertainment has taken so long to be recognized by game designers. Before I published my research in 2004, the common belief was that improving the graphics, building faster processors, and adding features to last year's best sellers was the way to create better games. There continues to be a lot of talk about creating "addicting" games. Many in the industry want their games to be as "addictive" as possible. There are significant limitations to this one-dimensional way of increasing engagement, because non-gamers who've had perfect access to games (for instance, someone living with a gamer) often avoid games precisely because they feel they are too addictive.

Back in 2000, my colleagues and I wanted to know what created engagement beyond loops of "stimulus, response, intermittent rewards" which many people use to design game "addiction" (and which you will learn more about in Step 3). I knew that there were healthier alternatives out there for creating engagement and a broader pallet of emotions being evoked in players, but I needed a deeper understanding of the psychology of play in order to discover what would appeal to a wider audience. You can't make better games without first understanding what players enjoy the most about games, and to do this you need to know the PX players really want.

MEASURING EMOTIONS

Because emotions are hard to see, the important role that they play in videogames was not widely recognized prior to my research. Whether or not "games can make you cry" was a lively debate for many years, since many people felt that games could only create the emotions of the sports arena. The starring role that emotions play in game mechanics was not widely understood.

Research was needed, and it needed to begin with externally, independently observable emotions, because emotions are fleeting and players frequently are either unaware of them, or often cannot remember experiencing them. This was the reason my qualitative research began by looking at emotion on players' faces as they played videogames, identifying the emotions they were experiencing as they were happening. This research was made possible by pioneering work conducted by one of the leading psychologists in the field of emotions.

Paul Ekman

Paul Ekman has done more to map out the human emotional terrain than almost any other researcher, especially in respect to facial expressions. Over the space of 40 years, he and his colleagues researched the muscles of the face and how they related to specific emotions. Similar to identifying the basic colors that everyone can see, they wanted to identify the basic emotions that all human beings feel [Ekman03].

Building on the work of the 19th century French researcher, Guillaume Duchenne, Ekman and his colleagues stimulated facial muscles individually in order to build a detailed map of all the muscles of the human face. This allowed Ekman to create what he termed a Facial Action Coding System (FACS), where each muscle has its own number. Using FACS, Ekman and his colleagues explored which muscles were involved in the facial expression of different emotions. It transpired that of all the potential combinations of muscles that could be used, only a small fraction is involved in producing the recognizable facial expressions associated with particular emotions.

This was already impressive work, but to be certain these facial expressions mapped to emotions across cultures, Ekman took this remarkable work even further. By using photos of different facial expressions, he and his researchers conducted studies in cities and towns in numerous countries around the world to discover which emotions had universally recognizable facial expressions. In these studies, researchers would tell a short story such as the loss of a child, or being asked to eat rotten food, and then ask the participant which of two facial expressions matched how someone in that situation would feel.

To ensure the facial expressions were truly universal and not just the result of watching television or movies, the researchers studied people around the world including the indigenous people of Papua New Guinea living in a traditional culture practicing subsistence-based agriculture who had no access to mass media.

This research contradicted the prevailing belief of anthropologists at the time that emotions were culturally determined. Ekman honed in on six key emotions that have facial expressions that are universally recognized by human cultures wherever they are in the world: happiness, anger, sadness, surprise, fear, and disgust. Table 1.1 summarizes these emotions. In later research, he expands the list of emotions to include emotions without unique facial expressions. There was such a variety of emotions that in naming them Ekman had to borrow words from various languages!

Table 1.1 Six Plus One Emotions with Universal Facial Gestures

Emotion	Game Example
Frustration (Anger)	Figuring out how to get a character off a roof in *Splinter Cell* (and created by usability issues that detract from the player's ability to play).
Fear	Falling into boiling lava, fast-moving projectiles aimed at the player in *Doom* (id Software, 1993).
Surprise	Using the linking books in *Myst* (Cyan Worlds, 1993) for the first time to transport to a new world. This is often followed by wonder.
Sadness	When the young magician Aerith in *Final Fantasy VII* (Square, 1997) is murdered.
Amusement (Happiness)	When two Sims get married in *The Sims* (Maxis, 2000), or rolling over and picking up sumo wrestlers in *Katamari Damacy*.
Disgust	Becoming a social outcast (social disgust) after losing the dancing challenge in *Sid Meier's Pirates!* (Microprose, 1997). This moment also creates contempt.
Curiosity*	Wanting to know what happens by driving the race track the wrong way in *Project Gotham Racing* (Bizarre Creations, 2001).

* Not all researchers (including Ekman) considered curiosity a universal emotion with a unique facial gesture. I include it here as a seventh emotion because of its importance in games and ease of observation.

Observing Emotions in Games

At first appearance players may seem emotionally detached during play—they may not be articulate, remember, or even be aware of the emotions they feel. Despite this, emotions have a vital role in creating that deep sense of engagement which is characteristic of highly enjoyable play. Watching players as they interacted with videogames, there was no doubt that the emotions were there—it was literally written all over their faces! Furthermore, careful observation revealed small facial movements (which Ekman calls *micro expressions*), that could be seen while players were doing what they enjoyed the most during play. Lasting barely a quarter of a second, these movements provide clues to changes in the players' mental state around choices they make.

FACS provided a means to measure the emotions expressed on the face during play, but as my colleagues and I were conducting this research it became clear that many emotions connected with players' favorite moments were not observable in this way. It became apparent that it was necessary to examine changes in the body as well as the face, to listen for sounds (such as laughter), and to watch which muscles were in use. Plus there were some emotions that were not included by Ekman, such as curiosity—a facial expression that can be recognized early in child development—which served an important role in play.

There were also some emotions that Ekman had identified that were peripheral to his work on facial expressions, but that were much more important in the context of videogames. One such emotion is *fiero* (an Italian word meaning personal triumph over adversity), which turns out to be intimately associated with games and sports. Everyone who has ever beaten a boss monster or won a Grand Prix race has felt this emotion, which produces a response in the whole body—the raising of the arms, punching the air, or jumping up from their chair. Some players and game designers even mistakenly think of this as the only important kind of fun associated with videogames. It is ironic that this emotion had no name in game design until this research on emotions and games made the need for a precise term clear.

Players feel emotions *before, during,* and *after* decisions. Nearly all decisions require the cognitive and emotional systems, but despite this, there is a tendency for game designers to employ just a fraction of the emotional tools available to them. For example, when the videogames industry first began to explore 3D representations, games filled themselves with situations and choices designed to increase anger, fear, and disgust, such as realistic blood splatters and boiling lava monsters, and choices like shooting and blowing things up. As you will shortly discover, there are many other emotions evoked by games, and designers who understand how to engage player emotions have a serious advantage when it comes to innovating new game ideas. First, however, you need to learn a little more about what happens when a game captures the player's attention.

CREATING ENGAGEMENT

Emotion is not the whole story of player enjoyment: gamers also love the deep sense of engagement they get when they play. More of a state of being than an emotion, "engaging activities" absorb attention and are self-motivating. The games that players enjoy the most are those that facilitate this self-motivating engagement, games in which the choices players make are rewarding in and of themselves. Examining the types of choices and emotions that go with these deep play experiences unlocks many secrets of how to create engagement.

The most influential psychologist working in the field of engagement is Mihály Csíkszentmihályi (pronounced "chick-sent-me-high-ee"). He was fascinated by what created optimal experiences—those that people remember most vividly, and that they prefer over other experiences. He conducted a series of detailed field studies that asked people to recall which moments in their lives were the most engaging. To increase the accuracy of his research, and to aid in catching his subjects when they were "in the moment," Csíkszentmihályi arranged for people to carry pagers that beeped them at random times during the day. The participants in this study would note in a journal any relevant details, such as what they were doing, their level of engagement, and the pertinent qualities of the particular activity.

Surprisingly, the moments that people enjoyed the most were not relaxing poolside vacations, but rather activities that required considerable effort such as rock climbing, dancing, gardening, and talking with friends. These activities call for significant mental investment and concentration, and provided opportunities for personal growth. Additionally, Csíkszentmihályi discovered that to maintain this deep sense of concentration these activities required clear goals and a perfect balance between skill and difficulty. Whether it was a woman gardening in Kentucky or a Japanese teen in a motorcycle gang racing through the streets of Tokyo, all of these disparate experiences had similar characteristics. Without a sufficient degree of challenge, people disengage and activities quickly become routine and boring. With too much challenge, a person becomes frustrated, suffers anxiety, and ultimately quits.

The concept from Csíkszentmihályi's research with the greatest relevance to game design is his model for *Flow*. Lasting much longer than Ekman's definition of an emotion, and having deep cognitive and behavioral properties, Flow engrosses a person in an activity. According to Csíkszentmihályi, optimal experiences are those where the person is balanced between the challenges they face and the skills they have acquired. He termed this the *Flow Channel*, the path between anxiety (too difficult) and boredom (too easy), as depicted in Figure 1.3 [Csíkszentmihályi90].

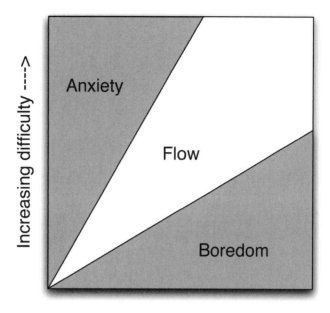

FIGURE 1.3 The Flow Channel.

Furthermore, Csíkszentmihályi found that people generally required that the level of difficulty increase over time (to avoid boredom as their skills improved) and often expressed greater enjoyment of these activities afterwards, upon reflection, than they did in the moment.

From this research Csíkszentmihályi created the Flow model, which characterizes people's optimal experiences. More of a state of being than an emotion, Flow creates a deep sense of engagement where a person's mind is filled by an activity that has an optimal balance of skill and difficulty. The activity increases in difficulty as the activity progresses. As a person's performance gets better, there is a sense of growth and improvement. Doesn't this sound like a game?

Requirements for Flow

The best way to understand how Flow creates engagement is to watch it in action. The conditions for the mental state of Flow are present in the design of most popular computer games, such as *Tetris* (Alexey Pajitnov, 1985), which create enjoyment from difficulty. One of the world's most popular games, *Tetris* captures attention with its simple rules and balance of difficulty with player skill. The game provides clear goals and plenty of feedback. The game rotates blocks in response to player input, and these blocks lock into place in a satisfying way. As complete rows are built, blocks get cleared with sound effects and animations. Like *Bejeweled*, all of these aspects work together to create a deeply engaging player experience.

Csíkszentmihályi identifies a number of requirements for the Flow state, and these can easily be applied to *Tetris*:

- **Clear Goal:** Position blocks in a row to clear them before the stack reaches the top
- **Achievable Tasks:** Position blocks one at a time
- **Immediate Feedback:** Indicate effect of controls (turn block), and show progress clearly (lines disappear)
- **Sense of Control:** Feedback creates satisfaction from success and "putting things in their place"
- **Increase in Difficulty:** The game gets harder (blocks appear and fall more rapidly) as the player progresses

Flow and Player Experiences

What Csíkszentmihályi describes as Flow clearly applies to player experiences. Flow characterizes a deep state of engagement and personal growth very similar to what gamers describe as being one of their favorite aspects of videogames. In addition to this, relief from negative emotions (such as the frustrations of everyday life) during game activities constitutes a major reason why people play.

Paradoxically, game players often characterize gameplay by how emotions vanish as they "get into the zone." And watching players this often appears to be true, at least at first glance. However, by watching closely for micro expressions, you can see that players clearly demonstrate emotional states connected to the choices that they make in games. Therefore, when playing their favorite games, players often cycle between states of deep engagement punctuated by powerful emotional moments. Csíkszentmihályi's Flow model is an excellent start for describing some of the engagement factors that games create. However, a more complete model of emotion and mechanics would capture more types of engagement seen in players' favorite experiences and thus give designers more tools to craft new kinds of gameplay.

My experiences of observing players demonstrated there were several aspects of player behavior not predicted by Csíkszentmihályi's model for Flow. Truly absorbing gameplay requires more than a balance of difficulty and skill. Players leave games for other reasons than over-exertion or lack of challenge. In players' favorite games, the degree of difficulty rises and falls, power ups and bonuses make challenges more interesting, and the opportunity for strategy increases engagement. The progression of challenges to beat a boss monster and the drop of challenge at the start of the next level help keep players engaged. Intense gameplay may produce frustration when the level of challenge is too high, but it can also produce many different kinds of emotions, such as curiosity or wonder. Furthermore, play can also emerge from decisions wholly unrelated to the game goal.

Additionally players spend a lot of time engaged in other activities such as waving a Wiimote to wiggle their character or create a silly avatar that require *no difficulty* to complete. Players respond to various things that characterize great gameplay for them, such as reward cycles, the feeling of winning, pacing, emotions from competition and cooperation. But to create great gameplay, designers have to adjust many aspects, not only in difficulty. Players clearly respond and seek out factors outside the Flow model.

Other Research

Before designing the study on why people play games, my colleagues and I looked at the groundbreaking work done by leading researchers and practitioners from diverse fields such as psychology, filmmaking, and drama about what creates enjoyable product and entertainment experiences, as well as prior research in the fields of play and videogames. Comparing these diverse frameworks provides an interesting perspective on the commonalities of creating human engagement. Most importantly, the majority of the prior research discussed at most one or two emotions, or looked solely at how to create emotions that are "positive" or "negative."

Perhaps the most relevant models of creating emotional engagement in general (after Csíkszentmihályi) are Tiger and Jordan's models of how products create pleasure—physio-pleasure, psycho-pleasure, ideo-pleasure, and socio-pleasure [Tiger92], [Jordan00], and Norman and Boorstin's three sources of engagement—voyeuristic eye, visceral eye, and vicarious eye [Boorstin90], or Norman's behavioral, cognitive, and reflective layers [Norman04]. However, examining players and the games they preferred showed there was more at work than just whether an emotion during play was positive or negative, or was arousing or relaxing as described in Norman and Boorstin's models.

There were also models that looked more particularly at software, such as those of Hassenzahl, Platz, Burmester, and Lehner, which consider ergonomic quality versus hedonic quality [Hassenzahl00] or the work of Wright, McCarthy, and Meekison, which considers spatial-temporal, compositional, sensual, and emotional threads, following an earlier conceptualization by John Dewey [Wright03]. However, none of these disparate researchers had mapped out the wide range of emotions that can be seen when people play their favorite games, and none of them broke out different factors for creating engagement from different kinds of choices.

Additionally, there was work that had specifically been conducted in relation to play, such as Jean Piaget's studies of childhood play and fantasy [Piaget62]. In specific connection with videogames there were pioneering studies such as those by Thomas Malone [Malone81] on the role of challenge, fantasy and curiosity in play (about which you will learn more in Step 3).

Not surprisingly much of the research on videogames had focused on challenge, and only a few recognized the importance of other factors or people during play. A notable exception was the work of Richard Bartle, which highlighted the interdependent roles that players naturally assumed in online worlds, for instance, providing places for players who like to socialize provides an audience for achievers when they return to town to boast about their accomplishments (about which you will learn more from Richard himself in Step 4) [Bartle96], [Bartle03a], [Bartle03b]. There was also additional work on the role of community for web designers by Amy Kim [Kim00], which was interesting and relevant, but narrow in focus compared to the wider goal of learning about emotions of play.

Ultimately, none of these frameworks focused on the creation of specific emotions during play, and none of the preexisting models identified specific game mechanics associated with what gamers most enjoyed about games. Additionally, the creation of visceral engagement and the use of games to change how players feel, or to improve their lives, were all subjects wholly absent from the body of research. This demonstrated a clear need for a model describing the relationship between emotion and gameplay that could ultimately inform game designers how to proceed in the task of refining player experiences.

Given the lack of research on this subject, my colleagues and I resolved to use a simplified version of Paul Ekman's FACS to identify which emotions were evoked by the games that players enjoyed the most. Watching the emotions on players' faces would lead to an understanding of how the emotions of play relate to the types of choices that players most enjoyed.

THE FOUR FUN KEYS

Back in 2000, my colleagues and I at XEODesign were thinking about the types of games we wanted to design, and those we wanted to play ourselves, and it was clear that the videogame industry lacked the language to describe (and the tools to create) new kinds of player experiences. The main focus of the industry thus far has been to perfect a small number of game styles.

For the past 10 years, a trip to the videogame store was like going into a toy store and seeing only six kinds of toys: GI Joe, *Risk* (Albert Lamorisse, 1957), sports equipment, Hot Wheels, *Dungeons and Dragons* (TSR, 1974), and a dollhouse (*The Sims*). Table 1.2 demonstrates how one-sided the market for videogames has been [NPD05]. Unless you were someone who could design intuitively, like Shigeru Miyamoto, Will Wright, or Sid Meier, there were no tools to describe and develop new player experiences that could break out of this cycle of imitation. The recent success of Nintendo's Wii and DS consoles, the *Guitar Hero* (Harmonix, 2005) and *Rock Band* (Harmonix, 2007) franchises, and downloadable casual games such as *Diner Dash* (gameLab, 2005) provide proof that a larger market exists for games that offer new play styles outside the game genres that dedicated gamers loved, the so-called traditional *hardcore gamer* market [Lazzaro08a].

Table 1.2 Top-Selling Games Offer a Limited Number of Play Styles

Type	Number of Titles	Percent	Definition	Example Games
Roleplaying and fighting	31	52%	Games where the primary interaction is fighting one-on-one or in small groups with a gun or fists.	*World of Warcraft* (Blizzard, 2004), *Guild Wars* (ArenaNet, 2005), *Star Wars: Battlefront II* (Pandemic, 2005)
War and strategy	5	8%	Games that simulate warfare where the player manages a whole battlefield of fighters.	*Age of Empires* (Ensemble, 1997), *Sid Meier's Civilization IV* (Firaxis, 2005), *Rome: Total War* (Creative Assembly, 2004)

continued

Type	Number of Titles	Percent	Definition	Example Games
Sports	9	9%	Games that simulate a real-world sport such as basketball or football.	*Madden NFL* (EA Tiburon, 1988 onwards), *NCAA Football* (Software Tool-works et. al., 1994 onwards), *NBA Live* (Hitmen et. al., 1994 onwards)
Racing	5	5%	Games where players compete by driving or flying.	*Gran Turismo* series (Polyphony, 1997 onwards), *Need for Speed* series (Pioneer et. al., 1994 onwards), *Mario Kart* series (Nintendo, 1992 onwards)
Other	10	10%	Games where players build or manage people and their relationships or run a business such as a theme park or zoo.	*The Sims 2* (Maxis, 2005), *Roller Coaster Tycoon* (Chris Sawyer Productions, 1999), *Zoo Tycoon* (Blue Fang, 2005)
Total	60	100%		

* Source: NPD 2005

Table 1.2 clearly demonstrates that over 60% of the best-selling games in 2005 focused on war games and the rest of the market only developed three other themes.

Having watched different emotions on players' faces for years in our play lab, I was curious how emotions related to a player's favorite moments in gameplay. Films, for example, have the language of cinema at their disposal—plus industry best practices such as concept statements, treatments, scripts, and story boards—all designed to design films that create more engagement. Without imitating these six common styles of game, what can designers do?

To measure engagement, attention, and motivation, it was necessary to identify the activities that players most enjoyed, and to do this my colleagues and I watched players play their favorite games from *Tetris* to *Halo* (Bungee, 2001) at home, school, work, and in the case of mobile games on the go. We interviewed gamers—men and women, young and old—to capture their experiences and enjoyment factors as they played and video-taped their faces so we could measure their emotional responses.

Inspired by Ekman, Csíkszentmihályi, Bartle, and others, our goal was to develop a framework for designing emotions in games based upon the types of choices players most enjoyed. This framework should do three things: target what players like the most about games, be measureable by researchers, and be controllable by designers. In essence, we hacked the "what's fun" problem from the player's perspective by looking at which moments in games players liked the most, which emotions they were feeling (by watching their faces), and noted what mechanics were involved. All together, we collected over 2,000 observations from 30 players in our original study and organized them by emotion into four main groups. By looking at the emotion first, we found which types of choices were present during the most engaging moments of play, and noted new relationships between mechanics that shared the same emotional space [Lazzaro 04a].

The manner in which gamers modify the way they play can be extremely informative about the play styles they enjoy the most. Further evidence for the mechanics behind different play styles can be found in the way players often alter the game and the way they play to offer more of a particular kind of fun that matches their mood. For example, players may revisit early levels of a game to wreak mayhem with their now overpowered character, they might use a game to provide a base line of engagement while doing another task (such as playing *Civilization* on easy mode while talking to a boyfriend on the phone), they might choose to play a game in order to help them resist the temptation to eat a muffin, or they might try to steer their car from the view on an opponent's screen in order to increase the challenge. The way people modify their play speaks volumes about what they most enjoy about games.

XEODesign's Research

Because game designers cannot design emotions directly, at XEODesign we first identified the moments players liked the most in games and noted which emotions were present. Through cluster analysis, we grouped together the moments that had similar emotions. Then—

working backwards from emotion to choice—we identified the four types of game mechanics that engaged players most effectively during play. Some emotions happened in a set sequences, such as curiosity leading to surprise, or amusement leading to social bonding. Grouping players' favorite mechanics by the emotions they created revealed four distinct play styles.   These groupings also showed that players' favorite mechanics often facilitated the transition from one emotion in a cycle to the next. Further examination of these emotion cycles revealed that, while in best-selling games they often occurred simultaneously, each group of mechanics created *different* player experiences formed around very distinct styles of play.

The results of this study showed that people play games in essentially four distinct ways, and each of these play styles is associated with a different set of emotions. Players seemed to rotate between three or four different types of choices in the games they enjoyed, and the best-selling games tended to support at least three out of these four play styles. In contrast to the common wisdom of the time, most players didn't want better graphics, or smarter AI. There were other factors far more important to players [Lazzaro 04c]. Recognizing the importance of delivering new player experiences helped fuel the success of Nintendo's DS and Wii game consoles.

Some players crave the increased heart rate of excitement from playing *Bejeweled* in timed mode, the skin-prickling sensation from wonder in *Myst*, the tension of frustration followed by the thrill of victory in *Madden NFL*, or the amusing conversation starter from rolling over sumo wrestlers in *Katamari Damacy*. For others, the draw of videogames was simply the exchange of worries and thought and feelings for relaxation and contentment, or a feeling of achievement from knowing they did it right.

What players liked the most about videogames can be summarized as follows:

- The opportunity for challenge and mastery
- The inspiration of imagination and fooling around
- A ticket to relaxation and getting smarter (the means to change oneself)
- An excuse to hang out with friends

The Four Keys to Emotion in Player Experiences

The four patterns that came out of this research were called the Four Fun Keys because each play style is a collection of game mechanics that unlocks a different set of player emotions. We found that rather than having one favorite play style, players rotated between any three of the four during a particular play session. Likewise, blockbuster games containing the four play styles outsold competing similar titles that imitated only one kind of fun.

Fiero from the Hard Fun of Challenge and Mastery

The most obvious play style is the *Hard Fun* of achieving a goal. Players favoring this Fun Key made comments about their play that focused on the game's challenge, strategic thinking, and problem solving. This Hard Fun generates emotions and experiences which lead to *frustration*, and then *fiero* (the emotion of "triumph over adversity" mentioned previously). Players utilizing this play style make choices in context of a clear goal, some obstacles to overcome, and an aim to make progress enhanced by the feedback delivered from the game. As with Csíkszentmihályi's concept of Flow, the game designer's biggest challenge in this style of play is balancing the game's difficulty with the increases in the player's skill. If the game remains the same difficulty, players may master the game and quit because they are bored. Conversely, if the game becomes too challenging too quickly, players quit because they become too frustrated. In addition to the level of challenge, the nature of the challenge must also change, because players who enjoy Hard Fun also like developing new goals, strategies, and puzzles to solve.

Curiosity from the Easy Fun of Exploration and Roleplay

Aside from challenge, players enjoy intrigue and curiosity. This Easy Fun is the bubble wrap of game design. Players become immersed in the game when it absorbs their complete attention, or when it takes them on an exciting adventure. Curiosity about a mystery, theme, or story holds player attention in a way that focusing on a goal does not. Easy Fun also keeps the challenges from Hard Fun feeling fresh and new. These immersive game aspects are collected under *Easy Fun*, which generates the emotions and experiences of *curiosity, surprise, wonder,* and *awe*.

Relaxation from Serious Fun

Additionally, many players enjoy the visceral, behavior, and cognitive experiences that games create. Players enjoying this *Serious Fun* play for internal sensations such as *excitement* or *relief* from their thoughts and feelings. Games become quick and easy escapes, a tool to blow off workplace frustration, and to achieve life goals. Treadmills for the mind, games become therapy and players appreciate games as a way to experience and express their values.

Amusement from People Fun

Players also use games as mechanisms for social experiences or—*People Fun*. These players enjoy the emotions of *amusement, schadenfreude* (pleasure in other people's misfortune), and *naches* (pleasure in the achievements of someone you have helped). These emerge from the social experiences of competition and teamwork, not to mention enjoying opportunities for social bonding and the personal recognition that comes from playing with others. People Fun increases social capital between friends, and creates social tokens, inside jokes, and shared experiences.

That's not to say that Hard Fun lacks excitement, or players don't feel curious when playing with their friends. In fact, players' favorite moments in best-selling games often involve mechanics from all four keys at the same time, and bring all the related emotions with them.

The most surprising aspect of these research findings was the dramatic contrast in emotional displays between one person playing alone versus several people playing together. Players in groups emote more frequently and with more intensity than those playing on their own. Group play adds new behaviors, rituals, and emotions that make games more exciting (you will learn more about social play in Step 2). We were also surprised at how aptly Flow describes challenge in videogames, and the promise this holds for making games that can improve quality of life. For the game designer, the Four Keys to unlocking emotion in moment-to-moment gameplay offer new opportunities for generating emotion through player choice.

HARD FUN

"I always know how my husband feels about a game. If he screams 'I hate it! I hate it! I hate it!' then I know two things. A) He's going to finish it. B) He's going to buy version two. If he doesn't say these things he will put it down after a couple of hours." —Wife of a "hardcore" PC gamer

The best understood aspect of videogames, that most clearly separates games from other activities, is the opportunity for challenge and mastery, or Hard Fun. In Hard Fun, players apply themselves to accomplish difficult tasks in the game world. The opportunity to win provides players the Hard Fun of overcoming obstacles and applying themselves. Hard Fun mechanics focus and motivate by requiring skill to complete a goal. For example, basketball would not be as much fun if the hoop were twice as wide and positioned at waist level. Simply pushing a button rarely feels like winning, so instead games challenge the player to achieve more. They are called Hard Fun because these game mechanics reward the player's hard work.

PLAYERS ON HARD FUN

What players like about the way games offer the opportunity for mastery:

- Playing to see how good I really am
- Playing to beat the game
- Having multiple objectives
- Requiring strategy rather than luck

Fiero and the Emotions from Hard Fun

The dominant emotions from Hard Fun mechanics are *frustration* and *fiero*. Fiero, the personal feeling of triumph over adversity, is seen by some designers as the Holy Grail of game design, because fiero is how players feel when they win. There is no word in English for this emotion, so following Ekman's lead I borrow one from Italian. Players cannot push a button and feel fiero; they must feel frustrated first because fiero is the reward for accomplishing something difficult. It is one of the most powerful and positive human emotions, although the quest to attain it requires considerable frustration!

To provide opportunities to feel fiero, videogames get the players so frustrated that they are almost ready to quit—but just before they quit, they finally succeed. When this happens, there is a huge phase shift in the body and players go from feeling highly frustrated to feeling very good about themselves. Like the denouement after a film's climax, game designers often reduce the challenge after a game's climax to enhance the player's feeling of power, to give players a chance to bask and reflect on their achievement. Unlike films, games provide fiero directly from choices that players make themselves. Games create emotion through developing a sense of player agency rather than empathy with a character on-screen. In other words, a film never hands the audience a jet ski to save the world from nuclear doom, but a game must do so because in games, *player choice matters*.

Figure 1.4 shows how Hard Fun generates fiero: during play, gamers often start bored, become frustrated with each attempt to overcome the challenge, then experience fiero when they finally achieve the win, before feeling relief that the challenge is complete. Looking for fiero during player testing is a good way to assess the Hard Fun in a game. Seeing fiero from trivial tasks such as being able to finally move a game character is also a great way to identify user experience issues that prevent play.

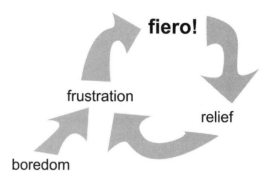

FIGURE 1.4 PX spiral—Hard Fun creates fiero.

Hard Fun Mechanics: Mastery

Videogames create Hard Fun through the use of specific mechanics, or types of choices offered to players. Most importantly, Hard Fun offers the player *a goal and a means to accomplish it.* As Csíkszentmihályi's model predicts, for Flow there needs to be a balance between the difficulty of the challenge presented and the skills available to the player to overcome that challenge. Long-term goals need to be broken into achievable steps, either explicitly, or by the strategic thinking of the player. Hard Fun mechanics provide goals, simplify the world, and offer enhanced progress feedback in the form of levels, points, and other achievements.

To maintain player engagement, Hard Fun mechanics must also vary the level of challenge. Games like *Doom*, *1942* (Capcom, 1984), *Golden Axe* (Sega, 1989), or *God of War* (Sony, 2005) offer a series of progressively more difficult enemies to defeat, ending each level with an especially challenging boss foe. Power ups are another tool that games such as *Pac-Man* (Namco/Midway, 1980) use to break up gameplay during a level, offering the opportunity for fiero in the middle of levels by offering temporary super powers as well as creating new options for changes in strategy. Extra bonuses during play also provide mini fiero-like experiences for players by offering the opportunity to win something mid-level (such as the fruit in *Pac-Man*). Games such as *Diner Dash* or *Zuma* (PopCap, 2003) reward repeat play by offering expert scores and side challenges such as hard-to-reach bonus coins, which keep the fiero flowing.

To keep players "in the zone" over time, games with very open worlds have to find different ways to provide Hard Fun. Virtual worlds such as *World of Warcraft* often structure challenge in the form of a quest whereby the player must overcome obstacles (such as killing deadly spiders) to earn a reward (such as a new piece of armor). The quest structure makes the goal state explicit to the player, and very large virtual spaces can then easily be populated with opportunities for achieving fiero by stuffing them full of quests. It is important to remember that game design requires more than Hard Fun. To maintain player enthusiasm for questing, *World of Warcraft* uses mechanics from all four of the Fun Keys.

Hard Fun mechanics increase engagement by requiring players to develop strategies to win. Hard Fun is more than beating more monsters in less time. For example, to earn enough bonus points by matching large groups of colored tiles to clear the level for *Collapse!* (GameHouse, 1999), a game in the popular casual *match 3* genre, players must pool large areas of one color. However, the introduction of a fourth color on level 4 breaks this strategy, thus requiring players to devise a new way to win. Players who enjoy Hard Fun love this!

Figure 1.5 shows how the challenge from the Hard Fun in a hypothetical game varies from level to level. To begin with, the player has little experience with the game, but the game has low difficulty to allow for this. In level 2, the player gets the hang of it, but the game increases the pressure (i.e. more foes, tougher challenges) to make it harder for the players to achieve victory. So when they win this level, they get the payoff of fiero. Level 3 begins with less challenge than the end of level 2, and the feelings of empowerment and relief from clearing the previous level carries players through the easy opening section of play and new experiences create curiosity to keep the game fresh. Then, once again, the challenge ramps up near the end, giving the players the fiero of victory at the end of the level. This pattern repeats over and over again in level-based games featuring Hard Fun.

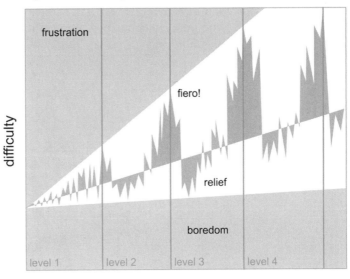

FIGURE 1.5 Navigating the Flow Channel in Hard Fun.

Often in later gameplay a game without enough Hard Fun feels flat because there are not enough challenges, or one strategy works for all levels. Likewise winning by luck rather than skill reduces players' sense of agency. A common source of this flatness can be the lack of an opportunity to devise new strategy. While players vary in how spiky and steep they want their play through the Flow Channel to be, in Hard Fun if there are not enough interesting obstacles, fiero is effectively denied. Because to overcome great challenge it is necessary for the player to face great hardship. This can necessitate changing game mechanics over time, not just by increasing the overall difficulty.

Players also look for a progression of new obstacles and the opportunity to develop new strategies as they play. A good rule of thumb is to require new ways to win every four or five levels and integrate new strategy into the rewards for Hard Fun. For example, in *Diner Dash*, the trophy for winning level four is a coffee maker which breaks player strategy for level five. Almost all players love to have a choice between several ways to play. After all, "choice" is what games are all about!

Summary of Hard Fun

The nature of the Hard Fun PX model is summarized in Figure 1.6, which shows how in Hard Fun player choice rewards effort with opportunities for mastery, which in turn provide fiero. Goals define challenge, or provide a sense of progress, strategies must be created and tested, and obstacles must be overcome. All of these deliver an experience of mastery which, when the challenge has been sufficiently tough, delivers the emotional reward of fiero.

FIGURE 1.6 Hard Fun PX.

Hard Fun PX Profile

The following table summarizes the choices and feedback that create Hard Fun, and the emotions that Hard Fun unlocks.

Choice and Feedback	Emotions
Goals	Fiero
Challenge	Frustration
Obstacles	Boredom
Strategy	
Power ups	
Puzzles	
Score and points	
Bonus scores	
Levels	
Monsters	

EASY FUN

"In real life if a cop pulled me over I'd stop and hand over my driver's license. Here I can run away and see what happens." —Player of *Grand Theft Auto III* (DMA, 2001)

Winning isn't everything. How true when we look at the emotions coming from videogames. In addition to the Hard Fun of challenge and mastery, games grab attention on a cognitive level from aspects that spark player imagination and surround the challenge. Easy Fun is the bubble wrap of game design. A seductive combination of mental Velcro and Fantasy Island. In addition to challenges provided by Hard Fun, games offer tools to support player fantasies, inspire creativity, and to simply allow players to fool around. Easy Fun frequently provides an emotional release when frustration from the challenge of Hard Fun becomes too intense. Games such as *Grand Theft Auto III* offer players a car—in fact any car that they want—and then offer them plate glass windows, innocent pedestrians, and conveniently positioned freeway ramps. It is up to the players to explore the relationship between these building blocks. Similarly, players enjoy Easy Fun in *The Sims* when they put their Sims in a swimming pool and then remove all the ladders.

PLAYERS ON EASY FUN

What players like about the way games engage their imaginations:

- Exploring new worlds with intriguing people
- Excitement and adventure
- Wanting to figure it out
- Seeing what happens in the story, even if I have to use a walkthrough
- Feeling like me and my character are one
- Enjoying the sound of cards shuffling
- Growing dragons

Curiosity and the Emotions of Easy Fun

The dominant emotions of Easy Fun are *curiosity, surprise*, and *wonder*. Curiosity is often the first emotion players feel from Easy Fun, and this can be experienced as an intense desire to find out what happens next. Curiosity is a unique emotion in that it has a strong cognitive component: the instant the unknown becomes known, curiosity evaporates. Surprise is also a unique emotion, a response to sudden novelty that opens up the sensory channels (ability to see, hear, and smell), which according to Ekman is neither inherently positive nor negative. It is one of the fastest emotions and dissipates quickly. The third of the Easy Fun emotions is wonder, which can be engendered by events that are extremely improbable yet that appear to be happening. Wonder is a full-body emotion, as powerful as the fiero of Hard Fun—it is the tingling sensation in their arms and the back of their neck that players say they felt when they first put a hand on a *Myst* linking book, or first saw the castle in *Super Mario 64* (Nintendo, 1997)—back when fully 3D games were still a novelty.

Curiosity is an emotion with a strong intellectual component. Once the mystery is solved curiosity disappears instantly. This is one reason movies are less compelling when someone "spoils the plot" by telling you the ending. If the outcome is known, the only curiosity left to hold your attention revolves around how the characters get there. Although wonder has the most intense emotional payoff of the Easy Fun emotions, curiosity is probably the most important, because it is the mechanism by which this play style motivates continued play. Wonder is a great reward, but players cannot anticipate that it is coming, and thus it cannot be a draw for play other than creating the desire to experience it again.

Wonder rivets player attention and is an emotion adults rarely experience but long to. This is why, when I designed *Tilt* (XEODesign, 2007), the first accelerometer game for the iPhone, I created a game mechanic that produced a strong sense of curiosity and wonder to continue and extend those feelings most enjoyed by people who owned an iPhone. To play, gamers rotate the iPhone to match different colored falling objects. Launched as a free web application two weeks after the iPhone was released, it won numerous awards including *Wired* magazine's Nine Best Hacks for the iPhone. People's curiosity about new things an iPhone could do drove over 250,000 people to visit the game's site. The game then enhanced people's fascination with the accelerometer built right in to the game mechanic. *Tilt* also offered a lot of social "over the shoulder play" as game iPhone owners could share this sense of wonder and impress their friends. Comparing this original free web app to the final *Tilt* game starring Flip the eco-hero who could offer the opportunity to identify the contribution of each of the Four Fun Keys.

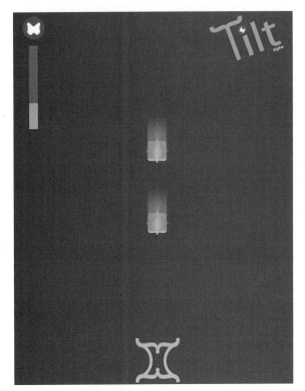

FIGURE 1.7 *Tilt* for the iPhone.
Design: Nicole Lazzaro, Code: Joe Hewitt, Art: Colin Toomey.
http://www.xeodesign.com/tilt

Figure 1.8 shows the PX spiral for Easy Fun. The players are drawn into the game by their curiosity, trying to poke in the corners and see what can be found. Then, when they encounter something unexpected they experience surprise, which gives way in turn to wonder (when facing the amazing) or awe (a blend of wonder and fear). In the case of awe, when the players realize that they are in no danger, they experience relief, at which point the game often offers them something new to be curious about.

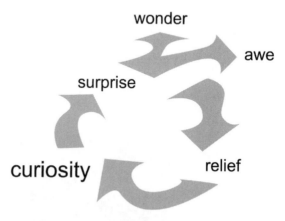

FIGURE 1.8 PX spiral—Easy Fun creates curiosity.

Easy Fun Mechanics: Imagination

Beyond challenge, players enjoy games for exploration, fooling around, and the sheer joy of interaction: the game situation has a degree of uncertainty and the player has a role in how it will work out. Easy Fun—the bubble wrap of game design—rewards players from the sheer joy of interaction and experimentation, roleplay, and simply fooling around. A core value proposition of Nintendo's DS and Wii game consoles comes from the fun of exploring physical movement such as swinging a tennis racquet in *Wii Sports* (Nintendo, 2006). The creation of Mii avatars that look like a friend or a famous iconic figure on the Wii provides a creative kick. The fact that cars in *Project Gotham Racing* handle differently than real cars makes them more fun to drive.

Games can build Easy Fun through the use of specific mechanics. Games such as *The Sims* use *ambiguity* and *incompleteness* to grab player attention: the Sims characters and the cartoon balloon language that they speak are open ended, which allows for player interpretation of what is going on—a big part of the fun of these games. Players effectively co-author stories during play where they make choices, their Sims respond, and then the players decipher what happens. The game strikes a deliberate balance and provides food for player imagination without being too specific. Much like real doll toys such as Barbie and GI Joe, the characters in *The Sims* are deliberately ambiguous so they more easily become vehicles for player imagination.

On the other hand, games such as *Myst* create Easy Fun by *offering the player more detail*. Instead of playing for points, players play for what film director/producer and game designer Hal Barwood calls, "the joy of figuring it out." For example, in *Myst* small details slow players down as they stop to examine the environments in a search for clues to solve puzzles as well as the overall mystery. A guiding design principle at Cyan Worlds, the developers of *Myst*, is that "the journey is the reward." The environments in this and other games they have made encourage players to linger and observe, rather than tear through them at breakneck speed. *Myst's* detailed surrealistic backgrounds such as Ship Rock Island pique player curiosity because they are different from real life, and reward players for careful exploration. The ring world in *Halo* has a similar effect.

A third way to approach Easy Fun is to provide *iconic situations and aspirational fantasies*, such as quitting one's job to run a restaurant in *Diner Dash* or fighting orcs in *World of Warcraft*. These situations suck players into a game in ways other than wanting to increase their score. The appeal of *Gran Turismo* is more than the ability to drive a race car, but also the fantasy of owning and kitting out high powered sports cars—something most players will never achieve in their real lives.

Great games engage the imagination as well as (or even instead of) the desire to achieve a goal from Hard Fun. Like improv theater, Easy Fun games offer players opportunities for spontaneous emotional responses. As in real life, in basketball games such as *NBA Street* (NuFX, 2001) in addition to making baskets and scoring points, players enjoy dribbling or doing tricks as if they were Harlem Globetrotters. *In Grand Theft Auto: San Andreas* (Rockstar North, 2004), players can steal any car they want, and also can go on a date, or jump out of an airplane and parachute to their front door step.

Videogames without enough Easy Fun feel overly directed. Players may lose interest in the game because the theme, controls, and other aspects surrounding the process used to obtain the score or complete the goals lacks engagement. Steve Meretzky calls the process of fleshing out this aspect of gameplay around the game's challenges as "putting meat on the bones." In designing *The Sims*, Will Wright looked for opportunities for "interesting failure states." In most games, there is a sheer joy of interaction that increases player engagement like waving the Wii controller, but the more predictable the attainable outcomes, the less likely it is the game will hold the player's attention.

Figure 1.9 shows how the balance between the expected and unexpected creates an ideal state for Easy Fun. If what happens is too strange and unexpected, the player experiences disbelief because what is happening is too far outside typical human experience. Conversely, if what happens in the game is too close to what players expect, the game feels predicable and players become disinterested. Striking a balance between these two extremes is essential to maximizing curiosity and keeping players involved with Easy Fun.

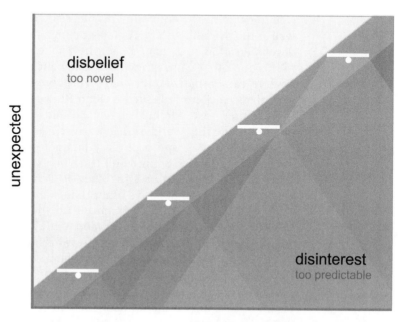

FIGURE 1.9 Novelty fills the player's attention.

Easy Fun is often found alongside Hard Fun. For example, in *Halo* once the Hard Fun is finished and all the aliens are defeated, players enjoy the novelty of running around blowing things up or exploring a surrealistic ring world where the horizon curves up overhead. When play becomes too stressful, players move between the Hard Fun of combat and the Easy Fun of exploration to prevent themselves from becoming too frustrated. Because these activities involve different emotions and kinds of choices, Easy Fun is both distinct from, and complementary to, Hard Fun.

Summary of Easy Fun

The nature of the Easy Fun PX model is summarized in Figure 1.10, which shows how in Easy Fun player choice rewards players with opportunities to exercise their imagination. Uncertainty, ambiguity, and iconic stories drive curiosity by providing interesting failure states (as suggested by Will Wright) and the joy of figuring it out (Hal Barwood). Additionally, players express their creativity through roleplay and player-created content and experiences, while detail encourages the players to explore the game world, providing opportunities to stumble upon surprising things which can evoke wonder and awe.

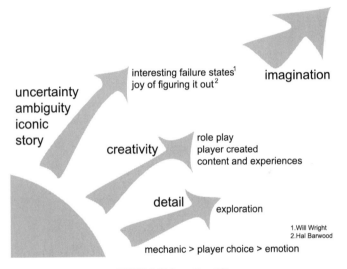

interesting failure states[1]
joy of figuring it out[2]

imagination

uncertainty
ambiguity
iconic
story

creativity

role play
player created
content and experiences

detail

exploration

1. Will Wright
2. Hal Barwood

mechanic > player choice > emotion

FIGURE 1.10 Easy Fun PX.

Easy Fun PX Profile

The following table summarizes the choices and feedback games use to create Easy Fun, and the emotions that Easy Fun unlocks.

Choice and Feedback	Emotions
Roleplay	Curiosity
Explore	Surprise
Experiment	Wonder
Fool around	Awe
Just have fun with the controls	
Iconic situations	
Ambiguity	
Detail	
Fantasy	
Uniqueness	
Easter Eggs	
Tricks	
Story	
Novelty	

SERIOUS FUN

"I play after work to blow off frustration at my boss." —A hardcore *Halo* player

In addition to the Hard Fun of challenge and the Easy Fun of cognitive engagement, games also grab attention through visceral engagement and cognitive intent. Games often offer interactive visceral stimuli that grab the player's attention. In this Serious Fun, players also play with a sense of purpose, often to change how they feel on a very deep level, improve the world in which they live, or to express their beliefs. Gameplay becomes therapy when it changes how players feel or creates something of value to them, and becomes part of their identity when it lets them express their values. Players often use the fun of games to motivate otherwise boring tasks, such as training or exercise. Offering a more visceral form of engagement than the curiosity-driven mechanics of Easy Fun, Serious Fun uses sound, visuals, and player choices to create a more robust PX when these mechanics respond to player actions in a rhythmic way. Players fall into a groove made more robust by engaging all of the senses. Having real-world impact increases player enjoyment and commitment to gameplay such as playing *Grand Theft Auto* to blow off frustration from work, *Brain Age* (Nintendo, 2005) to get smarter, *Dance Dance Revolution* (Konami, 1998 onwards) to lose weight, or playing a quiz game that donates rice to fight world hunger [FreeRice].

PLAYERS ON SERIOUS FUN

What players like about the way games create value:

- Clearing my mind by clearing a level
- Feeling better about myself
- Avoiding boredom
- Being better at something that matters

In Serious Fun, players use the fun of games to change how they think, feel, and behave. A player preferring this key loves the transformative power of games that create value for the player's real life. It adds another thing to love about the games they play. Games that provide Serious Fun engage player attention and desire to play through tasks that involve matching, completion, and big visual payoffs. The game experience adds to who they are and helps them change their world.

Relaxation, Excitement, and the Emotions of Serious Fun

The dominant emotions evoked by Serious Fun are *excitement* and *relaxation* and these are emotions that players frequently want out of their play experiences; they want to feel excited, they want relaxation, or they want some combination thereof. Players may begin play frustrated or bored, and play with the express intention of the game changing how they feel. Serious Fun mechanics also create other emotions when the reward for actions inside of the game spill out into the real world such as alternate reality games (ARGs), training simulations, or games that do real work such as the *ESP game* [ESPgame]. In the ESP game, conceived by Luis von Ahn of Carnegie Mellon University, pairs of players try to guess the same words to describe an online image. The game then tags the images with these words, making it possible for human beings to label nearly all the images on the Internet by playing a game. Players "feel good" about playing this game because it helps others [Ahn04]. Similar emotions drive much of the participation in many "web 2.0" applications such as Wikipedia and YouTube.

Figure 1.11 shows the PX spiral for Serious Fun. Players come to the game either because they are frustrated (by things that have happened to them in the real world) or bored. The game may throw intense visual and auditory stimuli at the player paradoxically causing further frustration, but this in turn leads to excitement (rising to the demands of processing the new threats and opportunities) or relaxation (once the stimuli decline or the set feels "complete"). Alternatively, the player may enter a state of Zen-like focus to ignore the increased stimuli (similar to Flow, again where the challenge is to process what is happening in the game world). This produces an inherently relaxing brain state—in this way, the game is functioning as a form of meditation, in that it focuses an individual's attention in order to produce relaxation.

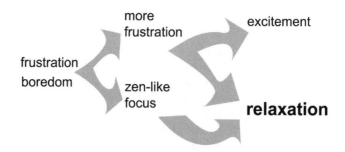

FIGURE 1.11 PX spiral—Serious Fun creates relaxation.

Serious Fun Mechanics: Stimulation and Value

Games create Serious Fun through several mechanics that provide visceral stimulation such as *repetition, rhythm*, and *bright exciting or relaxing colors and sounds*. In *Guitar Hero* players play along to the beat. In *Dance Dance Revolution* they do all this and also get valuable exercise or lose weight. The bright colors of *Bejeweled* or the cross-fire in *Halo* grab player attention by making the game screen more visually interesting than the player's surrounding environment. In games such as *flOw* (thatgamecompany, 2006), the meditative state created from the music, images, and rhythmic gameplay dominate the emotions from the mechanics from the other Fun Keys.

Virtually all games can increase engagement through adding *collection* and *completion mechanics*. Like gathering shells on the beach, Serious Fun mechanics often tap into simple, visceral, highly motivating activity loops. Game platforms such as Xbox 360 and EA's Pogo casual games portal recognize player advancement on personal profile pages. They also reward special events in-game such as a 100-yard pass or a 360 spin-out with a badge of achievement. Motivated by achievements, players often go back after finishing the game to gather all the badges. Other game mechanics and even game user interfaces can increase their engaging quality through collection and completion. For example, the map in *Diner Dash* becomes filled in with expert stars and new restaurants as the player advances. Beyond a high score (Hard Fun) or solving a mystery (Easy Fun), completing a set offers a reward all its own.

Serious Fun can also occur in the absence of the usual trappings of gameplay (such as challenges with goals requiring the exercise of specific skills). In games of pure chance such as slot machines and pachinko, the opportunity to earn real money increases player engagement. For these games, intense stimuli (spinning wheels, dropping balls) and establishing a rhythm (between each pull) make up for the lower levels of Hard Fun (players still have a goal to win money and have many strategies for choosing the right machine to increase their chances). Many slot machines allow players to stop wheels individually, decide whether to play multiple lines, and video slots offer bonus rounds with more interactive play. Furthermore, the stakes in a gambling game can be such that even though the challenge from Hard Fun relates to beating the odds rather than skill, the player still gets fiero from a big win (you will learn more about this in Step 3).

Games that deliver Serious Fun transform players, or create real value for them. Serious Fun mechanics such as badge collection *create perceived value*, but other mechanics can create value as well. In *Rock Band* and *Guitar Hero*, players enjoy learning about music. In *Bejeweled*, players gather as many diamonds, rubies, and sapphires as they want. Even if it is only a fantasy, the experience of obtaining something valuable to the player generates rewarding emotions and is at the heart of Serious Fun.

The Serious Fun in games can also create *real* value for the players when the excitement and enhanced feedback from a game encourages practice or helps players learn. The opportunity for a mental workout feels less like a waste of time and makes players feel good about themselves and the game. Figure 1.12 summarizes how in Serious Fun players *play with a purpose*. They use the fun of games to change how they think, feel, and behave or to accomplish real work, and through gameplay they can express or create value.

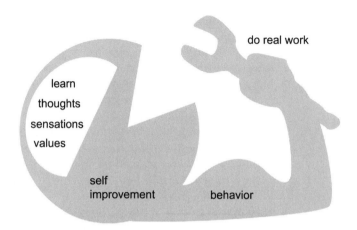

FIGURE 1.12 Serious Fun—Purposeful play changes self and real world.

In games that express Serious Fun, the game mechanics are the moral expression of the game in the same way that every story expresses a moral idea of some kind. This allows players to *express their values* in play. Whether it is the idea that hard work pays off in *Diner Dash* or the satisfaction of cleaning one's room in *Katamari Damacy*, people feel better about games that express who they are and what is important to them. Elderly people may play crossword puzzles not only because they believe it prevents Alzheimer's, but also because they enjoy how it allows them to express the value they hold in respect of taking good care of themselves and feeling smarter.

Players may express this part of the Serious Fun of a game in conversations with others who share their values, which increases the word of mouth and marketability of the game. For example, so-called hardcore gamers enjoy talking with others about the fact that they enjoy those games they consider to be "hardcore." These games reward dedication and practice through increasing complexity paired with strong negative emotions, and those who master them enjoy sharing their passion with others—it strengthens their sense of identity to fraternize with other players with similar values. Plus any emotion shared with others often intensifies that emotion.

People play *Brain Age* to feel smarter, exercise their mental faculties, or to ward off Alzheimer's, or play *Dance Dance Revolution* to lose weight or keep fit with aerobic exercise. Players blow off workplace frustration, relieve boredom standing in line, and laugh themselves silly by playing all manner of different games. Some prefer games such as *Wii Sports* over violent games because this reflects their moral values. The repetition and collection mechanics in games like *Bejeweled* create emotions and increase engagement in a visceral way. If instead of rubies and diamonds, players matched dirty broken glass and animal droppings, the game would feel very different! With Serious Fun players feel good about the value that the game creates *before*, *during*, and *after* play. Games with more Serious Fun offer more for the players to appreciate after they put down the controller.

As a result of all these factors, games without enough Serious Fun feel like a waste of time—the rewards the games offer do not spill over into the players' real lives with valuable personal consequences such as improving their mood, learning something interesting, keeping them fit, or validating their moral outlook.

Summary of Serious Fun

The nature of the Serious Fun PX model is summarized in Figure 1.13, which shows how in Serious Fun player choice rewards players with opportunities to create something of perceived value. Stimulation produces excitement, which can be a value in and of itself, and can also engender relaxation, or allow players to dissipate work and life frustrations. Practicing skills produces learning or health improvements, or constitutes "real work" if the players are learning things that apply in other contexts. The use of rhythm and similar techniques allow players to "Zen out" (that is, enter a deep state of Flow without overt challenge). These deep Flow states also serve the goals of eliminating frustration, alleviating boredom, or producing relaxation, all of which can connect deeply with the player's chosen values.

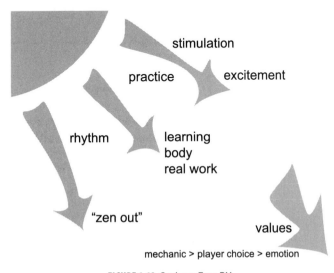

FIGURE 1.13 Serious Fun PX.

Serious Fun PX Profile

The following table summarizes the choices and feedback associated with Serious Fun, the emotions that it unlocks, and the values it may connect with.

Choice and Feedback	Emotions	Value
Rhythm	Visceral	Relax
Repetition (practice)	Relax	Excite
Collection	Excite	Kill time
Completion	Learn	Relieve boredom
Matching	Meditate	Lose weight
Stimulation	Self-learning	Get smart
Bright visuals	Esteem boost	Practice
Music	Express values	Create real work product
Learning	Pleasure from doing real work	Develop skills
Simulation	Meditation	
Work out		
Study		
Real-world take away		

PEOPLE FUN

"People are addictive, not the game." —Bob, a hardcore sports game player

Many games add to the fun by offering the opportunity to spend time with friends. This expands upon the engagement created by the other Fun Keys, and increases attention and motivation through social interaction, which in turn enhances and intensifies the emotions from the other Fun Keys. The emotions from winning, goofing around, and dancing together all are more intense when experienced in the company of others. There are several reasons for this (which you will learn more about in the next step), but in broad strokes the fun of social play comes from players adding content, working together, competing, teasing each other, outdoing each other with witty commentary, and laughing each other silly.

PLAYERS ON PEOPLE FUN

What players like about the way games bring their friends closer:

- It's the people that are addictive, not the game
- I want an excuse to invite my friends over
- I don't like playing games, but it's a fun way to spend time with my friends
- I don't play, but it's fun to watch

People Fun is characterized by a high degree of emotional expression. People playing games in the same room express a wider variety of emotions and experience a greater intensity of emotion more frequently than when they play the same game in different rooms (via LAN or Internet play, for instance). In collocated group play, the game shrinks to the corner and the whole room becomes the stage for play. The experience of playing with friends can be so intense that many people are willing to play games they don't like, or to play games even though they don't really enjoy playing games, because they want to spend more time with their game-playing friends. There are many more emotions from People Fun mechanics than there are from the other three Fun Keys combined.

Amusement and the Emotions of People Fun

"You can discover more about a person in an hour of play than in a year of conversation." —Plato

Emotions play a vital role in communicating and coordinating action between people as they work to accomplish tasks. People Fun offers many emotions that are possible only when two or more people interact, such as *gratitude* and *schadenfreude* (pleasure in the misfortune of others), as well as intensifies emotions that can occur in single player games but that can be observed much more readily in social play, such as *amusement*. This provides videogames a unique edge over media such as films, which by default are passive, single-person experiences, where emotion is experienced through empathy with a character rather than by direct interaction. Again, in games, player agency is king.

The dominant emotions associated with People Fun are amusement and the variety of emotions associated with social bonding. During player observations, amusement is the easiest way to detect People Fun in a videogame, and the intense sense of closeness that occurs after shared laughter is perhaps the most valuable emotional experience of this kind of play. Players laugh even at negative events—a spectacular failure becomes a source of fun and nearly always triggers a light-hearted response from the group! Amusement in a social context intensifies social bonds, and the psychological state that occurs after communal amusement is the feeling of camaraderie and admiration that comes from social interaction. Again, there is no good word in English for this emotion.

Another important emotion is *naches* (pronounced "knock-us"), a Yiddish term for the pleasure and pride in the accomplishment of someone a player helped, such as a child or mentee, and this is another frequently observed emotion, especially when playing videogames with more experienced players.

In People Fun, players interact and cycle between many emotions. These cycles of emotions offer what players like about hanging out with friends and increase social bonding. Figure 1.14 shows the PX spiral for People Fun: social interaction with other players generates amusement, which enhances social bonding, which encourages further player interaction. Generally speaking, the more people play together, the more they want to play together. People Fun is the difference between eating a grilled cheese sandwich and sharing fondue with friends. The game structures social actions to create more emotions whether it is helping someone with a long string of cheese or fighting over the piece that fell off someone's fork [Lazzaro 08b]. Wherever there is a lot of amusement between players, social bonding and People Fun cannot be far behind!

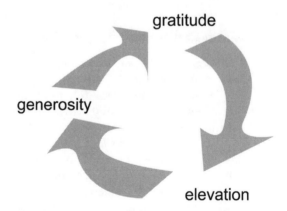

FIGURE 1.14 PX spiral—People Fun creates amusement.

People Fun Mechanics: Building Relationships

The most popular and obvious examples of People Fun mechanics are *high score boards, profile pages, avatars, gifting, emotes,* and *chat.* All these mechanics share one thing in common: they connect players in some way, either through communication (emotes, chat, profile pages), showing off achievements and creativity (custom avatars, high score boards) or by sharing social tokens (gifting, or items and events that obtain special meaning such as inside jokes) [Lazzaro08c]. However, these features only scratch the surface of the opportunities for fun between players. Games can structure social interaction in a number of different ways, and players love the excuse to hang out with friends. When people play side-by-side, they can deepen their enjoyment of the gameplay by adding commentary, making up house rules, and adding content—but very few videogames are built to take advantage of this.

Games build People Fun through the use of specific mechanics. Most common to multiplayer games such as *Top Spin Tennis* (Power and Magic, 2003) is the opportunity for cooperation on one side of the net and *competition* over it. Similarly, *Halo* offers more People Fun mechanics by offering competitive head-to-head death match play (player versus player or PvP) as well as cooperative modes where players work together to overcome the environment and computer-controlled characters (player versus environment or PvE). Massively Multiplayer Online games (MMOs) use even more elaborate cooperative and competitive mechanics such as interdependent player classes, chat, emotes, guilds, and player versus player combat to encourage interaction between players. The ability to compare and communicate also increases the connection a player will feel with other players of the same game.

Figure 1.15 illustrates the three basic draws of People Fun—competition, cooperation, and communication. The more lines of interaction a game provides between players, the more opportunities for People Fun there are.

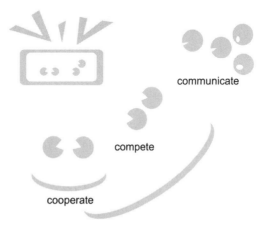

FIGURE 1.15 People Fun—choices with others increase social bonds.

Opportunities for *mentorship* and *leadership* from People Fun mechanics broaden the emotional spectrum for play. In games like the *Oddworld* series (Oddworld Inhabitants, 1997 onwards), *Pikmin* (Nintendo, 2001), and *Nintendogs* (Nintendo, 2005), players take pride in the accomplishment of others that they mentor towards success creating naches. In *Mario Kart: Double Dash!!* (Nintendo, 2003), players can introduce a friend to the game by having the friend ride in the back seat and throw things. Later they feel naches when the friend they introduced to the game later graduates and wins a race driving a car of their own. Teaching others how to play and sharing their love of gaming is something many players enjoy—it validates their own choice of hobby, as well as builds bonds with other people.

People Fun mechanics are highly effective at adding more emotion to games, because player interaction increases the number of emotions that can be evoked by a videogame. Increasing the number of ways players can interact with each other increases the range of emotions during play. In addition a single mechanic can rotate between players to generate more emotions. For example, a player who gives a health pack in a combat game feels generous while his or her companion feels gratitude. A third player witnessing these events feels elevation from this demonstration of human kindness in the middle of battle. The emotions are swapped later in the game when roles are reversed and the first player now needs help. This provides the opportunity for multiple emotions to be evoked from a single health pack mechanic.

In *World of Warcraft*, many mechanics can *only* be used on other players, such as a spell that bestows increased health for 30 minutes but that can be cast only upon other characters. This forces player generosity and seeds the opportunity for group dungeon raids and social bonding. In *Rock Band*, teammates can use their star powers to rescue a player who has fallen behind and is in danger of losing, aiding in the sense of camaraderie, inter-dependency, and teamwork.

All games offer an excuse for social interaction and forming social bonds—multiplayer games do so explicitly, but even a single-player game can form a social experience with several players contributing to progress through taking turns at the controller or other forms of explicit cooperation. This can be especially pertinent when the videogame skills of all the players are at different levels—for instance, two friends might come together to play a survival horror game such as *Resident Evil* (Capcom, 1996 onwards) even when one of them finds the game too difficult to control. They both cooperate on solving the simple puzzles and deciding where to go next, and both share in the shocks and surprises the game uses to scare the player. Another way that single player games can leverage People Fun is via non-player characters (NPCs), that is, characters controlled by the game—as you will learn in the next step, NPCs can fool the player into feeling that they are dealing with real people. Additionally, caring for and training virtual pets in games such as *Nintendogs* can generate many social emotions.

People Fun enhances the emotion from the other Fun Keys, as indeed they all do. For instance, for *Diner Dash* Nicholas Fortugno, the game's designer, incorporated the People Fun from managing customer emotions directly into the Hard Fun game mechanic. If the player makes customers wait too long, they get angry and steal from the tip jar on the way out. In this way *Diner Dash* multiplies player engagement by integrating Hard Fun and People Fun into the same game mechanic [Lazzaro05].

Games without enough People Fun are lonely experiences that players are less likely to show and share with their friends. Not all games need to include other players or NPCs, but those that manage to include these opportunities well can create a significant amount of engagement from doing so, because players then care on a number of additional levels.

Summary of People Fun

The nature of the People Fun PX model is summarized in Figure 1.16, which shows how player choice rewards players with opportunities for social interaction. Player interaction creates cooperative and competitive situations, as well as chances to mentor, lead, or perform. Personalization and creation of custom content allows for self-expression, and the creation of personal spaces (such as profile pages) and fan communities. Finally, even when the player is interacting with NPCs, the same suite of social interaction opportunities can be facilitated. All this serves to allow relationships to be built in or around the game, and this is the ultimate goal of all People Fun.

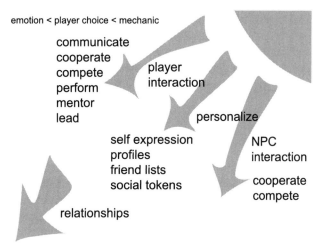

FIGURE 1.16 People Fun PX.

People Fun PX Profile

The following table summarizes the choices and feedback associated with People Fun, and the emotions that they as a whole unlock.

Choice and Feedback	Emotions
Cooperate	Amusement
Compete	Social bonding
Communicate	Schadenfreude
Mentor	Naches
Lead	Envy
Perform	Love
Spectacle for others	Gratitude
Characters	Generosity
Personalize	Elevation
Open expression	Inspire
Jokes	Excite
House rules	Ridicule
Secret meanings	Embarrass
Nurturing pets	
Endorsements	
Chat	
Profile page	
High score board	
Avatars	
Gifting	
Emotes	

CONCLUSION

To innovate and evoke more emotions in videogames, designers must first develop both the language and the tools to craft specific emotions around gameplay. A videogame's core value proposition involves player choice, and choices are impossible without emotion. This makes the design of emotion central to game design, because without emotion players lack the motivation to play. Players rotate between these different types of engagement offered by the Four Fun Keys as they play. Delivering games with a rich set of mechanics from all four Fun Keys helps players stay engaged, allows them to enjoy deeper emotional experiences, and offers a wider range of emotions from play. Figure 1.17 summarizes all the ways mechanics can be used to generate emotion covered in Step 1.

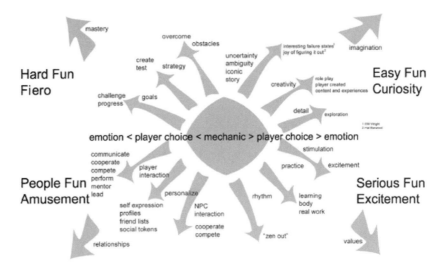

FIGURE 1.17 Summary of the Four Fun Keys.

When working with the Four Fun Keys keep the following points in mind:

- The interplay between player actions, choices, and feedback from the game creates a series of internal sensations called Player Experience (PX).
- Remember that the Four Fun Keys often occur together. It's not that Hard Fun lacks excitement, or players don't feel curious when playing with their friends. Players' favorite moments in best-selling games often involve mechanics from all four keys at the same time, and bring all the related emotions with them.

- To focus player attention, games simplify the world, enhance feedback, and suspend negative consequences. This maximizes the effect of emotions coming from player choices. In the simplest terms, game mechanics engage players by offering choices and providing feedback.
- According to Csíkszentmihályi, optimal experiences are those where people are balanced between the challenges they face and the skills they have acquired.

By planning an emotion profile at the beginning of the game-design process, game designers can target specific emotions with different game mechanics. Prototyping and testing these mechanics with players can help gauge the success of these decisions. Offering emotions from all four types of fun broadens the opportunity for player emotion in the game, not just in response to a game event, but also during and after play as well—the fun of a game does not end when they stop playing it, as fan communities and player profile pages demonstrate. Videogames already evoke strong emotions, but by intentionally crafting and heightening the emotions in player experiences, the videogames of the future will evoke more emotions than any other medium.

UNDERSTAND SOCIAL PLAY

by Katherine Isbister

Examining the emotions that players seek in videogames gives you a first step towards understanding play. Now you will explore what happens not just with a single player, but also among several players as they experience a game together. The principles discussed in Step 2 are taken from two areas of social science that have a lot to offer in terms of assessing what is happening between people moment-to-moment: social psychology and communication. This step begins with an overview of why social interaction matters for game designers, before looking at the specific mechanisms at work when people play together, recommendations for design choices that encourage and heighten social interaction, and considerations of player differences to keep in mind while designing games.

WHY SOCIAL INTERACTION MATTERS FOR GAME DESIGNERS

Game designers and developers might find that they focus most of their efforts on thinking about how an individual player will react to what has been created, moment-by-moment (unless they are designing what they know will be a multi-player game). Certainly there are tremendous challenges at this level of analysis, and this step is not meant to say it isn't so. Rather, it's meant to point out a whole additional layer at which a game is being experienced by players, which is fundamental to how they experience the world, and even, fundamental to why they play games in the first place. This is true even if you are designing a single-player game!

How could this be? Well, the fact is, human beings are social creatures at heart. We are not solitary animals—we live in social groups from the very beginning of our lives. Being social and figuring out how to do it well takes up a tremendous amount of our time in life. Biologists and neuroscientists tell us that the basic ways in which we perceive the world—what we notice, how our senses function, even what is happening in the neurons in our brains—is colored by our social nature. Examples of evidence gathered to support this claim include the following:

- Even infants orient very quickly to the sound of a human voice. They can recognize their mother's voice and face at two weeks old, and seem to prefer the sound of their mother's voice even in the womb [Kisilevsky03].
- Because of experimental research confirming that people can recognize faces even when they are at a great distance or highly distorted, researchers have concluded that humans most likely have a neural resource that is specialized for and devoted to facial recognition [Sinha06].
- When we see another person experiencing and demonstrating signs of an emotion, we automatically mimic that emotion in our own face, and in our brain, it seems to be the case that special *mirror neurons* are firing with sympathetic imitations of the muscle movements of that person [Iacoboni99].
- Most communication between people is happening not in the semantic content of the words, but in what are called "paralinguistic cues"— body language, facial expression, and tone of voice. So we all have to become experts at reading these signals in everyday life [Knapp02].

This means that anytime there is a social situation going on in combination with the playing of a game, players will be heavily involved in interpreting and reacting to that social situation, and it will color how they experience your game. And more often than not, the player will be in a social situation when playing.

Although most designers are familiar with the growing popularity of multi-player online games, many designers may not realize that most gaming is done in social groups—the Entertainment Software Association 2008 report [ESA08] says that "59% of gamers play games with other gamers in person." That's over half of the time!

Why is this so? Perhaps because playing with others is often simply more fun. Some interesting research done using biosensors (hooking up heart rate, sweat, and other monitors to players) showed that players had more emotional signals when they scored a goal against a real human being as opposed to a computer opponent [Mandryk07]. Playing games is not just a form of individual entertainment; it is something that people seek out as a way to be together doing something fun. This means most gameplay exists within a social context. A group of friends is doing all kinds of social "work" when hanging out playing a game together—becoming closer to one another by building trust and shared experience, establishing hierarchies of skill and dominance, letting off steam safely from conflicts among the group, carrying out tensions or grudges within gameplay, and so forth. This was what Nicole introduced in Step 1 as People Fun. Designers ignore all this at their peril, because it can have profound implications as to whether a game will turn out to be fun.

Another powerful reason to care about social play, even when designing a single-player game, is that researchers have shown that people have what you might call an overactive social sense. That is to say, that people end up making use of their social skills even with technologies that act as if they were human. This happens instinctively and despite a person's conscious awareness that they are dealing with a machine, not a person. Reeves and Nass demonstrated this phenomenon in a series of studies that they called the "Media Equation" [Reeves96]. They tested out findings from Social Psychology using computers. They would replicate a study, substituting a computer for a person in the study, and see if they got the same results. Time after time, they did. For example, they demonstrated that people can't help being polite to a computer. In one study they had a computer tutor a person, and then that person gave feedback on how well the computer did.

In one condition of the experiment, the participants gave feedback directly to the computer they were tutored by. In the other condition, they went into another room and told a second computer how the tutoring computer did. Reeves and Nass showed that people rated the tutor more positively when telling it to "its face" how it did, as opposed to when they told another. This mimics politeness norms in human interaction. The participants in the study denied that they thought the computer was at all human and certainly were not consciously being polite to the computers. They simply couldn't help it.

This means that anytime a designer makes a game social at all, such as when there are non-player characters (NPCs) on-screen, they are evoking the player's social skills in a powerful and unconscious way. It thus becomes even more vital that designers understand the building blocks of social play and social interaction when making design choices.

WHAT'S HAPPENING WHEN PEOPLE PLAY TOGETHER

As Nicole already noted in Step 1, when people play together it evokes all kinds of emotions and behaviors. Here, you will discover some of the key elements of social play.

Emotional Contagion

On a very simple, primitive level, social play introduces a powerful effect among players called *emotional contagion* [Hatfield94]. Because people are so easily influenced by seeing how others feel, suddenly all of the emotional effects discussed in Step 1 become magnified among players. Someone watching a friend play a round of *Katamari Damacy* (Namco, 2004), for example, will vicariously experience the emotions of the player as he unfolds in body language, exclamations, and facial expressions (if they can be seen). The spectator will also be influenced by the emotional cues (music, movement, and the like) in the game that are directed at the player. In turn, the spectator's emotions will have an effect on the player, creating a loop of emotional contagion that designers can take advantage of.

As mentioned, this can also occur when a player encounters NPCs (or has a view of the avatar in a third-person game). Such players will pick up and begin to feel the emotions they see on-screen without realizing it.

Performance

Communication and Social Psychological research has shown that a person's actions are fundamentally altered simply by having someone else observing [Cottrell72]. If a person is already good at something, her performance in the task may get even better when others are watching. If she is not so good, it may make her performance worse. Some people really enjoy performing for others, and get more of a charge out of playing for an audience. Designers can create opportunities for this kind of showing off. Designers can also use the embarrassment of performance to heighten the fun of play—the Wii game *WarioWare: Smooth Moves* (Intelligent Systems, 2007) is a great example of a game that leverages social embarrassment to powerful effect in terms of fun. Everyone gets embarrassed making the silly gestures that drive the game mechanics, and this can even be a bonding experience among players to share such a vulnerable moment. Interestingly, this kind of social facilitation effect also seems to occur when the watcher is a computer character [Rickenberg00]. So even an NPC audience in a game might enhance a solo player's experience.

Learning

One very important advantage of being social animals is that human beings do not have to learn everything from scratch all by themselves. Instead, each of us gains a tremendous amount of knowledge about the world not just from our own senses, but also from the people around us who already know many valuable things. One way this happens is through explicit teaching—people are mentored by parents, educators, and friends. This happens when people play games together, too. Part of the fun of mastering a game is being able to show off through teaching other players how it's done. And teaching others to play helps to ensure that the player has others to play with later.

People also learn very effectively merely through observing what others do—Bandura called this social learning [Bandura77]. He demonstrated that small children in a room where a video was being played of a teacher hitting a doll with a mallet, would be more likely later to hit such a doll in this way during their play, compared to children who had not seen this video. Watching is a powerful part of learning how to play a game—making it possible for a person to learn "over the shoulder" should increase the number of new players who find it easy to take up this game.

Relationship Building

When people play together, they are usually not just there because they want to engage with the game itself and its challenges. They are also there because they want to be social with the people with whom they are playing. Games provide opportunities for people to achieve important social aims such as:

- **Building trust and friendship.** Working closely on a shared goal, or even fighting one another but in a setting with close interaction, helps build trust and friendship and warm feelings toward others [Tschannen-Moran00]. So at a very basic level, playing together helps to deepen relationships. In a physical sense, gameplay puts people close together and may also synchronize their movements and lead them to share some powerful emotional experiences [Capella96]. All this adds to the deepening of relationships.

- **Establishing power relationships and alliances.** Social groups have internal dynamics that games can support and sustain [Shaw81]. For example, there may be power struggles going on in a group as to who is a leader. The group may work on this question in the context of gameplay—who leads the group in collaborative play? Who wins in competitive play? How do the group members treat one another as they play? Perhaps gameplay becomes a way for some group members to let off some steam or set someone down a notch in a safe context, if they have been tipping the power balance in an unwelcome way, or have done something to irk the group.

- **Trying on social roles and identities.** Gameplay also allows people to do some social identity exploration [Turkle95]. Players can select an avatar that has different social qualities than they do, and can play out those qualities in social gameplay. This kind of play can end up deepening relationships as co-players learn other aspects of one another that may not come across in everyday life and get to try on different ways to relate that may actually enhance their core relationships with one another.

SOCIAL MECHANISMS TO USE IN DESIGN

All this has some very practical and tangible implications for game design, and you will now see some of the ways that you can leverage the understanding of social play for the benefit of the development process.

Designing for Emotional Contagion

As you already saw in Step 1, part of what game designers aim to do is to create interesting emotions from play. Emotional contagion can be a powerful tool for doing this. If people are in the same room playing in front of a shared screen, a designer can definitely take advantage of that in thinking through the emotional cues in the game, like NPC and avatar actions, music, camera angles and cuts, and figure on the player audience being affected by these as well, which shifts the mood for all the players in a room. Even without a shared screen, when players are playing in the same room (for example, when a group gathers with Nintendo DS systems for a play session), the designers can assume they are hearing one another and seeing one another's frantic actions out of the corner of their eyes. One important thing to keep in mind is that one can't always predict how emotions play out socially from observing solo players. It is crucial for designers to watch groups of people playing the game, in order to get a feel for how emotional contagion will play out. Ideally, the team will want to do group playtesting internally among the development team (as Harmonix does [Kohler07]), to really get a feel for these dynamics and how to maximize them. This is true for all of the social effects in this step, and I'll touch on this again at the end.

Designing for Performance

In a social group, there is likely to be one or more people who really enjoy performing for others, and whose performance is enhanced by having an audience. Building improvisation, extra moves, opportunities for finesse, and the like into a game allows these people a chance to show off for the group, which will enhance everyone's experience. True performers will of course find unexpected ways to show off in the game—like the vehicle jumping in *Halo: Combat Evolved* (Bungee, 2003)—and designers can capitalize on this by spreading the word about how to do these things once they've been discovered.

Designers can also reduce the embarrassment of anyone who is especially shy in the group, surprisingly, by requiring *everyone* to do something that is embarrassing but fun. Performance games like *Karaoke Revolution* (Harmonix, 2003), *Rock Band* (Harmonix, 2007), or the aforementioned *WarioWare: Smooth Moves* require everyone to perform embarrassing actions, and thus end up building trust and affiliation by causing people to become vulnerable in front of one another. Creating variant difficulty levels that are easy to access helps to ensure that people whose performance is impaired by having an audience can still take part and improve at their own pace.

Designing for Learning

The best possible scenario for quick learning is when players can use social learning and observation—in other words, simply by watching, they can figure out a lot about how the game is played. Games with physical movement linked to game mechanics, like the *Dance Dance Revolution* series (Konami, 1999 onwards), have this quality. So do games with well-thought-out menus and without intense time limitations, such as *The Sims* series (Maxis, 2000 onwards).

This may not be possible for complex, real-time focused games without physical controllers. In this case, creating a great tutorial level that offers social learning for observers (for example, through the voice-over instructions and menus that can be seen by the audience) can help. Designers might also consider incorporating a mentor mode in which one player can coach and assist another as that person gets up to speed on a game's mechanics—something like those cars for driver education that allow teachers to co-pilot when needed. It's also helpful to create web space where players can upload replays for others to learn from.

If the development team wants a very broad audience for a game that includes casual gamers, it is very important to design for and to test out over-the-shoulder learning, as well as tuning the game for individual player learning curves.

Designing for Relationship Building

Building relationships is a side effect of playing together—few players choose to play a game with the goal of working on their relationships, but whenever people play together it is inevitable that these interconnections will form. When designing with this aspect of social play in mind, a few key points should be considered:

- **Build in breaks.** This may sound obvious, but isn't always taken into account—designers need to allow room for socializing to occur in the first place. That is to say, a game that has relatively short play cycles, with breaks in between for things like avatar selection or other selections (for example, a new minigame to try out) allow people to take a break, get a snack, talk about how the last round went, and the like. If designers are working on a game with longer play cycles, they should think about natural break points for groups of players, and how they might handle finishing asynchronously. It's boring in a group to sit out a very long period in which one has been knocked out of play. This is something the team will want to test out with groups of players pretty early on.

- **Form factors matter.** As discussed earlier, it's important to think about how the platform a game is played on impacts what people can share. A console game with a big screen that players share allows for more common input than individual handheld machines. A game with physical controllers changes social dynamics as well. Designers should use what they have well!

- **Encourage trust.** There are some social actions that end up contributing to trust and affinity between people, which can be built into a game. For example, getting into synchrony (performing the same action at the same time), being on the same team, not to mention standing close together or having to do some kind of shared physical action. Nass, Fogg, and Moon conducted an interesting experiment in which people were induced to view computers as their teammates, for instance [Nass96], which demonstrates that a game design could help induce a cooperative and trusting environment.

- **Let the players form their own power relationships.** Social dynamics are complex, and far beyond any game designer's ability to anticipate, but fortunately most games support the establishment of power relationships and alliances better than many of the other aspects of social play. Providing team dynamics that include competition among teams as well as among individuals allows social groups to explore their own power dynamics and alliances fluidly through gameplay. It's still wise to do group playtesting to see how these dynamics will play out, and to tune the offerings, of course.

Trying on Social Roles and Identities

Another aspect of social expression in videogames is the opportunity for players to roleplay different identities and try on roles that they would perhaps not normally explore in real life.

Creating a Custom Self

The explosion of avatar customization in recent games is a tribute to the importance and value of this social aspect of games. Investing in socially interesting opportunities for customization of avatars for your target audience is one way to encourage and enhance social play. There is little academic research as of yet on the particulars of which specific avatar qualities are more valuable than others, but there has been some preliminary research about how avatar choices are made and what they may mean socially, such as Nick Yee's Daedelus project [Yee04]. Development teams are probably best off doing some initial prototype testing with the target player groups to see whether they are really offering the right set of "knobs and sliders" to encourage people to forge really interesting and compelling social identities in the game.

Picking a Race, Joining a Guild

Providing multi-layered built-in social groups such as clans or races, as well as guilds, is another way to allow people to try on alternate traits at a broader level than personal appearance and characteristics. It also provides ready-made team-building support in the game world. Although the races in games are usually not directly correlated to real-world groups, of course this brings up issues and challenges (as well as opportunities) related to everyday experiences and understanding of race—there's a helpful introduction to this topic in the book *Race in Cyberspace* [Kolko00]. Researchers who study social interaction in games confirm that these kinds of social groupings provide important points of entry and ongoing value in play [Taylor06].

PLAYERS ARE DIFFERENT

When designing for social play, it is important to keep in mind that the player community is probably not made up of identical hardcore players of the same age and expertise, but more likely, of a range of people with widely varying qualities. Part of designing for social interaction is taking this into account.

When designers are aiming at a heterogeneous group of players, with different interests, aims, and skills, they need to design the game to appeal to this range. They can even use this to establish a niche social gaming market for the game. Two commercial examples are *Go, Diego, Go! Safari Rescue* (High Voltage, 2007) for the Wii, designed from the beginning to appeal to preschoolers, with some special parts of gameplay that parents direct with a second controller [Bryant07], and *LEGO Star Wars* (Traveller's Tales, 2005 onwards), a highly successful series of games known for their family-friendly co-op mode. In the Wii game, the preschooler's level of motor control is taken into account and the motions are very simple; pressing any button leads to the same action. This is not the case for the parts where the parents step in and play. In *LEGO Star Wars*, reviewers on the Amazon website report that the combination of the appeal of the *Star Wars* and LEGO characters, and the approachable difficulty level, make playing co-op mode a great diversion for themselves and their children.

There is also an interesting game created by a research lab entitled *Age Invaders* that is designed for three generations—grandparents, parents, and children [Khoo08]. In this game, based upon *Pac-Man* (Namco/Midway, 1980), the grandparents and grandchildren play together, and the parents can monitor from a remote location if they want and make adjustments. The children must stick to tougher timing and more complex mechanics than the grandparents, to keep things fair. Both groups enjoy the physical activity involved in the game. You'll learn more about difference in player skills in Steps 8 and 9, but it's always worth bearing in mind that no two players have the same competencies, and this is especially true with games that are intended to be played by players from different age groups.

Designers may also want to consider the various types of player personalities and how they may impact play. I touched a bit on performance and how some people really enjoy showing off for others—there are also personality characteristics that people bring to social interaction that will affect how they want to play in a game. Designers may want to consider personality profiling players, and building in types of play that suit multiple types of players within a single game—an idea explored in an interesting fashion in Alessandro Canossa's work on play personas [Canossa08].

THE IMPORTANCE OF TESTING SOCIAL GAMES SOCIALLY

Although it was mentioned earlier, I would like to reiterate the importance of testing designs early and often in a social setting that is as close to the one the development team thinks the game will be in when released as is possible. It is simply impossible to predict how a game will "read" in a group without seeing it unfold, and this will also allow the team to discover and capitalize on unexpected social dynamics that arise in play. It doesn't have to be more trouble for the testing team, and it's possible to include testing among internal team members in early stages to help with this. Such a process can give everyone on the team a good feel for how the game plays in a social context and what needs to be enhanced, fixed, or simply kept true to the end of the development cycle. Companies like Harmonix, which has really succeeded in the social gaming area with multiple hit titles, swear by this method [Kohler07]. Larger commercial game companies have begun doing social testing with players in their labs—for example Microsoft [Amaya08]. It can be done. Developers, please make social testing a part of your team culture!

CONCLUSION

Over half of all gameplay occurs in social situations—designers ignore them at their peril, even if they think they are designing a single-player game. I hope this step has convinced you of the importance of designing for social play, and given some concrete steps to take to ensure that a game has strong social appeal.

3

UNDERSTAND PATTERNS OF PLAY

by Chris Bateman

Having learned about emotions, player experience, and extroverted play, you are now ready to look at the patterns that occur in games of all kinds (not just videogames). These patterns of play were first identified by the eclectic French intellectual Roger Caillois in the 1950s, but thanks to advances in modern biology we can now relate them to mechanisms in the human nervous system. The third step towards making better videogames is understanding how your brain responds to these patterns of play, so you can see how other players might react to your games.

ROGER CAILLOIS

In his 1958 book *Les Jeux et Les Hommes* (usually translated as Man, Play and Games), the noted sociologist and intellectual Roger Caillois introduced a terminology for considering patterns in games [Caillois58]. He used the term *game* in a very wide manner, applying it to all play activities, partly as a consequence of his native language, French, where the term "jeux" and "jouer" express the concepts of both *play* and *game* in English.

Caillois' interest in games was sociological: the second half of *Les Jeux et Les Hommes* is an account of how societies relate to the patterns of play he identified, and is fascinating reading. However, the principle value of Caillois' work for modern game design is that his framework for considering games provides us a unique perspective for examining play.

The term "patterns of play" was not used by Caillois, but I have coined it to provide a means to refer to his system. Caillois was keen to observe that it is not meant as a taxonomy, which is to say, he did not intend that his descriptions would cover all kinds of play—he was simply trying to provide cross-cultural descriptions of play that picked out the common elements.

At the center of Caillois' system are four distinct patterns of play, which I will describe in this step. Caillois' choice of terms can be a little off-putting at first, because he chose words from various different languages in the hope of getting as close to the concept he was trying to define as possible. However, each of the terms has a simple translation that will help you get to grips with the basic patterns of play. The four patterns are:

- **Games of challenge**, which Caillois calls *agon* after the Greek word for a contest.
- **Games of vertigo**, which Caillois calls *ilinx* after the Greek word for a whirlpool (which is also the root of the Greek word for vertigo).
- **Games of chance**, which Caillois calls *alea*, after the Latin word for dice.
- **Games of imagination**, which Caillois calls *mimicry*, to stress the link with biological mimicry, such as when a creature mimics another's appearance.

Additionally, Caillois suggests that games can be considered to lie at various points on an axis between free creativity and rule-bound complexity, and coined two terms to refer to these poles. Thus, play can be seen to vary between the following two extremes:

- **Unstructured play**, which Caillois calls *paidia*, because its root is the word for child.
- **Structured play**, which Caillois calls *ludus*, after the Latin word for a game.

In the rest of this step I will discuss how Caillois describes these patterns, before looking at how those patterns relate to modern games—and how these can be linked to mechanisms in the brain and nervous system to explain why there are discernable patterns of play. Before I can talk about the biological side of the patterns of play, however, I should introduce a few major parts of the brain that have key roles in play.

The Brain

One way of looking at the patterns that emerge in play is to consider the mechanisms in the nervous system that relate to those patterns. This is not a full explanation of play—the player experience is arguably more important, and certainly more varied, than the biological explanation—but it is helpful to understand how the brain and so forth responds to play situations in order to see why there are recognizable patterns to be found.

Fortunately, I only need to give you a very brief tour of the brain to prepare you. Figure 3.1 shows the major regions of the brain.

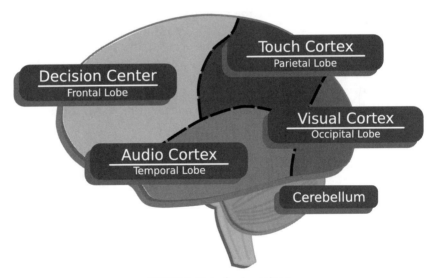

FIGURE 3.1 Major brain regions.

The main part of the brain—the "grey matter" we are all familiar with seeing—is the cortex. This is conventionally divided into four key regions, known as lobes:

- The *frontal lobe* is associated with cognitive function and decision making, especially a region known as the *orbito-frontal cortex*. I call the orbito-frontal cortex the *decision center* of the brain, as this is easier to remember than its technical name.

- The *parietal lobe* is associated with spatial sense, navigation, and the sense of touch. I call this the *touch center*.
- The *temporal lobes*, at the sides and below the frontal lobe, are associated with audio sense (speech and hearing), hence I call these the *audio center*.
- Finally, the *occipital lobe*, near the midline and beneath the parietal lobe, is where the processing of visual sensory information takes place, so I call this the *visual center*.

A final region of note is the *cerebellum*, which is situated beneath the occipital lobe and is involved in coordinating motor control, and in motor learning. Dr. W. T. Thach conducted research on the parts of the brain activated when playing *Tetris* (Alexey Pajitnov, 1985) and discovered that the cerebellum was heavily activated while learning the control skills involved, but became less active once these skills had been acquired [Thach96].

The Limbic System

However, the main part of the brain you need to be aware of is the limbic system, which lies deep inside the brain structure, sitting atop the spinal cord. It is sometimes called "the reptile brain," because it is assumed to have evolved at a time when reptiles were the most advanced form of life on the planet, although recent research places it even further back in time [Bruce95]. Suffice it to say, this was one of the first parts of your brain to grow as your embryo developed, which suggests it is a very ancient brain structure.

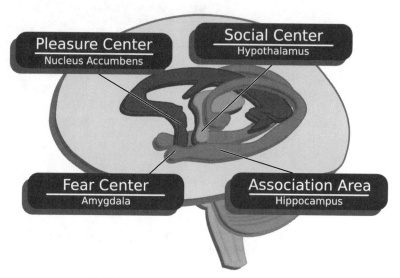

FIGURE 3.2 Key elements of the limbic system.

The limbic system is largely responsible for releasing chemicals (neurotransmitters) that correlate with our emotional experiences. Figure 3.2 shows the key elements of the limbic system, which have the following main functions:

- The *nucleus accumbens* is associated with the formation of habits (and thus behaviors). It is sometimes called the *pleasure center*, and I will use this term for simplicity.
- The *amygdala* is associated with emotional memory, and in particular with fear. I call it the *fear center*.
- The *hippocampus* seems to have a major role in coordinating associative memory, and the part of the brain it connects with is sometimes referred to as the *association area*, which serves as a slightly simpler name.
- Finally, the *hypothalamus* regulates a number of bodily functions (such as appetite), but the primary interest here is its role in affecting anger and trust. Although it is slightly misleading, I call it the *social center*.

Before moving on, I want to comment on the differences between brain regions from one person to the next. In 2000, researchers at University College London discovered that London taxi drivers—who have to acquire a considerable volume of spatial knowledge of the city streets (known as "the Knowledge")—have larger posterior hippocampi than other people [Maguire00]. This fascinating research shows that the parts of your brain that you use regularly may get bigger! In this way, every person's brain is different—not just because of background genetic variations, but as a result of what you have learned to do, and which skills you have acquired.

Having now examined some key areas of the brain that are affected by play, you are ready to explore the patterns of play further.

STRUCTURED AND UNSTRUCTURED PLAY

Caillois terms unstructured play *paidia*, and structured play *ludus*, defining them as follows:

> *[Games can] be placed on a continuum between two opposite poles. At one extreme an almost indivisible principle, common to diversion, turbulence, free improvisation, and carefree gaiety is dominant. It manifests a kind of uncontrollable fantasy that can be designated by the term paidia. At the opposite extreme, this frolicsome and impulsive exuberance is almost entirely absorbed or disciplined by a complimentary, and in some respects inverse, tendency to its anarchic and capricious nature... I call this second component ludus.*

He refers to *ludus* as "a taste for gratuitous difficulty" and this corresponds to some degree with what we usually mean by gameplay, whereas *paidia* can be seen as the absence of those formal game rules that we would consider to be game mechanics. In *21st Century Game Design* the term *toyplay* was coined to describe more or less what Caillois connotes with *paidia*, and I shall use this term here on the assumption that it will be slightly easier to understand [Bateman2005].

Toyplay

When people are engaged in *toyplay*, they play without rules and without limits. Toyplay is amusing, creative and chaotic, but it is also short lived, because when the natural play of a toy becomes formalized, it becomes a game. Children find toyplay in every corner of their lives, while adults may struggle to ever make it back to a place where they will permit themselves the freedom to play. But if we can construct games that harness toyplay, we might become able to make games for a wider audience than we ever thought possible.

I frequently accuse games designers (myself included) of being remiss in overlooking certain ways that people play, and toyplay is something game designers are prone to overlook entirely. This is not surprising: the game designer's craft is generally about producing the framework of play, which is to say the rules and abstractions that define the game world and its gameplay. It's not surprising given this situation that most game designers are more focused on the structured aspects of game design and less interested in toyplay. Yet toyplay is vitally important to modern videogames—when Will Wright notes that *Sim City* (Maxis, 1989) is essentially a toy, he underlines this point, and it is even more relevant to his most successful title, *The Sims* (Maxis, 2000), which has sold some 16 million copies, making it the most successful PC game in history.

One can see toyplay most clearly when a group of children enter a playground or a garden. It begins with exploration, the examination of everything that the play space contains. The components of the play space can include physical objects (a ball, a stick, a daisy), physical spaces (an open field, a long path), logical spaces (the lines drawn out for a sporting match, for instance) and other people (typically a child's peer group). Different children will approach these potential toys in different ways.

In some respects, this moment is the purest expression of toyplay, because the instant a course of action evolves, structured play begins to express itself. Indeed, play is arguably always on a journey from toyplay to gameplay (from paidia to ludus in Caillois' terms), although it would be wrong to think that it cannot also travel back towards toyplay again—

as when a group discards a tedious board game rule because it doesn't suit the way they want to play.

What may happen in our hypothetical playground? A child picks up the stick. It has heft and weight. He may begin to hit things with it, or may see it as a sword and begin to act out a little fantasy. A daisy may invite a child to pull off its petals, one by one—perhaps chanting "he loves me, he loves me not" or some similar rhyme. A child in an open field may be filled with a spontaneous desire to run (especially downhill!), which might evolve into a form of competition if other children decide to join in with her running, or they may use the space to spin around rapidly. Lines on the ground may invite a child to try and walk and balance along them, or suggest simple games.

Some activities will prove more fun than others. Hitting objects with a stick is more fun if everyone around you is laughing about it, for instance. The infinite possibilities of toyplay become mediated by the pragmatics of interaction. If the same group regularly returns to the same playground, patterns of play will develop. Expressions of game rules will gradually mediate the initial anarchy. Indeed, if the children have already learned simple games, they may turn straight to these structured patterns (depending, of course, on their personality, mood, and inclinations).

Pure toyplay, then, is short lived—but the impulse for unstructured play can exert itself in all manner of situations, even when formal rules are already in place. Whenever you are given a set of rules for play, it can be fun to explore what happens when those rules are bent, overlooked, or replaced, although the group must be willing. The more that a form of play is repeated, the more likely it is to become more formally expressed— this is the journey from toyplay towards gameplay—but toyplay can re-exert itself as a temporary escape from the rules at any time.

The journey from toyplay to gameplay arguably culminates in sports, which are constrained by rules so formalized that there are professionals hired to enforce them (referees). Sports are so rigidly defined that they contain rituals such as anthem singing, coin tossing, employment drafts, and so forth, which have insinuated themselves into their social structure.

The urge towards toyplay may diminish as a human ages, but it still exists. It is noticeable that those with a technical bent indulge in a kind of toyplay when they get a new gadget. Although a small few will read manuals first, many will launch themselves into experimentation: what does this do? I wonder what happens if I do this? Is there a way I can do this? This is a form of toyplay, at least until the structure of the device's interface or controls become apparent—until the user learns to play the gadget's game.

If you take the time to observe people interacting with things for the first time, you will have opportunities to see toyplay in everyday life. Sometimes the "game" is not fun, people become frustrated (especially with elaborate productivity tools), and all sense of playfulness is lost. But other times—playing with an iPhone for the first time, for instance, or perhaps driving a new car—you can see something of the child's inventive play in everyday life.

Toyplay in Videogames

When players sit down at a videogame for the first time, they will engage in exploratory toyplay, feeling out what the game does—but again, only if they feel safe to experiment. This safety can come from *game literacy* (experience with games), or from a friend or relative standing by to provide advice and support, or just from personal self confidence. Any budding game designer should spend the time to see people with very little videogame experience tackle a game for the first time. When players begin to play, they commence with the toyplay that evolves naturally from experimentation.

At the Game Developers Conference in 2005, Ramon Romero of Microsoft's Games User Research showed footage of various random people playing games for the first time [Romero05]. I was particularly touched by the middleaged man who drove around in *Midtown Madness* (Angel Studios, 1999) as if he were playing a driving simulator. "This is a great game," he said, as he stopped at a red light and waited for it to change. He had not interpreted the game world as a place exclusively for competitive racing, but had instead automatically tended towards toyplay, *and was having fun playing this way*! That the game was expecting him to race had not even occurred to him.

In the hypothetical playground, the children develop from pure toyplay to some basic game mechanics in an organic fashion. In a game world, the transition from toyplay to gameplay is mediated by the game design. The players find their avatar in an area with certain elements. They experiment. If they are highly game literate, they may immediately know what to do, because most games are highly derivative of one another, but as a general case this is unusual.

Suppose the players come across a ball as the first thing they find in the game world. They want to pick it up and throw it. But how do they do this? They experiment. They push buttons at random and see what happens. If the game is effective at supporting toyplay, fun things will happen—they may or may not end up throwing the ball, depending upon the design of the game. They might find that one button causes the ball to roll along the ground, and this might be entertaining in itself. If throwing the ball is an easy action to deduce, they will eventually do it. If not, they may conclude that it cannot be done. Gradually, players learn the game rules: game mechanics are enforced upon them (if throwing the ball is essential to progress, players may have to be taught to throw it).

It follows, therefore, that to support toyplay, game designers need to encourage and allow for the player's capacity to experiment freely, and assist the player to express the most obvious implied actions for each game element. This is an unusual situation—a videogame requires formal rules or procedures to exist, but if you want the players to play freely, you need to construct these rules in a form that supports self-expression (or the illusion of self-expression, created by anticipating the most likely free choices and implementing them). There are two principle ways I believe this can be achieved: simplicity and exhaustive attention to detail.

Simplicity

If the game is simple enough in its conception that free play is automatically supported, toyplay naturally results. This arguably happens with *Katamari Damacy* (Namco, 2004): there is nothing especially complex to learn, so players have the freedom to play (at least until the goal-orientation of the game's structure imposes). *LEGO Star Wars* (Giant/Traveller's Tales, 2005) similarly benefits from its simplicity (it had to be simple if a parent and child were to play together, because most parents are rubbish at videogames). The players do not actually have the freedom to do whatever they want, but rather the natural tendencies suggested by the game elements encourages players to act in a manner consistent with the intended play. Both games are considerably more expressive of the toyplay spirit than we have come to expect from the current videogames industry.

Attention to Detail

Alternatively, the makers of the game can invest the time and money to add additional play elements wherever they naturally occur. Part of the success of the recent *Grand Theft Auto* games (DMA Design/Rockstar North, 2001 onwards) is that attention has been paid to supporting the natural toyplay of the environment. A taxi suggests the play of being a taxi driver—so this behavior is added via formal rules (taxi missions). Bystanders and weapons suggest murderous carnage—and behavior is added to the game to support this form of toyplay (only suitable in a game!). Sadly, a great deal has been added with excessive emphasis on challenge and fiero, so the appeal still has its limits, but nonetheless, the playground world that the team builds with each successive *GTA* iteration supports more and more toyplay—more and more free play. This approach is devastatingly expensive, however.

There is nothing wrong with making videogames with complex mechanics, and these kinds of games will always have an audience, but if we truly wish to aspire to the mass market audience that AAA game budgets imply, we need to spend more design and implementation time focusing on the issues of minimizing how much the player must learn and maximizing how much the player can simply play. This involves simplifying the interface as much as is humanly possible and (perhaps) the addition of intelligently organized context-sensitive elements. It may also involve adding behavior to the game elements to support any obviously implied play actions—thus transforming the game world into a play world. This latter process is not principally a game design problem, but a game tweaking problem, ideally requiring observation of new players with the game (what is often called *blind testing*).

The videogames industry has an urgent need to recognize the sheer number of people who lack any kind of game literacy, for whom picking up a new game is not fun but instead is a baffling ordeal. I do not believe that videogames can be enjoyed solely by a certain type of person—I believe it is possible to make videogames for any and all people. But to do so, game designers need to learn new skills. They need to learn how to support spontaneous play, to discover how to construct game worlds as play worlds, and to present the game so that the player's transition into game mechanics can be a journey from toyplay, and not merely the process of patiently learning the rules of the game.

Toyplay, or *paidia* in Caillois' terminology, is the anarchic nebula from which all play originates. This unstructured play is fun (for most players, at least)—it is arguably the very definition of fun—but it is a short lived kind of fun. It is exuberant amusement, but it eventually gives way to structured play and to other kinds of enjoyment.

RULES

As we move away from toyplay and into gameplay (from paidia to ludus in Caillois' terms) the essential difference is the addition of rules. These rules can take many forms, but each serves to provide a constraint of some kind—rules about where you can go and how you can move, rules about what actions you can take, rules about how you gain rewards, and rules concerning what benefits you acquire for gaining those rewards. A detailed discussion concerning the nature of the rules that can be applied in the design of a game is far beyond the scope of this step, but two specific points are worth considering.

- The rules of the game provide structure to the play of that game—whereas in the playground the child can go anywhere and do anything without restriction, in a game situation this is rarely the case. Consider, for instance, the typical convention that the player must defeat a boss in order to proceed. This rule structures the play by creating a choke-point: you must rise to this challenge if you want to continue.

- The more rules the game features the more complex the game will be. In this regard, you can imagine a continuum of games from the incredibly simple, such as *Tic Tac Toe*, to the incredibly complex, such as the *Sid Meier's Civilization* series (MPS Labs, Fireaxis et al, 1991 onwards). This continuum is effectively the same as the one proposed by Caillois—you could say that *Civilization* expresses ludus more strongly than *Tic Tac Toe*.

Game designers are very focused on how to construct the rules of a game, and most have very different ideas about the best practices in doing so, but one aspect of the rules more than any other affects the nature of the player's experience: the reward structure. To understand this, it is useful to look at what goes on in players' brains when they attain a reward of any kind—be it a collectible, a power up, a critical victory required to progress, or simply the unlocking of a new cut scene.

Dopamine

I introduced the nucleus accumbens previously as the *pleasure center* of the brain, and this rather simplistic label is quite apposite: this region is strongly associated with generating pleasurable sensation. In the 1950s, James Olds and Peter Milner conducted a fairly distasteful experiment involving rats. The rats had electrodes implanted into their brains wired up to an area including their nucleus accumbens, and were placed in "Skinner boxes" which allowed them to press a lever to receive an electrical impulse. The rats preferred to press this lever—with its associated jolt to their nucleus accumbens—than to eat or drink, and in many cases died as a result [Olds54].

The pleasure center produces a neurotransmitter known as *dopamine*, which recent research has tied to the formation of habits [Faure05] and addictive behavior [Everitt01]. In essence, whenever a person experiences a reward of any kind—whether a natural biological reward, such as food or sex, or a rewarding experience, such as winning a bet or purchasing a desired object, dopamine is released. When a reward is experienced as being greater than expected, a greater amount of dopamine is released, increasing the motivation towards pursuing that reward again. This mechanism is believed to be the principle factor in the addictive behavior generated by drugs such as cocaine, which block the reuptake of dopamine and work on neurons that form part of the dopamine mechanism [Arias07].

It will not come as any great surprise that dopamine has been tied to videogames. A group of researchers at Imperial College London published a paper in 1998 linking the release of dopamine with goal-oriented behavior in videogames. The game in question was quite basic and involved moving a tank across a battlefield by using a joystick, but even with such a simple game the results were clear: rewards in games trigger a significant release of dopamine [Koepp98].

This research caused editor of *PC Magazine*, Dan Costa, to comment [Costa07]:

> *Video games are not like cocaine, your brain thinks they are cocaine. And if you doubt that, try to take the controller out of [my son's] hands before he reaches a save point.*

This is not the whole story concerning dopamine, behavior, and videogames (I will return to this point later), but it does underline the point that games are "addictive" precisely because they make use of the structures and mechanisms in the brain that serve a role in establishing new behaviors, and particularly reward-seeking behaviors.

Reward Structures

Even before dopamine had been singled out for its role in forming habits, psychologists had conducted considerable research into how reward structures mediate behavior in mammals (and presumably other animals as well). The trailblazer in this field was the psychologist B. F. Skinner, who as early as the 1930s was uncovering patterns in animal behavior and pioneering rate of response (number of responses per minute, for instance) as a tangible measure that could be used to generate scientific data in what had mostly been discussed in general terms previously [Skinner38]. This later led to the development of the idea of a *schedule of reinforcement* which is the formal, psychological version of reward structures in games [Ferster57].

What do I mean by a reward in the context of videogames? The answer to this depends on the player in question. For instance, players with a love of challenge experience a reward, namely fiero, when they defeat a difficult boss. Players for whom challenge is of lesser interest might experience relief when they defeat the same boss—still a reward, but considerably less motivating. Although fiero is probably a heady cocktail of different hormones at the neurobiological level, it seems very likely that dopamine is among the key chemicals released in these kinds of situations, which helps explain why players who are challenge-oriented find videogames so addictive.

There is almost no limit to what might be considered a reward in a videogame, but some obvious examples are gaining advantages within the game mechanics such as extra damage, narrative rewards such as cut scenes and the satisfaction of helping an NPC in need, new "toys" to play with (such as a new type of vehicle, or a new tool), access to new locations, the satisfaction of completing a collection of some kind (such as finding all the collectibles in a platform game), or the acquisition of game currency (allowing the players to purchase rewards from a shop— a second layer of reward).

Although I had studied Skinner's work at university, I first encountered the idea of schedules of reinforcement in the context of videogame design at GDC 2004, where John Hopson delivered a thorough presentation on the subject [Hopson04]. One of the key points to consider is the nature of the schedule of reinforcement behind the reward structure, which can be categorized as to whether they are based on a number of actions (*ratio schedules*) or on the passage of time (*interval schedules*). These can be further divided according to whether the schedules have a fixed pattern or a variable pattern.

In general, ratio schedules produce high rates of activity—"the more you do, the more you get." In a *fixed ratio schedule*, rewards are provided after a set number of actions. These are easy for players to understand ("collect 100 coins"), but after the reward is achieved, there is a natural pause, because the player may naturally think twice about attempting the same sequence of actions a second time in a row. Experience points in computer RPGs are a good example—although the gearing of experience systems is usually exponential, the intent is that the player is constantly moving up to tougher foes, thus keeping a constant ratio of kills to level. After gaining the level, the player may stop playing for a while.

In a *variable ratio schedule*, rewards are provided after a random number of actions—this is how a slot machine works. You keep putting in coins, because at some point it will pay out. These also produce a high rate of activity and interest, but they tend to block exploration since players will stick with the reward schedule until it is exhausted, or until they burn out on it.

Conversely, an interval schedule provides rewards after an amount of time. In a *fixed interval schedule*, the time interval is constant, which provides good control over the rate of reward, and comes with the same post-reward pause as a fixed ratio schedule. An example is the new items available in the shop each day in Animal Crossing (Nintendo EAD, 2001)—players come back on future days to see what's new, and the time interval (one day) is constant.

When the duration between rewards varies, a steady rate of activity with no pauses is generated—this is a *variable interval schedule*. However, the experience is considerably less intense than the variable ratio schedule because players quickly learn that their actions are independent of the reward. This kind of structure is good for encouraging a player to come back to certain places in a game, for instance, by having a reward appear in certain places "at random".

Both types of variable schedule produce a constant level of activity because "everything has a chance of reward"—something that can be seen, for instance, in the cutting of grass for rupees in the *Legend of Zelda* games (Nintendo, 1986 onwards). When the high rate of activity from a ratio schedule combines with the constant activity of a variable schedule (variable ratio schedule), the result is highly compulsive (something Vegas leverages in its slot machines)—but the player will eventually burn out.

In summary:

- Ratio schedules produce high levels of activity ("the more you do, the more you get")
- Variable schedules produce constant levels of activity ("everything has a chance of reward")
- Interval schedules produce paced behaviors ("your next reward will come later")
- Fixed schedules create a pause after reward ("you must do it all over again for your next reward")

The pause after a fixed schedule need not be seen as a negative. For example, to keep the player's interest in a computer RPG, the "pause" after gaining a level frees the player from the treadmill of leveling up to go and carry out other housekeeping activities in the game, offering a refreshing change of pace. Conversely, if players leveled up with a variable ratio schedule—they have a percentage chance of leveling up after killing a creature, for instance—they could rapidly get burned out.

A simple game can use a reward structure featuring just one kind of schedule, for instance, a lottery is based on a variable ratio schedule: you will be rewarded eventually if you keep buying tickets.

Most videogames have multiple schedules forming their reward structure: consider *Pac-Man* (Namco/Midway, 1980), which is based primarily on a fixed ratio schedule, namely collecting all the dots to clear a level. However, there are two other kinds of reinforcement schedule in this game—the interval schedule associated with the appearance of fruit (a reward in the form of intermittently appearing opportunities for bonus points), and the additional fixed ratio schedule associated with the power pills (the reward of turning the enemies into bonus points—satisfying for many different reasons).

Certain computer RPGs can have absurd numbers of reinforcement schedules imbedded within their design. *Disgaea: Hour of Darkness* (Nippon Ichi, 2003), for instance, has dozens of different mechanisms for powering up characters, including traditional character leveling up, the leveling up of the individual abilities of those characters, powering up items, acquiring specialists, capturing monsters to add to your party, gaining additional bonuses from the special mini-game (the Dark Assembly), and reincarnating characters in order to gain compound benefits. The game is too complex for many players, but those who enjoy complicated games find themselves easily addicted to the Nippon Ichi games.

Stopping Play

All of this comes to a head in how and why the player stops playing. The pauses associated with fixed schedules allow and encourage quitting. Players are constantly evaluating the very next thing they can do in a game, and if their level of interest drops below the draw for another activity, they will stop. If this happens through burnout, they may not go back—the gamble with variable ratio schedules like slot machines—but if they stopped because of the pause after achieving a sufficiently large reward in a fixed schedule, they are much more likely to come back. In this regard, one must be careful that the rewards themselves maintain at the very least a constant level of reward, or in the ideal case, an escalating degree of reward.

Of course, the best case is that just playing the game is inherently enjoyable to the player—that the core play is its own reward, which presumably happens when the core play allows the player to reach a state of *flow* [Csikzentmihalyi90]. Still, even when this is the case, players are likely to stop playing when they "have seen everything". This is when multiplayer elements can extend the play window of a game, of course, by providing new rewards—provided players are motivated by competition.

If one creates a game which is inherently fun for the player, an exponentially structured fixed ratio schedule can be sufficient framework to keep playing. This is most commonly seen in the exponential experience systems of a typical computer RPG, but can also be seen in other games, such as the monuments in *The New Tetris* (H_2O Entertainment, 1999). In this game, players are told that the lines they clear are contributing to building "Seven Wonders," and are rewarded after the required number of lines have been cleared with a short cut scene about the completed monument. Despite being wholly cosmetic, this structure remains quite effective as a high-level reward structure. Interval schedules lack the connection with player action, and variable schedules work only until the rewards are exhausted, but diehard players of *The New Tetris* routinely reset the monuments and start over again, with little loss of interest. Perhaps it is the exponential gearing that drives the appeal, pulling the players forward by gradually increasing the jump to the next reward, perhaps it is simply that the core activity is entertaining and the monuments provide a framework for pursuing that enjoyment.

I said earlier that the reward structure might be the most important aspect of the rules of a game in terms of determining the player's experience. This is because the reward structure determines whether the player stops playing, or comes back to the game again and again. Even a thoroughly enjoyable game activity loses the player's interest if it cannot provide adequate rewards (and even repetition of the same rewards may suffice if the core play is sufficiently compulsive, as *Tetris* shows).

This also serves as an explanation for why games with what may appear to be poorly balanced game mechanics can still entertain players, especially if they are at least easy to learn—provided a game provides rewards to a reliable schedule, it will keep the player's attention, at least until the game runs out of rewards, or repetition of the same rewards ceases to engage the player. High-quality game mechanics can aid a game by eliminating rough edges and inconsistencies, and certain players are actively drawn to elegant game mechanics, but it is the delivery of rewards, and not the quality of the game mechanics, which maintains a player's interest.

Competition (*Agon*)

Having looked at the axis of complexity that varies from toyplay to gameplay, that is, from *paidia* to *ludus* in Caillois' terms, you are ready to examine the first of Caillois' patterns of play—the pattern of competition and challenge he refers to as *agon*, after the Greek word for a contest.

Caillois described agon as follows:

A whole group of games would seem to be competitive, that is to say, like a combat in which equality of chances is artificially created, in order that the adversaries should confront each other under ideal conditions, susceptible of giving precise and incontestable value to the winner's triumph. It is therefore always a question of rivalry which hinges on a single quality (speed, endurance, strength, memory, skill, ingenuity, etc.), exercised, within defined limits and without outside assistance, in such a way that the winner appears to be better than the loser in a certain category of exploits.

Competition has been made so central to the videogames industry that many people consider "game" to be almost synonymous with the notion of competitive play. We play to win, the presumption states, and this indeed describes the way a great many of our modern videogames have been constructed. But as I will show later, there are other patterns of play that can be just as compelling.

Competitive Videogames

Videogames allow players to engage in games of competition against virtual opponents, and this seems to evoke many of the same kinds of behavior as facing a living opponent. Facing the game, players first size up their capacity to compete. People who cannot throw do not, for instance, enjoy participating in field events based around throwing. Similarly, people who cannot operate a first person shooter (a style of game with a particularly codified form) do not play FPS games in a competitive style. But those who have capabilities in a particular type of game frequently then enter the state of wishing to test themselves against a degree of challenge. This could be against other opponents—which is quite obviously a fit to what Caillois means by agon—or it could be against pre-set challenges, such as the main gameplay of a single player game.

Competitive play occurs in certain distinct forms that are worth identifying briefly, if only to provide a wider foundation. Firstly, there are games of *one-versus-one* competition, such as a fighting game. Such games are the most intensely competitive form, and most recognizably fit Caillois' description of agon. Then, there are *one-versus-many* games, such as the single player FPS, which (squad variants not withstanding) place a lone player in contest against many opponents. Still, the underlying assumption is that the challenge has been balanced fairly (although pragmatically, few games are so well tweaked for this to emerge). Finally, *many-versus-many* games, such as strategy games with whole armies fighting, are akin to team-based sports offering competition between equally matched sides. These distinctions, while notable, do not fundamentally alter the nature of competitive play, although they may alter the appeal.

The asymmetric case of the one-versus-many scenario is something that most people are highly familiar with in videogames, but that might have seemed strange to Caillois. Even in the case of one-versus-one and many-versus-many you can see asymmetry in games: playing a fighting game in single player mode, it is not possible for the computer opponents to be a balanced challenge for all players. Instead, the game presents a variable degree of challenge; the player climbs the curve of difficulty inside the game. Similarly, a strategy game often has scenarios of increasing difficulty. Instead of presenting a perfectly balanced challenge, the game starts easily (in principle, at least—few games balance themselves to be sufficiently easy for all comers), and then increases the degree of challenge until players encounter the biting point where they know they will have to perform at the best of their abilities to achieve victory. This is when Caillois' conception of agon in terms of testing oneself really takes hold: prior to this point, one might imagine the players' actions have merely been training. There is a parallel in sport: Olympic athletes must still rise through many qualifying rounds against opponents of differing capabilities until they find they are competing against competitors of their own caliber.

These rising degrees of challenge facing players are intended, arguably, to ensure that at some point players will face a challenge worthy of their abilities. There is a clear relationship between the emotion of triumph over adversity, fiero, and competitive play. Fiero, after all, is associated with the physical gesture of holding arms aloft in victory, which is something you can readily observe whenever an athlete wins an event, a bowler gets a strike, a sports fan's team scores, or a videogame player beats a difficult boss. This emotion is intimately connected to competitive play.

Hard Competition

When competition is tough enough for the player to earn the emotional reward of fiero, we are in the territory of Nicole Lazzaro's Hard Fun [Lazzaro04c], which was discussed in Step 1. I consider this to represent a subset of all the games of competition, and call this *hard agon* (in a cross between Caillois' and Lazzaro's terms) or *hard competition*. The focus in this pattern of play is giving the player sufficient challenge such that when victory is eventually achieved, it will come with the reward of fiero. Players who are especially focused on this kind of play fit the template of the Conqueror in the DGD1 player model [Bateman04], [Bateman05].

Games of hard competition seem most popular with gamer hobbyists (that is, hardcore gamers), although this is not to suggest that casual players don't also enjoy this style of play (possibly younger males in particular, although this is far from proven). Fiero can be a tremendously rewarding emotion, and therefore can be a tremendously *addictive* emotion. Why else would certain players pit themselves against challenges of such depth of adversity that they must endure nearly constant frustration as they pursue with dogged determination the repetitious play intrinsic in most games of this kind? When victory is achieved, the fiero "pays for" all the pain experienced on the way. Indeed, the greater the depths of pain endured, the larger the fiero for some players. For others, and especially for more mature players, the residue of frustration reduces the fiero to less engaging relief.

Games of hard competition *dare* players to beat them. Some are so punishing in the demands they ask of their players, that they practically reach the boundaries of becoming an ordeal. But, provided the fiero payoff is there, ultimately, it becomes worthwhile—as long as players have the dedication (or obsessive-compulsive tendencies) to overcome the struggle, they will be suitably rewarded. This is a drama that we are very familiar with—the *Rocky* films, for instance, made millions out of fiero fantasy.

I argue that many players often do not notice the (debatably) ramshackle design of many games because when a game is offering hard competition, shoddy game design (bad control mechanisms, poor mechanics, and so on) are just friction adding to the frustrations that are endured on the path to victory. This places a much greater burden on games that do not use competition and challenge as part of their core play to have superior game design, delivering a smoother play to their audience.

All this connects with the idea that games of hard competition are not just about fiero—although this is effectively the reason why players who fit the Conqueror archetype prefer this kind of play—but also about *anger*. The frustration that often precedes the emotional reward gained in final victory is an expression of anger. I will return to this point later.

Easy Competition

At the opposite extreme of the trials of hard competition are those games that offer trivial victory over opponents. Some of these games are diluting the competitive play with random factors (which I will talk about later in this step). Consider, for example, party game franchises like *Mario Party* (Hudson Soft, 1999 onwards) or *Bishi Bashi* (Konami Sapporo, 1996 onwards). These are ostensibly games of competition—players are certainly thrown into competition—but are really a heady mix of competition and chance. It is not the chance to prove superiority versus one's foes in these games that provides all the fun, but the random chaos of the mini-games. More commonly, players are invited to enjoy being strong relative to their opponents—practically the opposite of the fiero-related enjoyment delivered by hard competition. This can be seen in games such as *Rampage* (Bally Midway, 1986) and to a certain extent *Gauntlet* (Atari, 1985), which give the players control of avatars who must overcome vast hordes of (weaker) opponents.

These games can be considered *easy agon*, that is, games of *easy competition*. Some players may consider there to be little of interest in play when it has been made so unchallenging (perhaps reflecting the importance of fiero to such a person), but personally I find nothing problematic in exploring such child-like escapism against virtual opponents. Such play is amusing and entertaining, and far more suitable for stress release than the tension of fiero. It is notable that many of the games that push in this direction rely on multiple players to add to the fun (drawing on People Fun instead of Hard Fun), but this is not strictly necessary.

A player's experience of a competitive game is determined almost entirely by the strength of the player (determined in part by the player's own abilities, in part by the game parametrics) relative to the strength of the opposition. Games of hard competition are at the very least evenly matched, and more commonly are biased *against* the player, so that the player must work even harder to win, and thus achieves an even greater payoff in fiero. Conversely, games of easy competition begin when the player's strength is weighted higher than the opposition—indeed, these games are arguably at their most fun (and by fun in this case I mean the fun of amusement, not the fun of fiero) when the players are ludicrously overpowered with respect to their opponents. This was surely what made *Rampage* fun to play when it first came to the arcades—players enjoyed the power fantasy of smashing up a city.

It is also worth noting that the vast majority of these games rely on playing with other players. We saw in Step 1 that People Play focuses on amusement, and in Step 2 that playing with other players can enhance one's enjoyment of amusement via the social contagion mechanism, thus this connection is not entirely surprising. It is likely that a study of brain activity while playing such games would involve the social center (hypothalamus) in some manner, but this has yet to be investigated.

Because it is the relative difficulty that determines which space the player is in (hard competition, through the "true agon" of equally matched opponents, and finally to easy competition), games can deliver both kinds of play by simply having a large enough range of difficulties. The *Dynasty Warriors* games (Omega Force, 2000 onwards) demonstrate this facet particularly well. On their higher difficulty settings, they provide hordes of tough troops and even tougher officers that lure the players to overcome the odds stacked against them and earn fiero. On their lowest difficulty settings (and perhaps after some judicious powering up), players can enjoy the feeling of effortlessly cutting down hundreds of enemy troops, and knocking enemy officers about the battlefield like they were stuffed toys. Both can be intoxicatingly entertaining, but in general terms, these two different settings appeal to different players.

The implications for game design are that for games wishing to court a wide audience, there may be much value in beginning by balancing the game for easy competition, or at the very least, for *including* this pattern of play among others. This may be the harder task; it is very easy to conceive of means to make a game harder, but generally difficult to conceive of means to make a given game easier without subtracting game mechanics (and thus changing the nature of the gameplay). However, I suspect that game designers who work on highly competitive games might argue that balancing for hard competition is an equally challenging task, if for no other reason than the audience for games of fiero is extremely demanding and particular in its tastes.

Difficulty Settings

The nebulous notion of game difficulty seems to be important when considering games of competition. I used to believe that it was possible to build self-calibrating games that could adjust to match the level of difficulty desired by the player. However, it is becoming readily apparent that the level of difficulty desired by the player is not something anyone can reliably presuppose. Some players want to be met at about their level of challenge (they desire "true agon"), some want to be met with very little level of challenge (desiring easy competition), and some secretly yearn to have the game beat them into a bloody pulp so that they may later emerge victorious and aglow with fiero (desiring hard competition).

Perhaps it will be necessary for games with dynamic difficulty mechanisms to identify the player's desire with respect to competitive play from the onset. Sorter questions may be the easiest option to implement; something like: "Do you want to: (1) Play for amusement (2) Face a reasonable degree of challenge (3) Triumph against overwhelming odds?" Wrangling the language on such questions so that they can be presented to players without confusion is a difficult task, but I remain confident that sorter questions are a viable means by which a game might establish the nature of play that the players desire. More elegant solutions to these kinds of problems will emerge the more game developers and researchers pay attention to this issue.

The fact that different players desire to be in a different place with respect to the degree of challenge connects notably with the model of *Flow* [Csikzentmihalyi90], which Nicole Lazzaro explained in Step 1. The Flow Channel, where abilities and challenge are equal, is an area, not a line. Recall that when ability outstrips challenge, boredom results; when challenge outstrips ability, anxiety results. Hard competition therefore lies near the top of the Flow Channel—where players are close to their limits. Easy competition lies near the bottom of the Flow Channel—where the player faces just sufficient challenge to entertain. "True agon" lies in the center of the Flow Channel. Perhaps finding means to chart a player's position in the Flow Channel will allow for an automated game balancing system in the future.

Fiero, Puzzles, and the Brain

Competition with an opponent is not the only way to generate fiero. There is another key way that a player can find this emotional reward, and that is by solving difficult puzzles. Just as with the experience of triumph over adversity that is experienced when a player is victorious in some kind of visceral struggle, players will receive a reward of fiero when they complete a difficult puzzle (when they "beat" the puzzle).

Tellingly, the part of the brain that is active when solving puzzles—the decision center (orbito-frontal cortex)—is very closely tied to the pleasure center (nucleus accumbens) [Rolls00]. This isn't entirely surprising given what I have already discussed in connection with Skinner's work: If behaviors can become habitual, the part of the brain that makes decisions must have a key role, and indeed the decision center is associated with addiction as well [Volkow00]. Dopamine seems to be released in connection with making rewarding decisions.

Recall that when a reward is experienced as being greater than expected, a greater amount of dopamine is released: this may explain the intensity of the fiero response. To experience fiero one must have struggled against great hardships; in these situations failure is expected, so when success is achieved the intrinsic reward is correspondingly stronger (more dopamine is released). This also suggests that games of hard competition may be more addictive than other kinds of games, but this point is tangential.

So the same pattern of emotional response I have described in connection with games of hard competition recurs with games of hard puzzles, for example classic adventures epitomized by the Magnetic Scrolls games such as *The Pawn* (1986) and *The Guild of Thieves* (1987), or the LucasArts games such as the *Monkey Island* franchise (1990 onwards) and *Maniac Mansion: Day of the Tentacle* (1993).

In Step 8 I will explore some of the reasons why these games used to be a core part of the market for videogames, but have been in steady decline since full 3D worlds first appeared. For now, it is sufficient to note that solving hard puzzles is a kind of biological analogue to hard competitive play.

It is also interesting to consider the parallels between both these kinds of Hard Fun and fixed reward schedules—games of agon appear to correspond to fixed schedules. Both create a pause after the reward of victory (or solving the puzzle), after which the players expect their next reward to come when they next win (or solve the next puzzle).

Beyond Competition

Competition, Caillois' agon, is a noble pursuit; the desire to improve one's abilities and to face others in challenges in order to see who will emerge victorious is a motivating force behind all sports and many games. Videogames have expanded the historical remit of games of competition to include a wider array of challenges, beyond the central ground of equally matched opponents, and into asymmetries of ability that manipulate the emotions of their players, either through the addictive challenge of fiero when the challenge is high, or through the trivial escapism of amusement when the challenge is lower.

So endemic is competitive play to the gamer hobbyist culture that we often forget that there are other ways to play (three of which I shall talk about shortly), and indeed the impression of non-gamers is often that this is what the hobby is all about. The illusion that competition is necessary to videogames springs from the importance placed on fiero by challenge-oriented players (those who fit the Conqueror archetype), since the most powerful fiero rewards are achieved in the most demanding of situations.

However, this grossly overlooks the fact that most players in the modern market for videogames are unwilling to strive against impossible odds simply for an ultimate payoff in fiero. Indeed, when placed in the play situation that would normally deliver fiero (defeating a tough boss, for instance), a great many players are more likely to experience mere relief when the goal is achieved. Fiero has been the backbone of the videogames industry up until the dawn of the 21st century, and will probably always provide a sizeable component of its income, but it is not the only way to organize games.

VERTIGO (*ILINX*)

We tend to think of *vertigo* in connection with that unsettling feeling one gets leaning over a tall cliff. Some people have great anxiety about this situation, whereas others find it exhilarating. The same emotions—excitement and fear—lie beneath both experiences, but different individuals respond to identical situations in different ways, because everyone has had a lifetime of unique experiences that prepares them in different ways.

Caillois calls games that evoke vertigo by the name *ilinx*, which is a Greek word meaning whirlpool. These kinds of play activities are associated with the momentary destruction of perception—this can be the vertigo of speed or of spinning, or it can be the intoxicating allure of petty destruction—the pleasure of stomping on a sandcastle, for instance. He described ilinx as follows:

> *Ilinx... includes those [games] which are based on the pursuit of vertigo and which consist of an attempt to momentarily destroy the stability of perception and inflict a kind of voluptuous panic upon an otherwise lucid mind. In all cases, it is a question of surrendering to a kind of spasm, seizure, or shock which destroys reality with sovereign brusqueness. The disturbance that provokes vertigo is commonly sought for its own sake.*

This experience, where players are thrown into experiential disarray by what is happening around them, is quite distinct from the competitive play described by Caillois' agon, yet, as I will discuss shortly, there are strong biological connections between the two patterns.

The Fight-or-Flight Response

The fight-or-flight response is a basic biological stress mechanism found in most vertebrates and many other animals, and first described by Walter Cannon in 1915 [Cannon15]. Cannon observed that animals reacted to threats with an arousal of the sympathetic nervous system, priming the animal either for fighting the threat or fleeing from it. The two responses—fight or flight—are chosen by the animal in question based on its instincts and individual personality. (There is also a third response—freeze—but this is of less interest to examining play.)

The response was later linked to the hormone and neurotransmitter epinephrine (adrenalin), which raises the heart rate and triggers a host of other biological responses that prime an animal to take action when facing a stressful situation. The stress response relating to adrenalin provides the emotional feeling of both *excitement* and *fear*. Psychologically, these feel like different states, but biologically, the physiological response is in essence the same (being driven internally by the same chemical).

The difference between excitement and fear is subtle, and many psychologists have remarked on their similarity (for instance, Nina Bull's study of hypnotically induced fear [Bull51], and Smith and Ellsworth's examination of emotional responses in the 1980s [Smith85]). Indeed, the key distinction is the individual's expectations: when negative outcomes are expected, fear occurs (you might term it anxiety, but it's the same emotion), but when positive outcomes are expected or no conscious expectation exists, excitement occurs. In the case of the choice to flee, fear is the dominant reaction.

In both cases—fight and flight—adrenalin is involved, but in the fight response there is another factor. In the 1950s, a researched named Albert Ax discovered that the physiological states associated with the emotions of fear and anger could be artificially generated by administering injections of particular neurotransmitters. Fear, as I have already discussed, was linked to epinephrine (adrenalin). Anger was linked to a combination of epinephrine and norepinephrine [Ax53]. This anger stimulates the aggression that allows the fight response to win out over the flight response.

The fight-or-flight response is thus tied intimately to the neurotransmitters epinephrine and norepinephrine, both of which are produced in the adrenal glands (which sit above the kidneys in humans). The fear center in the limbic system (that is, the amygdala) appears to play a key role in managing this behavior: it assesses the sensory information that an organism is experiencing to see if there is any cause of fear, and if so triggers the release of epinephrine, thus readying the animal for either fight or flight. This response is entirely subconscious.

The fight mechanism may also involve the social center (that is, the hypothalamus)—presumably this is the part of the limbic system that initiates the release of norepinephrine from the adrenal glands. It may seem strange that the part of the brain involved in trust would also be the part to affect anger, but then, when are we angrier than when our trust has been abused? Whatever the precise mechanisms involved, we can connect anger and the fight response on the basis of the current research.

The two parts of the fight-or-flight response thus correspond to games of competition and games of vertigo respectively. The desire to fight is motivated by anger overcoming fear—this is the emotional pattern of competition which, after all, are generally about conflict and violence. Conversely, the desire to flee (flight) is motivated by fear overcoming curiosity and occurs in the absence of anger. This is the exact emotional pattern associated with games of vertigo—excitement (which is a form of fear) in the absence of anger.

Caillois' ilinx, therefore, are games of stress without anger—games of adrenalin, which need not involve competition or violence. Stress creates excitement (modified fear) and when the stressful situation passes, the player experiences an endorphin rush of one of two kinds: in the case of simple survival through the stressful episode, *relief* (the physiological signs of which are exhalation and muscle relaxation), and in the case of a sense of achievement or victory, fiero (the physiological signs of which are hands suddenly held high, and a possible intense vocal exclamation, such as "Yes!").

Both responses are intrinsically rewarding, which suggests that dopamine is released when they are achieved. On the basis of informal observation, fiero seems to be clearly a stronger and more pleasurable experience than relief, which suggests that a greater quantity of dopamine is released during fiero than during relief. This also reiterates an earlier point: that competitive games may be more addictive than other kinds.

It follows, therefore, that Caillois' agon and ilinx—games of competition and games of vertigo—represent the two sides of the fight-or-flight response when it is activated in the context of play (although Caillois didn't make this connection himself).

Now that I have described the biological underpinnings of ilinx (and agon), you are ready to explore some examples.

Rushgames

I call games that evoke ilinx *rushgames* as this captures the essential element of the experience, namely excitement or fear; play experiences in which the players must maintain concentration and control against a background of stressful events. This nickname naturally draws upon the way people talk about an "adrenalin rush" in the context of exciting and fear-inducing activities. There are many kinds of rushgame, depending upon the source of stress being applied—including high speed, vertigo, situational pressure, instinctive terror, or wanton mischief.

In terms of the emotions concerned, these rushgames embody both Caillois' ilinx and Lazzaro's Serious Fun, which in Step 1 was described as being connected with excitement and relief—the same emotions that relate to games of vertigo. There is a sense in which these two very different descriptions are in essence related, and this can be seen as a result of their common grounding in the fight-and-flight mechanism just described.

Although competitive play is often assumed to be what videogames (and games in general) are about, rushgames may actually be more popular—both *Tetris* and certain *Mario* platform games sold more copies than any obviously competitive videogame yet made. However, this kind of claim can be difficult to enforce as many competitive games evoke excitement, and hence may appear to qualify also as rushgames. However, it is possible to have rushgames that include neither competition nor violence, whereas videogames that fit Caillois' agon contain at least one and often both of these things. There are other distinctions between these patterns of play, which I shall return to shortly.

As the graphical realism of videogames has increased, the potential for supplying the play of ilinx, that is, an experience of vertigo, has similarly expanded. In early videogames, the graphical power was extremely limited, and it is arguably only recently that the games industry has fully begun to explore the powerful effect of vertigo on players. It can be seen most clearly in any games with the illusion of speed, such as high-speed racer franchises like *Need For Speed* (Pioneer Productions et al, 1994 onwards) or *Burnout* (Criterion, 2001 onwards), and also in snowboarding franchises such as *1080 Snowboarding* (Nintendo EAD et al, 1994 onwards) and *SSX* (EA Canada, 2000 onwards). In these games, the sensation of high-speed movement (which is often enhanced by special effects such as "speed haze") serves to heighten the players' enjoyment by artificially inducing a state of vertigo.

Of course, the vertigo I speak of here is not the nausea-inducing kind referred to in medical circles, but rather a vertiginous experience; an experience that evokes excitement or fear. A rollercoaster produces physical vertigo, but a video of a rollercoaster still produces a certain sensation akin to vertigo provided the viewers suspend their disbelief.

Perhaps the clearest indication of this is the power of a car chase when seen on a cinema screen—one can become swept away in the speed of the imagery. Physical vertigo is included in Caillois' category of ilinx, but it can be extended to cover many peripheral situations, and it is these fringe cases that are perhaps most pertinent to videogames.

In order to deliver vertigo, it is necessary first for the game to deliver a convincing simulation of the experience in question—which is to say, that *mimicry* (a pattern I will describe later, and which can be understood as a kind of sensory simulation or illusion) is a requirement for videogames to deliver ilinx. However, as I will also demonstrate later, almost all modern videogames rest in this way upon the delivery of mimicry. It is important to note this connection here, however, as it was not true of agon. A player of Chess or Othello, for instance, can get the full competitive experience with very little in the way of mimicry.

This raises an interesting point, which is the various patterns of play can and do support each other: in fact, Caillois' ilinx can perhaps best be understood in the context of videogames as an experience enhancer. As I will talk about when I describe the many ways in which vertigo can be evoked, there are many ways in which the play can be enhanced by the addition of rules that create tension and excitement.

Vertigo can be seen acting as an experience enhancer in games of competition quite clearly: the satisfaction (fiero) of winning a race in the *F-Zero* games (Nintendo EAD et al, 1990 onwards) is surely enhanced by the mad breakneck speed dash for the finish line—a few seconds of total consciousness-destroying vertigo, followed by victory. Similarly, in the final avalanche levels of *1080 Avalanche* (Nintendo Software Technology, 2003), where the player is asked to escape from a rapidly looming wall of snow, the sense of vertigo achieved is palpable, and makes the eventual victory seem all the more sweet.

Videogames can also draw upon vertigo in a literal sense—using the player's natural fear of falling to create excitement. A prime example of this are the *SuperMario* games (Nintendo, 1987 onwards), which evoke excitement by dizzying the players with the consequences should they miss their next jump, coupled with the additional pressures of compensating for momentum. The high-scroll speed of the *Sonic* games (Sonic Team, 1991) is perhaps even more obviously vertiginous in nature, and combines elements of speed with literal vertigo.

Note, however, that platform games need not necessarily be rushgames. The *Mario* games are inherently more stressful than many of the 3D platform games that occurred during their heyday in the 1990s, for instance—games such as *Spyro the Dragon* (Insomniac, 1998) or *Banjo-Kazooie* (Rare, 1998). This is because many of these kinds of games are using the platform game structure, but are really offering players opportunities for exploring an imaginary world and other more relaxed forms of entertainment (which I shall talk about later).

Destructive Vertigo

Speed and fear of falling represents just a part of the full scope of experiences of vertigo. Returning to Caillois' description of ilinx:

> *In parallel fashion, there is a vertigo of moral order, a transport that suddenly seizes the individual. This vertigo is readily linked to the desire for disorder and destruction, a drive which is normally repressed... In adults, nothing is more revealing of vertigo than the strange excitement that is felt in cutting down the tall prairie flowers with a switch, or in creating an avalanche of the snow on a rooftop, or, better, the intoxication that is experienced in military barracks—for example, in noisily banging garbage cans.*

This aspect, which might be called *destructive ilinx* or *destructive vertigo*, correlates with the reckless abandon that is allowed by a game such as *Grand Theft Auto: San Andreas* (Rockstar North, 2004) and its many relatives. I contend that one of the reasons the *Grand Theft Auto* games have been so successful at tapping into this side of Caillois' ilinx is that they have not been wholly realistic. This can be seen in the shrewd choice of a non-photorealistic art style, and also by the presence of "game-like" elements in the game world, such as "power up" tokens. This is real, but it is also a game. The unreal situation that results empowers the players to, for instance, go on murderous killing rampages, and laugh as they do so. The most recent title in the franchise, *Grand Theft Auto IV* (Rockstar North, 2008), has a somewhat more realistic art style and no visible tokens, but the underlying sense of irony remains.

I do not believe there is anything morally wrong with this kind of escapism, and the unreal quality of the game facilitates this freedom to misbehave. This can be understood in terms of what Johan Huizinga (who directly inspired Caillois' work) termed "the Magic Circle," that is, the special space within which play occurs, which is not quite the same as the normal world [Huizinga55]. Whatever happens inside the game space is not a part of everyday life, and normal considerations are temporarily suspended. Those who attempt to replicate GTA in more realistic tones should think twice about their approach: some players may crave a grittier edge, but a light-hearted attitude often encourages play more effectively.

It is possible to find elements of destructive vertigo in all manner of games—such as the amusing pleasure of causing gigantic pileups in the crash mode of *Burnout 2: Point of Impact* (Criterion, 2002), or the reckless devastation of architecture in *Blast Corps* (Rare, 1997), *Mercenaries: Playground of Destruction* (Pandemic, 2005), *Rygar: the Legendary Adventure* (Tecmo, 2003), or *Otogi: Myth of Demons* (FromSoftware, 2003). It can even be found in a more innocent fashion in a tree-chopping rampage in *Animal Crossing*. Destruction is fun—it is exciting not only because it is a visceral experience, but also because you are not usually allowed such license and this violation of the normal social order is inherently thrilling.

It should also be noted that you don't need to be violent to appeal to destructive ilinx. The *Katamari Damacy* games (Namco, 2004) are built upon the vertigo of rolling things up—you are "destroying" the environment, but not in an overtly violent fashion. Some adults scream when you pick them up on your Katamari, but most children laugh—it's good natured chaos, not bloody carnage, and as the narrative elements of the game underline, no one gets hurt. And again, it can make you laugh, especially when you pick up (say) your first cat, or you become big enough for people to run away from you.

The important factor in this approach to creating the experience of vertigo is that the players do something that they normally wouldn't (or couldn't); something disruptive and chaotic, and often destructive.

Pressure

As well as the use of speed, fear of heights and destructive mischief to bring about vertigo, it is also possible to put the players into a state of stress by reducing their capacity to respond to game situations. This can be achieved either as a result of increasing pressure to act ("time is running out"), or decreasing freedom to act (an ever-increasing number of obstacles, or an ever-decreasing set of options). You see this very commonly with puzzle games, and the most successful game of this kind is *Tetris* itself, which is a quintessential pressure rushgame, placing stress on players to deal with problems that occur before the play field fills up.

The most obvious way to create pressure on players is to place them under time pressure—challenging the players to complete the required actions before time runs out. This has two immediate effects: it adds excitement, of course, but it also creates the possibility of fiero (by creating a challenge to overcome). This technique is also well known from story writing, and indeed has acquired the name "the ticking clock" among Hollywood writers (a narrative device rendered with blunt literality in the TV show "24"). However the time pressure is generated (whether by the narrative or by the game mechanics), the net result is the same: players are placed under pressure to act. In the case of games with timers, this manifests as an ever-increasing pressure to act, which in turn can generate escalating excitement.

Arcade games in particular have made use of timers to add tension, although often this originates in the need to get the players to keep adding coins, rather than a conscious attempt at increasing the excitement of the play. Sometimes the timer is rendered literally as an on-screen counter, as in *Out Run* (Sega, 1986), but many of the older arcade games used a more tangential approach. For instance, *Joust* (Williams, 1982) sends an "unbeatable" pterodactyl to attack players when they take too long to clear a stage, serving as a timer but without the literal display of a clock.

A different approach to the same kind of play can be found in "plate-spinning" games (also known as *time-management* games), such as *Diner Dash* (Gamelab, 2005) and its antecedent, the arcade game *Tapper* (Bally Midway, 1983). In these games, situations requiring player response occur with increasing frequency, thus creating the stress situation. For example, in *Tapper* a number of irate and thirsty customers need to be provided drinks, and as the game progresses more and more customers appear, adding to the mounting pressure. Clearing each barroom challenge in *Tapper* gives the players the reward of relief—they survived the crisis situation. *Diner Dash* and similar time-management games are one of the three commercially successful casual game genres [Irwin08].

Vertically scrolling shooters in the "bullet maze" style also generate vertigo by decreasing the player's freedom to act, in this case by increasing the number of bullets on-screen such that the task of maneuvering the player's ship safely requires complete and total attention (produces a state of flow). Games of this kind include the *DonPachi* series (Cave, 1995 onwards), *Gunbird & Gunbird 2* (Psikyo, 1994 & 1998), and Treasure's console-based *Radiant Silvergun* (1998) and *Ikaruga* (2002).

Another related means of applying pressure is to have the players' overall performances index-linked to their capacity to accurately complete actions in succession—commonly achieved via the use of an exponential combo multiplier that dramatically inflates the score the players achieve as a result of many successive successes. In a combo-focused game, *one mistake breaks the chain*—it is this undesirable outcome that provides the nail-biting excitement, because to reach the highest scores requires few if any breaks in the combo chain.

This approach can result in hugely popular games, and is very common. The recently released *Link's Crossbow Training* (Nintendo EAD, 2007) is the latest of a long tradition of shooting galleries based on this form, and the classic *NiGHTS: Into Dreams* (Sonic Team, 1996) became highly chain-focused after the player mastered the basics. Most successful of all the games of this kind, however, are rhythm-action games such as the *Dance Dance Revolution* (Konami, 1999 onwards) and *Guitar Hero* franchises (Harmonix, 2005 onwards). Both of these games function as pressure rushgames in general terms, and (once the player becomes fully cognizant of the scoring mechanism) as chain rushgames.

A final approach to engendering vertigo is to move beyond excitement and attempt to provoke fear directly—often by use of traditionally "scary" monsters (zombies, alien creatures, spiders, snakes, and so on). The survival horror game, of which the *Resident Evil* franchise (Capcom, 1996) is the most commercially successful, represents a special kind of rushgame in which terror is encoded into the narrative setting of the virtual world.

These games usually add an additional source of pressure, namely the conservation of ammunition and healing items. Indeed, this element is crucial to the general feel of this kind of survival rushgame—decreasing resources increases the stress upon the player, making the surprises the game triggers to cause the player to jump with fright all the more effective. A great number of tricks from the narrative language of film can be gainfully employed in this style of rushgame, which is perhaps the only kind in which fear is expressly more important than excitement.

I have one last observation concerning the emotions associated with rushgames. It is the nature of the play of these games—which generally involve attempts to maintain control under difficult conditions—that they can also lead to *surprise*. This is a brief emotional response, probably also related to fear (the emotions expert Paul Ekman makes this connection [Ekman03], for instance).

In a rushgame that creates tension by the use of a long combo chain, if players break the combo by making unexpected mistakes, they will often display the open mouth, wide-eyed expression that corresponds to surprise (although competitive players may suffer frustration instead), and similarly a survival horror game may plan shocking events to evoke surprise. Interestingly, surprise can often be followed by relief—especially if the shock doesn't turn out to be as serious as first assessed—which means surprise can also be a route to the emotional reward of relief. Because surprise and fear seem to be quite similar (apart from duration), this reinforces the idea that games of this kind are ultimately about fear, usually experienced as excitement, and the related reward of relief.

The Value of Vertigo

Despite the focus on games of fiero by many gamer hobbyists, vertigo is perhaps a more important commercial force in videogames. Many games can be identified that are not heavily biased towards the competitive pattern of anger and fiero, but few that do not draw upon excitement in some form (although in this regard, I still have something more to report).

In fact, a recent study of 1,040 gamers (both hardcore and casual) revealed that 8 out of 10 players report that excitement enhances their enjoyment of a game, and a quarter actively seeks out games that give them this feeling. Only 1% of players say they don't like feeling this way [Bateman08].

Conversely, the same study revealed that only 1 in 5 gamers report anger increasing their enjoyment of a game, whereas a staggering 42% of those surveyed said they didn't enjoy feeling angry while playing a game, and that they avoided games that made them feel this way [Bateman08]. This suggests in general terms that hard competitive games are considerably less popular than games that focus more directly on excitement, but this conclusion overlooks the fact that the fans of games of hard competition purchase many titles during a year, and thus still represent a highly lucrative market niche.

Chance (*Alea*)

In reporting his four patterns of play, Caillois links the competition of agon with another kind of competition: that of alea, or games of chance. There is a reason for this: The same kind of emotions (anger and fiero) can be triggered by this alternative pattern—anger in the form of frustration (or disappointment) when we lose, and fiero when we win (especially when we win against all the odds). But despite the emotional similarity, the nature of this pattern is very different from the pattern I described in connection with competitive games.

Caillois describes alea as follows:

> *Alea is the Latin name for the game of dice. I have borrowed it to designate, in contrast to agon (games of competition), all games that are based on a decision independent of the player, an outcome over which he has no control, and in which winning is the result of fate rather than triumphing over an adversary. More properly, destiny is the sole artisan of victory, and where there is rivalry, what is meant is that the winner has been more favored by fortune than the loser. Perfect examples of this type are provided by the games of dice, roulette, heads or tails, baccara, lotteries, etc. Here, not only does one refrain from trying to eliminate the injustice of chance, but rather it is the very capriciousness of chance that constitutes the unique appeal of the game.*
>
> *Alea signifies and reveals the favour of destiny. The player is entirely passive; he does not deploy his resources, skill, muscles, or intelligence. All he need do is await, in hope and trembling, the cast of the die.*

Anyone who has gambled will recognize this description; those who have never understood why people gamble will similarly struggle to understand alea. Indeed, many narrow-minded intellectuals like to berate and belittle players of lotteries by calling such games "a tax on stupidity".

Caillois' view on lotteries is rather that they provide hope to those whose prospects in any given culture are limited. He observes that there comes a point in a person's life when they recognize that they cannot change the circumstances of their birth nor the talents they have been given. If their talents do not correspond to a means to make their own fortune in any given culture (and different cultures value different traits in this regard), they may still hold out hope for a life-changing miracle. As Caillois writes: "It is the [social] function of alea to always hold out hope of such a miracle".

At a biological level, it is worth considering the parallels between games of chance and variable reward schedules, to which games of alea appear to correspond. For instance, slot machines produce fairly regular activity out of players because they function as a variable reward schedule.

Games designers have a tendency to overlook or dismiss alea (chance), although in cultural terms it is a highly significant class of games. The global video games industry has around $28 billion turnover [AFP05], whereas the global gambling industry is worth a staggering $1,098 billion, 40 times as much [BBC02]. And gambling is merely the most profitable incarnation of games of chance; there are a wide variety of forms of play that focus upon alea, and even more games that incorporate random elements in their play.

For instance, TV game shows based on luck are phenomenally popular. For almost as long as TV has been around, Mediterranean nations have aired game shows that under the hood are essentially games of chance. Even in the United States, where the dogma of competition and meritocracy dominates all aspects of the culture, "Wheel of Fortune" remains the most watched syndicated show on television, and the successful export of Endemol's franchise "Deal or No Deal" to the U.S. shows beyond a doubt that luck sells.

The secret: universality. Only a competent player can be victorious in a game of skill, but *anyone can win a game of luck*. But there is more to chance in games than just this aspect of accessibility.

Games of Chance

What is the allure of games of chance? It is more than the potential to win money, since it is possible to enjoy games of chance without wagering upon them (although no doubt the rewards of victory become all the sweeter as the payoff increases!). There is a point in, say, a game of dice when the player experiences what might be described as the destruction of consciousness—time seems to slow or stop, and thought is impossible as they wait for the outcome to resolve. This experience can be compared to the Zen concept of "little satori," the temporary abolition of consciousness, which was introduced to the West mostly as a result of the work of Alan Watts [Watts57].

Sporting events are full of little satori—that moment of consciousness-destroying excitement when something might happen—when your team is close to being able to score, for instance. You are gripped in the excitement of the possibility and unable to think at all, lost as you are in the moment. When a lottery player is still enjoying the experience of playing (rather than playing purely out of habit), the lottery draw can bring about a similar little satori experience; there is a genuine tension and excitement. In my view, the cost of a lottery ticket is quite low provided it is still giving you this little satori experience—a ticket to a sporting event can cost you 20 to 40 times as much, and generally only affords you two or three such experiences. Seen this way, a lottery ticket is good value.

This experience can be found in many examples outside of sports and gambling. The excitement of unwrapping a mysterious present, checking the morning mail for something interesting, channel surfing, listening to the radio (hoping to hear a great song), unprotected sex, card or sticker collections (and their big brother, trading card games), toy capsule dispensers and chocolate boxes all have a certain appeal in this kind, which can be likened to Caillois' alea. Indeed, in the U.K. there is one particular brand of chocolate known as Revels, each packet of which consists of half a dozen different types of similar-looking chocolate with little more than luck determining what you will eat next, has realized that the mystery and chance of eating them is part of the appeal. A 2005 advertisement for Revels depicted two competitors playing a game of Russian roulette with a bag of the chocolates—who will pull out the dreaded coffee chocolate…? [Burnett05].

For the most part, chance is more important to tabletop games than to videogames. Almost all successful hobby games incorporate a chance element as a core mechanic, whether through dice rolling or drawing from a random deck of cards, and tabletop role-playing games (RPGs) rely extensively upon dice for their excitement. It is possible to play these games without a random element, as with *Amber Diceless Role-playing Game* (Erick Wujcik/Phage Press, 1991) but the most popular games—of which *Dungeons & Dragons* (TSR et al, 1974 onwards) is the paradigm case—rely upon the chance element to add to the tension.

The importance of the dice ritual in a tabletop RPG is in the sense of ownership over the narrative that it affords, what games researcher Ben Cowley has termed *imagined agency* in discussions with me on my blog. When the game requires the player to make a dice roll, the progress of the narrative depends upon the player's action. Players cannot influence it in direct terms, but via the dice, they have control of fate. Computer RPGs do not capture this element at all, and hence have a tendency to devolve into mindless progression through the core reward schedules, something which is beautifully parodied in *ProgressQuest* (Eric Fredricksen, 2002), which allows players to power up their characters with a variety of amusingly named equipment items without any action whatsoever on the part of the players.

It may be that this particular function cannot be transferred to videogames, as pressing a button and getting a random number lacks the tactility and imagined agency of throwing dice. Players in such a situation feel that the computer is determining fate—they just get to tell it when it can start. Indeed, transferring games of chance to videogames is a challenge, because for what Caillois denotes by alea to truly exist in a game the players must be willing to abandon the outcome entirely to fate. This is tricky for many game-literate players to accept, in part because of an (not wholly unreasonable) assumption that the game will grant the players control over saving and loading the game state.

Save game mechanisms are arguably key to the tension between videogames and the kind of experience of chance play expressed through gambling. How can one appeal to fate if the outcome of a random event can merely be repeated until success is gained by reloading and retrying? This is the reason that videogames that incorporate gambling elements necessarily override the player's access to save mechanisms. *Juiced* (Juice Games, 2005), for instance, is a car-racing game that attempts to build gambling into the heart of the game structure. It largely fails in this because players of videogames are largely conditioned to games giving them control over saving, and so the players sooner or later become compelled to circumvent the autosave mechanism, thus rendering the gambling elements irrelevant.

It thus seems at first glance that chance is not important to videogames, but I hope to demonstrate shortly that this is a misconception.

Sources of Play

There are essentially two sources of play that any game can draw upon: the first is *choice* (or design), which you see in any FPS game, for instance, that employs no random elements (except, perhaps, in the AI mechanics) and places the player in a tightly controlled environment. The second is *chance*, which can be seen most clearly with games like *Beggar-my-Neighbour* (AKA *Strip Jack Naked*) or *Snakes & Ladders*, which use only chance to drive play.

There are few if any card games that do not use chance as the source of play; this is inherent in the nature of card games. The player learns a small set of rules, and then operates within these mechanics to process randomly generated hands in a certain way, wherein the fun of play can emerge—either by offering interesting choices for play, or by generating interesting situations within the play. (Even though the player does not choose to play an Ace in a hand of *Beggar-my-Neighbour*—it is turned over as the next card—it is still fun to do so; there is the schadenfreude of making the other player suffer, for a start!)

In the context of board games, and in particular the hobby games that are the more interesting part of that commercial field (since selling "reskinned" *Monopoly* sets is more about marketing, not about game design [Berlinger08]), it is relatively clear that successful games in this market almost always draw upon chance. There are classic strategy games like Chess, Draughts, and Go that have no random elements, but these are invariably a smaller market than those games that do draw upon chance to drive play—a new non-random board game can't offer much more than Chess or Go already offers, so it would be competing with a dominating established brand. Most, such as the short-lived board game *Kensington* (Brian Taylor & Peter Forbes, 1979), vanish without a trace. I should perhaps acknowledge that chess sets probably do make up a big market share in the board game market, but the point remains: if you want to make a new commercially viable board game, it will include chance either via random tiles, a deck of cards, or by dice.

It is harder to find the same influence for chance in videogames, but it is still there. *Tetris*, the second most successful videogame of all time (33 million units sold on GameBoy, admittedly on the back of bundling with the handheld unit), uses chance as its source of play. Indeed, almost all puzzle games share this facet: *Bejewelled* (PopCap, 2001) and *Bust-a-Move* (Taito, 1994 onwards, originally published as *Puzzle Bobble*) also draw upon chance as the primary driver of play (although there is a strong design factor in the latter), and it is difficult to find exceptions. *Lemmings* (DMA Design, 1991) is a notable exception—although the appeal here can be traced in part to other factors.

What's interesting about this link to puzzle games is that the connection—both in terms of play and in terms of popularity—between card games and puzzle games becomes apparent. Both are formed around similar principles: a small set of rules that mediate the way the player deals with a randomly generated sequence of cards, tiles, bubbles, or what have you. I might go so far as to say that if you want to make a successful "casual game," you would do better to study the way people play solitaire card games than to study anything that happens on a Sony, Nintendo, or Microsoft console.

In general, the expression of chance in videogames can be seen in two distinct ways. Firstly, there is the trivial use of chance in, for instance, AI mechanisms, to prevent the player from predicting how things will behave, which I call the *noise function*. This is not very much to do with what Caillois denotes with alea, but it is an important role for chance in games. Secondly, there is the use of random numbers to generate unique playfields within which the player takes actions to sustain a process or achieve a goal (or both), which I call the *landscape function*.

The puzzles games I mentioned previously all rely upon a landscape function: *Tetris* has the landscape effect occurring somewhat in the background, as a consequence of where the player chooses to place the new (random) tetronimo, but *Bejeweled* has the landscape function front and center: the player makes decisions as to which two gems to exchange in a randomly generated (and randomly refreshed) playfield. Many of these moves result in intrinsically rewarding cascades, and thus the game has a variable schedule generated automatically out of its use of a landscape function. What's telling about *Bejeweled* (and the other "match 3" games which have cloned it) is how accessible the game has been made: it would be more exciting to play against the clock (an option is provided for this), but the main game mode has no time restrictions, and invites the players to act at their own pace. It is the genius of the team at PopCap that they stripped away all the challenge-assumptions endemic to the games industry in making this game, and in doing so triggered the casual games gold rush. "Match 3" games are the second of the three styles of casual game that attract a big audience [Irwin08].

This is not the only way the landscape function can be used, of course. Games such as *Sid Meier's Civilization* use this technique to create a space within which competitive play happens, but the function is still there. An example of something in a non-competitive style is Digital Eel's marvelous 2002 game *Strange Adventures in Infinite Space*, which randomly shuffles an internal "deck" of possibilities to create a miniature galaxy that can be explored in about 30 minutes or less. The landscape function here serves as the core interest for the game (although there is also another aspect that I shall describe in the context of the last of Caillois' patterns).

Despite these uses for chance in videogames, it is still usually relegated quite significantly to either the background (the noise function in AI) or the corners of the videogames marketplace. Why is chance not used more often in other videogame genres? The answer appears to be twofold: firstly, a widespread (but not universal) prejudice among game designers and programmers against chance that is probably connected to a micromanagement mentality, and secondly, a pragmatic quality assurance (QA) problem.

Games that use chance such as card games and puzzle games essentially represent atomic systems, which need to be tested and balanced in a variety of different ways. This is a viable QA task, because the scope is constrained. But consider what happens when subsystems in a larger game switch to random sources—consider (for instance) what would be implied in a subsystem that gave randomly generated monster distributions in the rooms of an FPS: the QA workload would be exponentially higher as a result of this. A single configuration could be checked in one pass, whereas a random configuration might not be fully checked in a thousand passes.

This resistance from QA is actually a powerful and necessary force inside the games industry, and arguably the reason that games drawing upon chance are found principally outside of the console market. Game designers love to posit design ideas that will generate "a different game every time"—but such games rarely make it through to the upper market. Games of this kind are much more commonly found as independent games, which by nature of their lack of budget have reduced scope, and thus inevitably fall into the comfortable arena of just one major randomly-driven system to balance and tweak—*Strange Adventures in Infinite Space* is a clear example.

One notable exception to this trend, however, is the use of random treasure tables in computer RPGs and MMORPGs, as in *Diablo* (Blizzard, 1997 onwards), the game that spring-boarded Blizzard into the big time. Here, I might argue that the players' stake is their time that is gambled against getting something impressive out of the random treasure. It's an equipment lottery, if you will. Games that use treasure tables of this kind do employ chance as the major driver, and the QA implications are bridged by the simplicity of the mechanics involved (which are rarely more than the equivalent of a dice roll compared to a table).

Similarly, *Animal Crossing* manages to use this same random "treasure" mechanic without any violent play elements, and has outsold all but the most successful computer RPG titles. In fact, this game is packed full of expressions of chance play—checking the (random) items in the shop each day, fishing, looking for insects, seeking buried treasure and the monthly lottery are just a few of the ways the game leverages random elements to create its play. In all these instances, the player faces not the threat of loss, but the potential for something wonderful to happen by chance. However, in order to make this work, it is necessary for the player to be denied the capacity to reload an earlier save, in order to lend validity to each random outcome. This may not suit every player, but there is no doubting that *Animal Crossing* has found its audience.

A final way that chance can manifest inside videogames, which is perhaps a special role of the noise function, is the use of chance to deliver a random sequence of mini-games and the like in party games such as *Mario Party* or *Bishi Bashi*, which generally target a very wide audience. As mentioned previously, although they are ostensibly competitive, much of what is delivered is fairly random chaos. This is fine—the players of such games enjoy the mayhem—and the influence of chance makes it easy for anyone to win, whatever their age or skills. Something similar must have influenced the random structural elements in the racing game *Kirby Air*

Ride (HAL Laboratory, 2003), which was also designed to cover a very wide age range of players. This returns to an earlier point, which is that in principle, anyone can win in a game of chance.

Emotions of Chance

I already discussed the importance of fiero to the competitive pattern of play (Caillois' agon), but this is not the only kind of play that can tap into this emotion. In games of chance (Caillois' alea), fiero is also a key emotion; if you watch gamblers, you will see the same tell-tale signs of fiero (screwing up of the face, raising of the hands in victory) when they pull off the big win. However, in games of chance, the accompanying emotions of boredom and frustration observed in Lazzaro's Hard Fun key do not occur. The only other similarity with the competitive play pattern is that excitement is once again the precursor to fiero—the pay-off of fiero does not occur unless the player is anticipating the possibility of victory or success, which necessitates some excitement.

An examination of the emotional patterns in connection with games of chance shows that there is something of a sequence involved: the player knows or discovers that they could be about to win (or gain great advantage towards winning) and experiences excitement. When the situation resolves, they experience either fiero in the event that they got lucky, or disappointment (sadness) in the event that they were unlucky. There is no frustration, because the player is not directly responsible for the outcome—in the competitive pattern of play, the players become angry because they could have done better; frustration spurs them to try again, but harder, heightening the eventual payoff of fiero if they persevere. In the chance pattern, the outcome lies solely in the hands of fate, so there is nothing to provoke frustration—failure instead causes varying degrees of disappointment depending upon the relative cost of that loss.

(One might still relate this disappointment to anger, however. Fritz Perls, the founder of Gestalt psychology, has suggested that "depression is anger turned inwards" [Perls69]. Because there is nothing that the player can do, having lost, the same mechanisms that would normally cause frustration, anger, might manifest as depression instead. If this insight were validated, it would mean that the experience of failure could be related to anger, just expressed in a different manner.)

To demonstrate this pattern in practice, consider the experience of play in a set-collection game such as Rummy or Mahjong. Think back to your most intense experiences of playing such games. When your hand is nearly complete—a few cards or tiles are needed to win—you become emotionally aroused as you draw your next card; you feel excitement because you know this card could allow you to win. When you see the card and it is not the card you need, you feel the mild sadness of disappointment. But if the card you see if the one you need to win—success! You flush with fiero as the enjoyment of victory hits you. The payoff may be less than with the anger-enhanced fiero of competitive play, but it is nonetheless highly satisfying (and if a sufficient sum of money has been wagered, the fiero may even be greater).

It is possible that you don't quite recognize yourself in this pattern—rather than sadness in the event of not drawing the winning card, you might instead experience mild anger. If this is your experience of such games, it is quite possible that your native play style favors competitive play—so much so that you bring elements of the competitive play pattern even into games of chance. In this event, it is quite likely that if the choice of game were up to you, you would favor a game with less elements of chance and more opportunities for direct competition—this doesn't guarantee that you are a gamer hobbyist, but the odds are greatly in favor of this interpretation.

There is also another form of the chance pattern that occurs in games in which the player is charged with the task of surviving as long as possible, for instance, *Tetris*. Here, Lazzaro's Serious Fun pattern is more apposite: players experience excitement as the tension of the situation heightens (and the body produces adrenalin in response), and relief when they pull themselves out of the worst scrapes. Because the play is continuous with no express goal, that is, process-oriented, there is no channel for fiero—although one can certainly reorganize such games to include a goal and thus allow for fiero. It is an open question whether doing so would widen the audience for such a game, or narrow it.

Games of chance have such universal appeal because they are absolutely fair. In a game of pure competition, whomever is more skilled will win every time (all things being equal), but in a game of pure chance anyone can win, regardless of who they are, how old they are, or what their skills might be. The greater the reward in a game of Caillois' alea, the greater the appeal—hence the draw of state, national, and international lotteries. The size of the stake the player could lose may intensify the experience, but it is what can be won that entices, whether that reward is money, a unique gift, a nice chocolate, or temporary ownership of the flow of the narrative.

IMAGINATION (*MIMICRY*)

Caillois' final pattern of play is mimicry, which he described in terms of games of simulation, but because this evokes images of fairly mechanical sim games, I prefer to consider Caillois' mimicry to represent games of imagination. He described mimicry as follows:

All play presupposes the temporary acceptance, if not of an illusion (indeed this last word means nothing less than beginning a game: in-lusio), then at least of a closed conventional, and, in certain respects, imaginary universe. Play can consist not only of deploying actions or submitting to one's fate in an imaginary milieu, but of becoming an illusory character oneself, and of so behaving. One is thus confronted with a diverse series of manifestations, the common element of which is that the subject makes believe or makes others believe that he is someone other than himself. He forgets, disguises, or temporarily sheds his personality in order to feign another. I prefer to designate these phenomena by the term mimicry...

The pleasure lies in being or passing for another. But in games the basic intention is not that of deceiving the spectators. The child who is playing train may well refuse to kiss his father while saying to him that one does not embrace locomotives, but he is not trying to persuade his father that he is a real locomotive... Mimicry is incessant invention. The rule of the game is unique: it consists in the actor's fascinating the spectator, while avoiding an error that might lead the spectator to break the spell. The spectator must lend himself to the illusion without first challenging the decor, mask, or artifice which for a given time he is asked to believe in as more real than reality itself.

Caillois was writing at a time before videogames, and his focus therefore was on conventional play activities and theatre (which also notably uses the term "play"), but mimicry is especially pertinent to digital entertainment. Where Caillois talks of the actor and the spectator, in a videogame these two roles can be the same person. Players are actors in the sense that they control their avatars, but they are also spectators as they are enjoying watching their avatars take actions.

Almost every videogame has elements of mimicry. When you sit down to play a game, you know that what is happening is not real; you suspend your disbelief in order to allow the game to sweep you away in its situation and world. The game is a tool for imagination—whether it is imagining that you are a heroic warrior-priestess, a gun-toting action hero, a hard-driven career woman, or a fluffy animal. People do not usually consider this aspect of the game to be at the center of the play, but is this as a result of being blinded by an excessive focus on challenge? Is mimicry more of a draw to play than it might first appear?

Mimicry in Videogames

The vast majority of modern videogames have a large component of mimicry. It added enormously to the appeal of all the *Prince of Persia* games (Jordan Mechner et al, 1989 onwards), for instance, although in this case the games were all designed and structured in such challenge-oriented fashion that they could never appeal solely for their mimicry. It might be the chief reason that *World of Warcraft* (Blizzard, 2004) radically outpaced the *EverQuest* (Verant Interactive, 1999) brand in terms of subscribers. It is also perhaps the principal reason for the astronomical success of the recent *Grand Theft Auto* games. Yet all of these examples are subject to easy objections, because although mimicry certainly contributed to their appeal, none of these games has mimicry at the center of its play.

The power of mimicry can be best seen in the success of games for which this is the primary form of play being offered. *Sim City* (Maxis, 1989) had impressive success for its day by offering the mimicry of building a working city, but was limited by its focus. Although creating a city was entertaining, it didn't engage a great many players for an especially long time, in part because of its inherent complexity and emotional distance. In creating *The Sims* (Maxis, 2000), Maxis offered a game of mimicry with a much wider appeal—and critically, a game with the potential to appeal to women.

It is not that mimicry appeals more to women than men, rather, it is that the types of mimicry that people are culturally indoctrinated into differ by gender. Boys tend stereotypically to play with toy cars and weapons—and games incorporating mimicry of vehicles and weapons tend to have a serious bias towards competitive play. Girls tend stereotypically to play with figures (dollplay) and domestic situations (playing house). These play activities had not been provided as the focus of play in videogames prior to *The Sims*, perhaps because prior to Will Wright few people with the necessary influence had considered women a worthwhile target audience—thanks in part to gender biases in games industry employment (which I will describe in more detail in Step 8). 16 million units and many satisfied customers later and (astonishingly) the industry as a whole still struggles to recognize the significance of mimicry to hitting a wide audience, despite *The Sims* being the best-selling PC game of all time [EA05].

Nintendo, more than any other platform-license holder, seems to recognize the value of this type of play. Whereas Sony and Microsoft still remain focused on challenge as the key drive in play, Nintendo has released games such as *Animal Crossing, Doshin the Giant* (Päräm, 2002), and *Nintendogs* (Nintendo EAD, 2005), all of which supply their play primarily in mimicry. *Nintendogs* in particular is a game of pure mimicry—the joy of the game is pretending to be interacting with a real puppy. Its success is timely, however; earlier sprite-based pet simulators required more suspension of belief. *Nintendogs* leverages the improvements of graphics power (specifically animation quality) and the touch screen and microphone functionality of the Nintendo DS handheld console to enhance the mimicry experience. It has sold 20 million units (more even than *The Sims*) and is the best-selling game for the Nintendo DS [Nintendo08].

You would think at this point that the value of mimicry would be proved, but there are still people who dismiss titles such as these as special cases, and who continue to believe that the only pattern of play worth pursuing in videogames is that of competition. To be sure, competitive games are a very strong market, and much easier to compete within thanks to the specialist press and the gamer hobbyists who buy many titles each year, thus creating solid cash flow. But competitive games represent a highly saturated market, and most titles of this kind fail miserably. There must surely be more opportunities for unique titles like *The Sims* and *Nintendogs* to break new ground.

There are many gamer hobbyists who claim that graphics are irrelevant to good games, and indeed there are a small number of players for whom this is the case, but it is categorically not true of all people that graphics do not matter. In fact, the converse is indicated: as a mimicry enhancer, graphics are absolutely critical to the success of games in the mass market. However, most games fritter away their graphical advantages by delivering play in a more competitive context—thus appealing to the players for whom the improvements in graphics are at best an added bonus. That said, the step up in graphics between each generation is becoming rather marginal. Innovative play design is likely to become progressively more important in the years ahead.

Note that in supplying mimicry, photorealism need not be a prerequisite (although it seems to be the case that for the U.S. market, photorealism might be preferred). Because mimicry is an imaginative process, the transformation into an experience of mimicry can originate in all manner of different art styles.

One can see this hinted at in Caillois' work. He considered theatre to be the ultimate formal expression of mimicry. Writing in the '50s, it wasn't that motion pictures didn't exist, but Caillois recognized that the masks, disguises, and tricks of the theatrical tradition were a more complete expression of the draw to mimicry (which uses imagination to suspend disbelief—what some might call immersion) than films, which aim to minimize the suspension of disbelief. It is possible, however, that those who find imagination difficult in adulthood (and this may be the majority of people) may only be capable of enjoying mimicry when the leap of imagination is minimized through realism. Box office receipts certainly exceed theatrical receipts, although one cannot ignore the effect of marketing in this.

Intrinsic Fantasy

I have said that almost all videogames provide mimicry—and indeed, it is hard to find a valid exception, except perhaps for a digital version of (say) the peg-based logic game *Mastermind* (Mordecai Meirowitz, 1970) or something similarly abstract. Before exploring the different kinds of mimicry that can be found in videogames, I would like to discuss perhaps the first investigation of the appeal of mimicry in videogames.

At the start of the 1980s, a researcher at Xerox Palo Alto Research Center explored what was appealing about the digital entertainment of the time. Thomas W. Malone was conducting research into games as tools for learning—now a very popular topic, but at the time, videogames were far from spectacularly impressive. To put this in context, the most advanced coin-op videogames at this time were *Asteroids* (Atari, 1979) and *Pac-Man* (Namco/Midway, 1980). Malone published a number of papers, all of which make for fascinating reading, which contained numerous ideas still pertinent to the games industry. In fact, what is most disturbing to me is that Malone's papers aren't cited more often, or indeed, required reading for game designers.

The papers are packed full of little observations that remain as poignant today as ever. For instance, in the 1980 paper Malone notes in the context of the way the game communicates success and failure to the player:

> *...performance feedback should be presented in a way that minimized the possibility of self-esteem damage.*

This is a lesson that a staggering number of videogames have never learned! Most players are easily discouraged, and yet a macho, Conqueror-style ethos is still quite prevalent, with failure being met with abuse and ridicule, even in an otherwise charming game such as *Katamari Damacy*—although at least in this case a touch of humor offsets the problem.

The most salient line in the 1980 paper states succinctly what should have been the mantra for the videogames industry for the past 25 years [Malone80]:

> *If computer game designers can create many different kinds of fantasies for different kinds of people, their games are likely to have much broader appeal.*

The same idea is reiterated in a later paper [Malone81]:

> *...fantasies can be very important in creating intrinsically motivating environments but that, unless the fantasies are carefully chosen to appeal to the target audience, they may actually make the environment less interesting rather than more.*

This is a claim I have been making with ever-increasing force in recent years, and when game researcher Ben Cowley first provided me with copies of Malone papers, I was stunned to read someone else making this observation back when the industry was in its infancy. How did Malone reach his conclusion? By analyzing the components of a specific videogame and the response that players had to the game with different elements removed [Malone80]. He found that the inherent fantasy of the game (the setting, or the focus of the mimicry) is the single largest factor in a player's enjoyment of a game—a fact that remains as valid today as it was in 1980.

This, in fact, is the key factor to consider when making any videogame: what is the intrinsic fantasy that the player will take part in?

Curiosity and the Brain

Almost inseparable from a discussion of mimicry is a consideration of the emotional behavior curiosity, which you were introduced to in Step 1 as part of Nicole Lazzaro's Easy Fun key. Malone actually has some interesting points concerning curiosity, which he presents in a preexisting psychological framework [Malone80]:

> *Curiosity is the motivation to learn, independent of any goal-seeking or fantasy-fulfillment. Computer games can evoke a learner's curiosity by providing environments that have an optimal level of informational complexity (Berlyne, 1965; Piaget, 1952). In other words, the environments should be neither too complicated nor too simple with respect to the learner's existing knowledge. They should be novel and surprising, but not completely incomprehensible.*

This observation ties up with recent research into a neurobiological mechanism for interest (which is to say, curiosity) by Biederman and Edward Vessel. Using functional magnetic resonance imaging, Biederman and Vessel conducted an experiment in which participants were presented with a series of scenes that had been independently rated in terms of how pleasurable (or interesting) they were. They then studied the activity in the brains of the subjects to see what was going on [Biederman06].

What they found was a possible neural mechanism for explaining perceptual pleasure, one which involved certain opioid chemicals, and in particular what are known as mu-opioid receptors. These are found in parts of the brain associated with the modulation of pain and reward. But the greatest density of these receptors is found in the association areas (that is, the region around the hippocampus), and what Biederman and

Vessel discovered was that there was a direct link between memory and perceptual pleasure.

The researchers identified a visual pathway in the brain, beginning in the visual center (occipital lobe) and terminating in the association area (around the hippocampus). All the areas in question contained mu-opioid receptors of the relevant kind—the neural pathways that interpret visual information in the brain were wired for pleasure! They concluded that people experience perceptual pleasure when experiencing images that are "novel and richly interpretable".

They note "perceptual preferences arise from the *connections* the brain makes with stored information," because the greatest density of the mu-opioid receptors are in the association areas where memories are formed. Thus, it is not enough for a visual image to be entirely novel—such an image would be hard to interpret, because of its unfamiliarity. Rather, images that produce the strongest response in terms of perceptual pleasure are those that are "richly interpretable," that is comprised of familiar content, but in novel and interesting ways. It is very likely that similar mechanisms are at work in the audio and touch centers for those senses.

Biederman and Vessel's research is a fascinating look at a possible neural mechanism for curiosity (or at least interest, which is related), but there are some contradictions. A well known effect in psychology is the tendency for familiar things to be preferred to unfamiliar (a fact well known in advertising and marketing). This *mere exposure effect*, first explored by Robert Zajonc in the '60s [Zajonc68] shows that people have a psychological preference for the familiar—which is part of the reason that brands are so valuable in the marketplace. People as a statistical whole would always rather purchase a known quantity than gamble that something new will appeal. Biederman and Vessel speculate that the mere exposure effect is constrained to the early stages of exposure, but it is less than clear that this claim will hold up to scrutiny: the evidence from the marketplace is decidedly to the contrary.

What does this mean for videogames? Firstly, it explains why branded videogames are so commercially successful—if the player has enjoyed a movie (say), they have the capacity to enjoy the game too, because this draws on familiar content (mere exposure effect) but presents new experiences that are richly interpretable in terms of the familiar memories that are activated in the association areas. The epitome of this phenomena is *LEGO Star Wars* (Giant/Traveller's Tales, 2005), which presents environments that are richly interpretable in terms of multiple familiar elements—there are all the recognizable characters, objects, and places from the *Star Wars* movies (which are very popular among videogame players), and the familiarity of the LEGO pieces as well. Every scene of the game allows the players to interpret it in terms of what they recognize from *Star Wars*, and to pick apart how it is constructed from LEGO blocks too.

That's not all. In a follow-up paper, published with graduate student Xiaomin Yue, Biederman and Vessel find evidence that the pleasure that comes from experiencing novel and interpretable activates the part of the brain that contains the pleasure center. Thus they conclude that "perceptual preference is a function of the conventional reward system". This is to say that this entire mechanism for interest and curiosity is ultimately tied to dopamine [Yue07]. The authors talk of the "click" of comprehension that happens when a richly interpretable scene is suddenly interpreted in its optimal light—this is presumably a small release of dopamine.

No wonder *The Sims* and *Nintendogs* have been able to attract such large audiences! They are activating the same reward system that challenge-based games tap into with the experience of fiero in victory, but via an entirely different set of mechanisms. This discovery should in principle end the debate (such as it is) as to whether games of mimicry are a viable marketplace, but since the case in favor of this conclusion was fairly robust even prior to the new research, it is likely that the games industry will stubbornly persist in its challenge-obsessed rut.

One last thought concerning mimicry and the brain concerns the recently discovered neural mechanisms referred to as *mirror neurons* [Rizzolatti04]. These were accidentally discovered by the researchers Giacomo Rizzolatti, Luciano Fadiga, Leonardo Fogassi, and Vittorio Gallese, who were experimenting on the neurons of macaque monkeys. They discovered neurons that activated whether the monkeys were doing a particular action, *or watching someone carry out that action* [Rizzolatti96]. A great number of hypotheses have since appeared concerning these, but whatever is eventually decided concerning their operation it is very likely that these are intimately tied up with our enjoyment of mimicry, not to mention our capacity to learn by imitation.

Types of Curiosity

Returning to Malone, he divides curiosity into two variants: *sensory curiosity*, which is about maintaining interest in the senses (and matches up with Biederman and Vessel), and *cognitive curiosity*, which is more about the semantic content of information. For example, one picks up a *National Geographic* because the photo on the cover is intriguing—this is sensory curiosity. One picks up a newspaper because of a surprising headline—this is cognitive curiosity [Malone80].

The idea of sensory curiosity is not enormously explored beyond the basic statement, although there is some discussion about Jerry Mander's 1978 work on television and TV commercials in particular. The discussion here focuses on "technical events"—that is, camera cuts, zooms, and other changes that apparently serve to keep the viewer's interest solely on the level of sensory interest. I believe there is considerably more work to be conducted in exploring sensory curiosity in videogames.

On the subject of cognitive curiosity, Malone makes an interesting (although intuited and therefore essentially unsupported) claim:

> *...people are motivated to bring to all their cognitive structures three of the characteristics of well-formed scientific theories: completeness, consistency, and parsimony. According to this theory, the way to engage learners' curiosity is to present just enough information to make their existing knowledge seem incomplete, inconsistent, or unparsimonious.*

There is much to explore in the context of videogames in terms of these three conditions: each suggests a way to sustain the interest of players. By comparison, Lazzaro's work highlights three aspects of curiosity that can be leveraged: *ambiguity*, *incompleteness*, and *detail*. Ambiguity seems to match Malone's inconsistency to some extent, incompleteness matches incompleteness perfectly, and Lazzaro's detail seems to match Malone's sensory curiosity. Only Malone's term unparsimonious (that is to say, ideas that violate the principle of Occam's razor that knowledge should be succinct) seems unmatched in this comparison. I'm uncertain to what extent players are interested in parsimonious game rules, or to be more precise, while I'm certain some players are interested in developing parsimonious knowledge, it's unclear how one leverages the absence of parsimony to provoke curiosity.

Curiosity and Chance

One final aspect of how Malone suggests making use of player curiosity is particularly intriguing. In the 1981 paper, he includes the following bullet point under the subheading of curiosity [Malone81]:

> *Does the interface use randomness in a way that adds variety without making tools unreliable?*

This matches up to our exploration of the landscape function. Malone is suggesting that randomness is useful in games because it can provoke curiosity—and on examination, it seems he is on to something here. It is undeniable that the benefit of randomly generating content in a videogame is that the chance-fuelled combinations will produce something intriguing, memorable, or simply bizarre. Malone even lists *randomness* as one of four factors most strongly correlated with a game's popularity (the other three being explicit goals, score-keeping, and audio effects—but since he was working in 1980 it is important to remember just how crude the games used in his studies would have been).

The idea that an uncertain outcome can fuel a player's interest is one of the most fascinating elements of the Malone papers, and suggests a link between chance and curiosity in videogames. Malone notes:

Randomness and humor, if used carefully, can also help make an environment optimally complex.

And also:

...if randomness is used in a way that makes tools unreliable it will almost certainly be frustrating rather than enjoyable.

Malone's observations that uncertain outcomes are inherently part of the draw of videogames warrant further investigation. It seems to me that there are games where the outcome is not really uncertain—in most RPGs, you know you're going to level up, you just don't know *how*, for instance—but even in these cases there is always a level of uncertainty at work. Consider how a player who has mastered a particular game produces a new uncertainty by adding a higher level goal (in speed runs, for instance)—thus restoring uncertainty to the situation.

Perhaps in uncertainty there could be a definitive link between chance and curiosity, something that will expand the emotions associated with chance in games and potentially suggest a whole new avenue of exploration in videogame design.

Types of Mimicry

There are many aspects to the expression of mimicry in games, although in broad strokes they can be considered to belong to a small set of themes:

- Games that facilitate a performance element
- Games that provide mimicry as a challenge
- Games that rely upon toyplay
- Games that are driven by curiosity
- Games that employ physical elements (kinesthetic mimicry)

I will describe the first four briefly before discussing the fifth in the next section.

Games that facilitate performance tend to be online and multiplayer. After all, one must have an audience in order to perform, and although this is conceivable in a single player game (imagine a child performing for a parent, for instance), the commercial advantages are most significant when the volume of spectators becomes sufficiently large. This is readily apparent in *World of Warcraft*, which shrewdly included commands, such as /dance, which allow for anyone to enter into ad hoc performance. However, thus far these elements of mimicry have largely been incidental, and no one has leveraged people's enjoyment of mimicry as a primary play element, although a case could be made for the massively multiplayer screensaver, *The Endless Forest* (Tale of Tales, 2005).

An example of a game that presents mimicry as a central challenge is the *Tokyo Bus Guide* (Forty Five, 1999 onwards) games. These pose the player with a very specific challenge: become a bus conductor in the city of Tokyo. Although there is a mode in which the player steers the bus, the game comes into its own in the mode in which the player controls only the indicators, doors, and tannoy system. In the play of this game, players "win" by acting as convincing bus conductors. They must stop the bus close to the passengers at the bus stop, indicate before pulling away—and don't forget to play an announcement so that the passengers know where the bus is going! Strangely compelling, the game is slightly too rigid for Western tastes, although the basic play can undoubtedly be exported in other ways.

Toyplay games are exemplified by *Animal Crossing*. Players are invited to play with the game elements however they wish. They are not placed in a structure that dictates goals and challenges to be overcome, rather they are placed in an imaginary world and empowered to play. There are small challenges in *Animal Crossing*, such as the fishing micro-game and the (optional) daily hunt for buried treasure, but these are elective components in a game that has, as its central activity, the decoration and expansion of the player's house. There is also a secondary interpersonal element—the player lives in a town with animals who become the player's friends (albeit at a very low level of sophistication). This is a quintessential mimicry experience—much akin to playing with a doll house (play also leveraged by *The Sims*), although it is worth remembering that the landscape function also provides variety to the play. The game probably also involves the social center (hypothalamus) because of its friendly reactions with the other characters, but research in this area is scant.

Games that focus on curiosity generally present a detailed environment, within which there are things to find. In the casual games space, this is represented by *hidden object* games exemplified by the *Mystery Case Files* series (Big Fish, 2005 onwards), which was the first successful game of the genre [Hillis07] (which is the third of the three most popular forms of casual games [Irwin08]). These games owe a debt to earlier book-based hidden object play, of which the best-known examples are the classic British puzzle book series *Where's Wally?* (Martin Handford, 1987), known as *Where's Waldo?* in North America. These clearly use the interest mechanism described by Biederman and Vessel: a richly-interpretable scene is provided, in which the players are invited to seek out a specific target person or object, or a collection of such.

Another approach to mimicry focused on curiosity is represented by explorable 3D environments, such as the diving simulation *Endless Ocean* (Arika, 2007), which allows players to explore a virtual sea at their own pace, seeking out new types of fish. The game is extremely laid back, and contains little excitement except for the discovery of new creatures (and the chance to swim with sharks), relying wholly upon mimicry for its play. Examining reviews for this game highlights the hostility among certain gamer hobbyists for games of pure mimicry (as opposed to games of competition or vertigo). Although *Famitsu* and *NGamer* gave it positive reviews, *Eurogamer* described it as "pleasant, pretty, bubbly boredom," whereas *GamePro* said "it lacks a crucial element: fun" (clearly equating fun here with either Lazzaro's Hard Fun or Serious Fun, and neglecting the possibility of Easy Fun being sufficient on its own). Furthermore, *Electronic Gaming Monthly* opted to spend its review space mocking the game, further highlighting that games of pure mimicry struggle for acceptance among many gamer hobbyists, despite their relative popularity in the mass market [WikiEO].

In recent years, the most successful commercial games have undoubtedly been the recent *Grand Theft Auto* games, particularly *GTA: San Andreas* which has sold a staggering 20 million units [Take-Two07]. Part of the appeal of these games is that the player is presented with a world to explore and play within, with an impressive lack of limitations relative to other games. Steal cars, beat up or run over pedestrians, knock over a liquor store, and engage in a high-speed police chase—these are the public face of the play of these games. But if one examines how people actually play the games, you will also find people driving around the cities for fun, getting dressed up and going out on a date (in *San Andreas*), and sitting on the beach, watching the sunset while the radio plays a nostalgic hit. These games deliver mimicry to a degree previously unrealized. However, Rockstar North achieved this only by virtue of game budgets on a scale previously unrealized.

It is an omnipresent fallacy within the games industry that it is necessary to spend ever more money in order to make profitable games. It is true that if you want to see sales figures on the scale of tens of millions you will need a big budget—either for development (*GTA*) or for marketing (*The Sims*), or more likely for both. But many of the games that are afforded vast budgets have no potential to tap the higher sales figures. Any game, like *God of War* (SCE Studios Santa Monica, 2005), *Prince of Persia: Sands of Time* (Ubisoft Montreal, 2003), or *Tom Clancy's Splinter Cell* (Ubisoft Montreal, 2002), that has challenge at the center of its play is probably going to top out around three to five million units or so. Any mimicry included in these games is stifled by a structure that is anathematic to the play needs of a wider audience: a series of challenges that must be overcome to progress. Of course, five million units is still a great sales figure, but the point is that adding more money isn't going to grow the audiences of these games significantly, and at some point adding to the development budget is going to result in a net loss.

The detailed graphics and animations that can facilitate mimicry are expensive, but games of mimicry need not be. *Animal Crossing* is a great example, as it uses rather dated graphics to limit its development cost. True, the audience for such a game is less than the audience for (say) *GTA*—but the economics of games simply require that games make more money than they cost to make. *Nintendogs* is another good example, enjoying popular success despite (I am assuming) modest development costs.

Kinesthetic Mimicry

The arrival of the Nintendo Wii has brought mimicry to the forefront of everyone's attention thanks to its phenomenal success in reaching out to a wider market. The Wii has become the best-selling console of its generation [Sanchanta07] despite an endless prophecy of doom from gamer hobbyists and industry professionals alike concerning the limitations of the console.

I have already discussed how mimicry can be expressed in many forms, but few have such wide appeal as kinesthetic mimicry—that which involves the players' sense of touch and motion. You can see it in small children who play with toys that mimic adult tools—plastic mechanics tools or cooking utensils, or mock weapons such as wooden swords and toy guns. The experience of mimicry is enhanced by the use of such props.

The earliest instances of the use of kinesthetic elements in videogames occur in arcade games and Atari (not to be confused with the modern publisher which has bought this name) were at the forefront in the arcade revolution of the 1970s. *Qwak!* (Atari, 1974) featured a satisfyingly sturdy shotgun peripheral that was integral to its cabinet, and extended the kinesthetic mimicry of a carnival shooting gallery game (which predate videogames) to an electronic form. (The earliest light gun game, incidentally, is considered to be the *Seeburg Ray-O-Lite*, from 1936.) In the same year, *Gran Trak 10* (Atari, 1974) used a steering wheel to add kinesthetic mimicry to a simple top-down driving game. (This game was also the first to use ROM memory.) However, the graphics of these early videogames were crude, and these early attempts were largely unsuccessful.

In the next decade, arcade games began to explore kinesthetic elements further, and games like *Out Run* (Sega, 1986) had a cabinet featuring not only a steering wheel, but a gear stick as well. *Hard Drivin'* (Atari, 1989) went one step further. Its steering wheel included forced feedback (a first for the arcade). The cabinet featured a gear stick and an ignition key, which the player turned to start playing. Coupled with its early shaded polygonal graphics (which were a sensation at the time), *Hard Drivin'* was a hit in arcades the world over. Similarly, gun play was catered to with new cabinets such as *Operation Wolf* (Taito, 1987) and its sequels.

By the 1990s, the arcade audience demographic had shifted considerably. For some time, the rise of the home consoles and the PC as a gaming machine had taken the gamer hobbyists out of the arcades and back into their dingy bedrooms. Arcade games were increasingly required to draw upon kinesthetic mimicry to pull in a broader audience, and the games of the '90s illustrate this neatly. Namco built elaborate control devices into their games *Prop Cycle* (Namco, 1996), *Alpine Surfer* (Namco, 1996), and *Rapid River* (Namco, 1997). *Prop Cycle* was the most successful of the three—its control mechanism was literally a bicycle, and its pedal-powered play had wide appeal (although players often lacked the stamina to play more than once a day!), whereas *Alpine Surfer* used a snowboard (coupled with a hand rail) for control, and *Rapid River* used a paddle to control its virtual dinghy.

Namco wasn't the only company pushing in this direction. *Sega Bass Fishing* (Sega, 1998) was not an enormous success in arcades, but was widely distributed around bars in the United States, whereas *Dance Dance Revolution* (Konami, 1999) was a runaway success with its dance platform which allowed players to literally move their whole bodies to control the game. All of these new games had one thing in common: they were good exercise as well as being good fun.

However, attempts to spread kinesthetic mimicry into the home were less successful. In fact, until recently the only form to make it into the home was the light gun. The NES Zapper (Famicom Light Gun in Japan) was shipped with the system from 1984 (and similarly with the less successful XG-1 bundled with the Atari XEGS system). These first light guns enjoyed success because they were bundled with the consoles, but as light guns began to be packaged separately the problem with getting kinesthetic mimicry into the home became more apparent: the cost of the peripherals was a barrier. Games were generally quite expensive; adding the cost of the light gun peripheral made them out of the reach of most families.

The Sega Dreamcast was the first console to really attempt to push other forms of kinesthetic mimicry into the home, most significantly with the excellent home version of *Sega Bass Fishing* (Sega, 1999), which captured the play of its arcade predecessor with the satisfyingly realistic fishing controller, and with the novel *Samba De Amigo* (Sega, 2000), which required special maraca controllers to play. But the same problem dogged these attempts: the cost of the game and controller together was prohibitive.

The first real success story of bringing this kind of play into the home was with Konami's *Dance Dance Revolution* brand. Although retailers were reluctant to stock the dance pad peripherals, the arcade game was so popular that the PlayStation and PlayStation 2 versions of the game (from 1999–2006) experienced unprecedented success through online sales. Part of the reason for the success was that the games targeted an audience traditionally considered out-of-bounds for videogames (namely a female audience, although the games were enjoyed by both genders).

Sony's EyeToy, released in Europe along with *EyeToy Play* (Sony, 2003) used visual and motion-recognition technologies to allow the players to control games with their entire body—while simultaneously showing the players themselves on-screen. Although a great commercial success, the general lack of sensitivity meant that it was not ideal as a control device, and was mostly only used for simple mini-games.

The success of both dance mat controllers and the EyeToy paved the way for the boldest step forward in bringing kinesthetic mimicry into the home. In 2006, Nintendo unveiled their latest home console, Wii. Its unique remote controller contained a variety of sensors, including a pointing suite equivalent to a light gun, tilt sensors, and motion sensors. This device offered something that was previously an impossibility: it could be used in multiple different roles to mimic multiple different activities. The Wii removed the barrier that had previously hindered kinesthetic mimicry from making it into the home: the expense of a separate control device. The Wii remote came bundled with the console.

Furthermore, with Nintendo packaging *Wii Sports* (Nintendo, 2006) with the console, it had produced a home electronic package ideal for a wide audience—five different experiences of kinesthetic mimicry, most of which were readily understandable by a new player (even one with low game literacy) since the actions of play were modeled upon the actions of the sports being simulated. The fact that the games are also great aerobic exercise only furthers their appeal.

However, the potential to bring experiences of kinesthetic mimicry into the home still depended upon games that leveraged this potential. Although *Wii Sports* succeeded admirably, the 50 mini-games in *Super Monkey Ball: Banana Blitz* (Sega, 2006) show the problems of developing for Wii. Many of the control mechanisms for the mini-games are difficult to teach the players (since they do not copy real-world motions), and consequently produce highly unsatisfying game experiences.

Nonetheless, the Wii represents the forefront of this form of mimicry, and has already succeeded in bringing a wider audience of players into the videogames market with its potential for highly intuitive control, and the ability to mimic any number of different activities. It is likely, however, that this wider audience will buy only a few games for the Wii, hence the majority of the cash flow in the games industry will remain focused on the gamer hobbyist (requiring new games every month and, in some cases, every week). Both Sony and Microsoft are hemorrhaging money on their hardware in an attempt to secure the support of the key demographics, whereas Nintendo is making sterling revenues on its console, selling it to a broader demographic and making a profit on every unit sold.

Although the chief activities emulated in videogames remain the same—guns, cars, and sports—the advent of a generalized control solution for kinesthetic mimicry finally breaks down the cost barrier of getting this form of play into the home. The chief question remaining is whether the success of the Wii is sufficient to spur Sony into continuing its copycat policy (almost every hardware or controller change that Sony has implemented, with the exception of the EyeToy and the Buzz quiz controllers, has been in imitation of Nintendo to some extent). Either way, the Wii represents a significant step forward in the kinesthetic mimicry of videogames.

The Imagination of Mimicry

I strongly believe (and the market data confirms) that there is a vast untapped market for games that present mimicry as their core play. Firstly, such games can invite the players to play in their own way and at their own pace. They need not place frustrations in the player's path and force the player to overcome them. This appeals to challenge-focused players but these do not appear to be in the majority (although as mentioned, they are still a significant niche market because they spend a considerable amount of money on videogames). The worlds of these games do not need to be as large as a *GTA* world to support play—instead of large but emotionally empty worlds, they can be smaller but more emotionally invested worlds by allowing more player customization, say, or by having non-player characters with personality.

In his book *The Blockbuster Toy*, Gene Del Vechio (a veteran marketer from major toy companies) provides eight different ways a toy can appeal to a child, all of which are based around his concept that a successful toy transforms the child in a manner which is emotionally on target. One of these is related to challenge and mastery, and one is related to collecting (a form of play not covered by Caillois' model, but which relates to Skinner's reward schedules). The remaining six are all forms of mimicry, with themes such as creating (*Sim City*), nurturing (*Nintendogs*), emulation (*Endless Ocean*), friendship (*Animal Crossing*), story emulation (film licenses such as *LEGO Star Wars*), and experience (*World of Warcraft*) [Del Vechio03].

Adult play is simply an extension of child play. Some of the themes and content may be expanded, of course. Sexual or intensely violent themes may emerge, and emulation of stories that have already been experienced may expand to full-blown storyplay (the spontaneous creation of new stories). At its core, however, much of play is about imagination, and games of mimicry are tools for enhancing imagination and reducing the degree of suspension of disbelief required. Adults may no longer be able to create spontaneous play out of little plastic figures, but place them in a vivid digital world and suddenly they all become like little children, eager to indulge their imagination and often desperate to escape the confines of the mundane world.

Mimicry is a powerful tool for play, but it is one that until now games have often harnessed only tangentially. When we recognize just how powerful mimicry can be; when we get past merely shackling players to repetitive play by designing addictive play systems that use reward schedules to maintain interest, or narrowly defining the world of games as those which supply fiero; when we watch how people play, and what they enjoy; perhaps then we will be ready to allow videogames to be all that they can be.

Imagination is unlimited. Games should be too.

Conclusion

Les Jeux et Les Hommes was the first attempt to consider the common cross-cultural patterns that occur in play and games, and remains as relevant and intriguing today as when it was first published in 1958. The four patterns of play (and the axis of complexity that accompanies these) provide a way of understanding how and why people play games of any kind, and as I hope to have demonstrated here is particularly relevant to videogames. As the games industry moves forward into the future, we are better equipped than ever to understand how to design games that people will enjoy, and we are finally beginning to comprehend the inherent diversity that is generated by the infinite possible combinations of the patterns of play first explored by Roger Caillois 50 years ago.

UNDERSTAND THE LIMITS OF THEORY

by Richard A. Bartle

The first player model to be published was Richard Bartle's framework for considering the relationship between different kinds of players in MUDs—the text-based virtual worlds which were the precursor to modern Massively Multiplayer Online games. Having looked at different aspects of player modelling and psychology of play from the point of view of emotions, social play, and Caillois' patterns of play, you are now in a position to consider the limitations of a theoretical approach to game design.

INTRODUCTION

Bartle's[1] player types model is the best-known and most widely used theory of virtual world design. However, it is frequently misunderstood and misapplied. This step examines the basic theory and describes how it tends to be used in practice. Then, it explains how it *should* be used.

ANECDOTE

One of *MUD2*'s players was called Dextrus.

Dextrus was among the most imaginative players[2] we ever had—very innovative, very exciting and *very* charming. She had something of a bad girl reputation, though: in a game where character death was permanent[3], people tended to be more than a little upset when Dextrus appeared out of nowhere, beat them up, and took their stuff. It was made all the more embarrassing because she was invariably at a lower level than her victims when she did this.

One day, Dextrus decided to abandon her killing ways. Tired of being treated as a pariah, she announced that she would thenceforth fight no other player characters except in self defence. Sure enough, that's what she did. In the weeks that followed, she redeemed her previous indiscretions by helping out other people unstintingly; she rushed to their defence when monsters caught them unawares, she gave them her own equipment to use, and she led thrilling expeditions to the more far-flung and dangerous parts of The Land. Because she was so charismatic and kept true to her word, in a short space of time she became hugely popular.

So it was that some three months later she volunteered to accompany another player, a mage, on his "wiz run". The way *MUD2* works is that once characters have sufficient experience points, they are promoted to the level of wizard/witch (or *wiz* for short); this means the regular game is over and they achieve immortality—it's effectively ascension to an administrator position. A *wiz run* is when you're trying to get those final few points you need, with everyone else in the game either cheering you on or hoping to stop you. It's often a player's most heart-thumping, exhilarating time in the virtual world, long to be remembered. Dextrus had generously offered to be the mage's bodyguard as he endeavored to rack up those last, remaining, precious points.

---

[1] Which is to say, my.

[2] Actually, she was a *character*, rather than a player. Her player was male—he's now a senior lecturer in computer games at the University of Portsmouth—but Dextrus was female.

[3] Yes, permanent: if your character died in combat, it was obliterated from the database.

The pair descended deep underground, to the realm of the dwarfs. The risks were high—there were a lot of dwarfs—but the rewards commensurate. The mage and Dextrus fought their way side-by-side through several heavily-guarded rooms until they finally stood on the threshold of the treasure chamber. The contents of this trove would be enough to push the mage over the finishing line and into wizardhood.

Suddenly, disaster struck! Dextrus went off to the Royal Bedroom to deal with the queen dwarf, but the king dwarf appeared before the mage could follow and immediately attacked! The fight went right to the wire, and it looked as if the mage—still injured from earlier fights—would lose. Then, in the nick of time, Dextrus finished off the queen, raced back, and took down the king.

And before the mage could even say thanks, Dextrus took him down, too.

She'd been tracking the king, knew where he was, knew when he was about to appear, and had deliberately left to kill the much easier queen knowing that the king would instantly assault the mage. Next, having despatched the queen in a timely manner, she waited until the mage was close to death and valiantly returned to save the day.

Then, in one exquisite moment, she killed a mage who was 30 seconds short of making wizard. It was exactly 100 days since she'd last killed another player character.

Moments passed, and a zero-points novice entered the game, bearing the same name as the deceased mage. He shouted a single, agonised word: "WHY?"

The reply was simple: "Because I'm Dextrus."

Everyone Thinks They're a Designer

Everyone who plays virtual worlds thinks they're a designer.

If you play virtual worlds, you, too, think you're a designer. You have opinions on why some things are just plain wrong, how other things could be improved with just a few minor tweaks, what's fun and what's not, and how the virtual world should be. If you were in charge, things would be like *this*!

However, unless you really *are* a designer, you're deluding yourself. What you *actually* want is a virtual world that you, personally, would wish to play. Designers don't create virtual worlds that they, personally, wish to play; they create virtual worlds that *people* wish to play.

Designers read up on every subject that they can conceivably find of relevance to creating virtual worlds. They'll spend six hours absorbed in details of the inner workings of the Palestine Liberation Organization in the 1970s because somehow they sense it will help their understanding of guilds, or orcs, or griefing, or terrain, or who knows what[4]. They build up an implicit understanding of how and why things fit together, and draw on it when they construct worlds.

It's not, therefore, unsurprising that designers will read every piece of academic work on virtual worlds that they can get their hands on[5]. Indeed, they're not averse to creating their own theories for use by other designers. Furthermore, other designers will sometimes use those theories if they think they're useful tools. After all, designers speak the same language, and know what the theories are saying.

Except... everyone thinks they're a designer. Players, journalists, academics, and game developers all think they're designers. If you ask them, well no, of *course* they won't *say* they're designers. In their very next breath, though, they'll be telling you why *PvP* is unfair, or how the crafting system is broken, or what can be done about real-money trading, or that warlocks need to be nerfed *right now*. They profess not to be designers, but then proceed to act as if they believe they are.

Now when these people read theories of virtual world design, a number of things can happen. Sometimes, they actually are nascent designers, and they understand the theories fully—this is not as uncommon as one might think[6]. Often, they're no kind of designer, but they still "get" what a theory is saying. The problems only arise with people who

- Don't properly understand the theory.
- Misapply the theory as a consequence of this.
- Take it upon themselves to trash the theory in public because it clearly doesn't work.

Sadly, this is not as uncommon as one might think, either.

In this step, I'm going to look at one of the most enduring theories of virtual world design, and describe the ways in which it has been misunderstood and misapplied. I shall then explain how it should be understood and should be applied. I get to do this because it's my theory[7].

---

[4] One of my students did this once, at a critical period when he should have been working on his final-year project. He felt very frustrated and angry, because how was he ever going to become a designer if he allowed himself to be distracted in this way? I told him that, on the contrary, it meant he was *destined* to be a designer, and related the occasion I spent two days reading up on pagodas when I should have been revising for a programming examination. Designers just do that kind of thing.

[5] They won't necessarily agree with its premise or conclusions, but they'll read it.

[6] The ability to design virtual worlds is not some rare gift handed out to the chosen few by the gods of creativity—like storytelling, many, many people have it within themselves.

[7] This makes it very painful for me—not because it hurts to say bad things about my theory, but because it hurts to say good things about it. It's just too close to self-aggrandizement.

Before I begin, though, I should perhaps say something that may surprise the non-designers among you: I *want* my theory to be superseded. I want it, because that means we'll get a better theory in its place, which in turn means we'll get better virtual worlds.

I really, *really* want better virtual worlds.

PLAYER TYPES

In 1996, I published a paper called *Hearts, Clubs, Diamonds, Spades: Players who Suit MUDs* [Bartle96]. In it, I examined the reasons why people play MUDs (as virtual worlds were known back then), and showed how the different playing styles were interdependent.

The paper was far more successful than I had expected it to be—I thought it was pretty obscure stuff that most designers knew intuitively anyway. I was probably correct in this view too, but because I'd actually written it down, that meant designers could make *non*-designers read it. In doing so, they could at last explain why, for example, it was not a waste of time to implement features that none of the programmers liked. Other people *would* like them—people who were just as important to the health of the virtual world as win-at-any-cost gamers. Although it may seem natural today to muse about how socialisers want one thing and how achievers want another, back in the mid-1990s this wasn't the case at all until *HCDS* appeared. Game worlds were essentially designed for developers, not for players.

Since then, the player types theory has been used to inform the design of many virtual worlds, including most of the large-scale game worlds from *Ultima Online* (Origin Systems, 1997 onwards). Designers always "got" it; all it really meant to them was that they could say things such as "the explorers will like that; okay, let's put it in" to one another when they couldn't before. Of course, given that I was telling them what they already knew, it should come as no surprise that they took the ideas of the paper on board fairly swiftly.

What was more of a revelation, though, was the extent to which players embraced the model. They could see themselves in it, they could see their friends in it, and it made sense. There was even a survey created, so people could find out what their "Bartle Quotient" was; it's still on-going, and over 500,000 people have completed it to date—making it the largest and longest-running gamer survey on the Internet [Andreasen99]. Countless blog and forum threads have appeared directly as a result.

The paper completed its passage into canon when it was reprinted in textbooks aimed at both the games industry [Mulligan03] and academia [Salen05].

And with that final hint at respectability, I can finally end the torture of singing my own theory's praises...

So what does the theory say?

Well, my having just extolled at length the theory's ubiquity, it would be rather contradictory to continue as if you had never come across it before[8]. I'll therefore only give a brief overview of it here—you can consult the original paper if you want to "refresh your memory" concerning its details.

The theory posits that people who play virtual worlds for fun don't all find the same things fun, but that their different ideas of what is or isn't fun can be captured using two parameters. The first of these is the degree to which they prefer to deal with the players of the virtual world as opposed to the virtual world itself (or *vice versa*). The second is the degree to which they prefer to act upon or interact with the first parameter.

The result can be expressed in the form of a graph[9], as shown in Figure 4.1. As you can see, the graph describes four *player types*:

- *Achievers* like acting on the virtual world. Their aim is usually to succeed in the context of the virtual world—to reach the highest level, for example.
- *Explorers* like interacting with the virtual world. They act in order to find out things about the virtual world and how it works.
- *Socialisers* like interacting with other players. They like talking, being part of a group, and helping others.
- *Killers* like acting on other players. Sometimes, this is to gain a big, bad reputation (whence the name), but other times it's to gain a big, good reputation (in guild politics, for example).

The theory goes further, in that it explains the relationship between each player type. Socialisers, for example, like each other's company, regard explorers as mostly harmless, have a mutually uneasy tolerance of achievers, and utterly loathe killers. Lowering the number of killers in a virtual world would therefore make it more attractive to socialisers—but only up to a point. Even though they don't like killers, socialisers do like having something to talk about, and killers perform that role for them.

---

[8] Altogether possible, but nonetheless contradictory...

[9] Back in 1999, I was designing on one of the earlier versions of *The Lord of the Rings Online* (one that never made it into production) and had cause to attend a meeting with the publishers and license holders. I was pleasantly entertained when one of the publishers drew this graph on a whiteboard and asked us how our design addressed each of the quadrants.

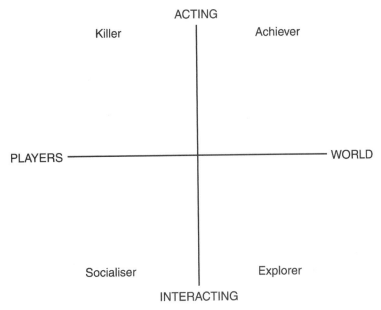

FIGURE 4.1 Player interest graph.

Put another way, if you take away all the killers, you take away the seasoning that brings out the main flavors of the dish that socialisers want to eat, leaving it bland and tasteless. However, having too many killers makes the dish too spicy to be palatable, and stops socialisers from tasting anything else.

So, this, in a nutshell, is the player types model. Some points to note:

- It applies only to people who play virtual worlds for fun. It doesn't apply to people who play virtual worlds but not for fun. This may be the case for groups such as journalists, academics, and designers, for example, who are playing for meta-reasons.
- Likewise, the model does not apply to people who play things other than virtual worlds for fun. More appropriate theories exist that should be used even for related game formats, such as face-to-face role-playing [Kim98], or for games in general [Koster05]. Some of these approaches do bear a passing resemblance to the player types model [Lazzaro04c], but their subject matter is nevertheless formally beyond its scope. Furthermore, although the precepts of the model have been found to be valuable in some non-game areas such as website design [Kim00], I make no claims as to its competence in those areas myself.
- It is intended to be used by game designers. If you want a theory for other purposes (such as studying player psychology), you may be

better served by a straight taxonomy that comes with data sets (such as Nick Yee's *motivations* [Yee07]).

- The player types described may resonate with groupings from other, earlier systems[10], but this wasn't done with any foreknowledge on my part. Any similarities are there either through coincidence or because I was inadvertently reinventing the wheel.
- It's a *model*, not simply a categorization system: you can "run" it to build a picture of how a virtual world will turn out with different balances of player types. This means it can be used predictively, and its predictions can be tested.

The model has continuing utility. This is important to mention, because unlike general scientific theories (which, the longer they last, the more they are trusted), there is among gamers a belief that what was true for textual worlds in 1996 can't possibly be true of today's vast graphical extravaganzas; the theory's mere longevity alone must therefore discredit it[11].

Unluckily, demonstrating that the theory is still both used and useful is not altogether easy in a formal academic context, because so few designers ever discuss their designs in a public forum. Thus, although it might be possible to discern from the questionnaire given to beta testers of *Pirates of the Burning Sea* (Flying Lab, 2008) that the developers wanted to know your player type, the actuality is not recorded anywhere that can be cited (and therefore the supposition could well be wrong). Likewise, the observation that *World of Warcraft* (Blizzard, 2004) awards experience points every time a character enters a new area seems strongly to suggest a desire to reward explorers, but this doesn't mean the player types theory was ever invoked. *WoW*'s designers have not gone on record as to what informed (or didn't inform) such decisions.

---

[10] For example, there was a Medieval theory of "four temperaments" (choleric, melancholic, phlegmatic, sanguine), based on a Greco-Roman medical theory of "four humors," which can profitably be used in theories of game design—see Step 8 in this book! It's very tempting to suppose that these temperaments must correspond loosely to player types, although the details of such a mapping are non-obvious (I've seen several different versions). This is unsurprising, because the only thing they *actually* have in common is a division of individuals into four types. Incidentally, the four temperaments theory fed into philosopher Carl Jung's work on psychological types, which in turn spawned other theories of personality type and led to psychometric tests such as Myers-Briggs; these later developments can also be used in game design, but again bear no relationship to the player types model [Bateman05].

[11] This is not a view limited to my theory, either. Large tracts of work done on textual worlds in the 1990s are routinely and deliberately ignored by new researchers, who don't seem to want to accept that the virtual world experience behind the interface is much the same for both textual and graphical worlds.

Occasionally, however, designers do mention their use of the model. For example, Paul Barnett, Creative Director for *Warhammer: Age of Reckoning* (Mythic, 2008), explained in an interview with the BBC how this game specifically targeted player types that other game worlds[12] had neglected [BBC08].

One particularly stand-out example of how the model had shown to be effective concerns *GoPets* (GoPets, 2005), a virtual world primarily for children that involves looking after interactive, virtual pets and kitting them out with "cool clothing and accessories." It's subscription-free, but players buy things in-world for (ultimately) real money. Initially designed to be entirely a social world, it (in the designer's words) "carpet bombed" the social quadrant of the player types grid [Bethke07]. It did reasonably well.

Then, the developers did some data-mining to see which virtual objects sold to heavy users (so they could make other objects along similar lines). They discovered that one particular object, a fruit tree available for only three weeks, attracted players who were 11 times more likely to be active than average users. Not only that, but when compared to other active users, these people were four times more likely to be heavy (profitable) users. Put another way, fruit tree buyers were 44 times more likely to be profitable than regular *GoPets* players [Schubert07].

The fruit tree was just about the only element in *GoPets* that had a goal-oriented behavior associated with it: if you looked at it for an hour, it produced a fruit (but the timer reset if you went away) [Woodard08]. The *GoPets* team realized that the people buying it were, according to the player types model, achievers. They therefore decided to add more game-like elements, in order to make play more attractive to the achiever mind-set. They began by putting in some simple cooking and farming activities.

Seven days later, this had *doubled* their revenue.

So yes, the player types model does still work and is still relevant (at least for *GoPets*).

INTERPRETATION

I'm now going to spend some time describing common ways in which the player types model is assailed, and explaining why these are (or are not) misinterpretations of what the paper says.

To some extent, what follows will come across as a classic "straw man" argument, in that I will give unsupported, generalized statements

---

12   Well, *WoW*...

of criticisms for the sole purpose of demolishing them. Now actually, I could name names and provide references—turning straw into flesh in the process—but I'd rather not do this because I don't want to give the appearance of being vindictive[13]. However, for the sole purpose of demonstrating that the arguments I am about to outline are not *entirely* the product of my wild imaginings, I will reluctantly point the finger at one paper [Karlsen04], which I have selected for such treatment purely because it is the one most often cited by other papers (including some heavyweights [Yoon05] [McGonigal06])[14].

So, the first thing to point out is that my paper does have some genuine flaws, and many of the criticisms levelled at it are not due to misinterpretations at all but to actual shortcomings [Bartle08]. Its main problems are:

- There seem to be two distinct groups of player in the killer quadrant. One type wants to act on players for bad reasons (the eponymous *killers*) and the other for more laudable reasons of group organization (what might be called *politicians*).
- Players are known to move between types over time, but there is no mechanism offered to suppose how or why this happens.
- The model doesn't account for the concept of *immersion*.
- The theory doesn't link to any established theories from beyond the games industry.

All these issues were addressed by a modification to the basic theory that adds a third dimension to the 2D graph [Bartle03b], [Bartle05], thereby turning the four-type model into an eight-type model. It is important to note, however, that this does not mean that the theory is validated— just that these particular holes in it have been fixed. Eventually, new holes *will* be identified which can't be patched, an understanding of which will hopefully form the basis of an entirely new theory.

Most of the mundane attacks on the theory, of the kind perpetuated in guild fora and other message boards, are relatively easy to dismiss. For example, "Where do gold farmers fit in? They don't!" is easily explained by pointing out that gold farmers[15] aren't playing for fun—they fall into the meta-player category—and that the player types model explicitly excludes such people from its categorization.

Another common tactic is the counter-example that isn't: "I like building/crafting/fishing, but that isn't one of the types!". Well yes, it

---

[13] You swine, you know who you are...

[14] Sorry, Faltin!

[15] These are people who play virtual worlds in order to acquire in-world currency that they can sell for real-world currency—usually against the wishes of the developer and the majority of the players.

isn't—but have you asked *why* you like building/crafting/fishing? Because you want to increase your fishing skills? You're an achiever. Because you want to give fish to your friends? You're probably a socialiser. Because you want to see what kinds of fish you can catch? You'll be an explorer, then. Because you hope to lure someone else into joining you so you can suddenly attack them while they're armed only with a fishing rod? Well, that would make you a killer. It's wholly possible, too, that you simply like the fishing mini-game, in which case you'd fall into the meta-player category: you're not playing the MMO because it's fun itself, you're playing it so you can play the fishing mini-game for fun.

A more interesting misunderstanding is one that accepts the theory but misapplies it. For example, a developer might read the dynamics section of the paper and conclude that if they want more socialisers (say) then they should add more socializing tools or create more common spaces where serendipitous social encounters can occur. Now while it is true that this will indeed make your virtual world more attractive to socialisers, that's not *all* it will do. It's a question of balance: if you attract more socialisers, you could also attract more killers (who love to wind up socialisers) and put off some achievers (who may conclude that the virtual world is "about" chatting, rather than "about" killing things to get stuff so you can kill bigger things to get better stuff). It's the overall package that is attractive or not, not just the individual components. Changing the components will alter the balance, but that doesn't mean it will increase the absolute number of players overall—it could even lead to a numbers-decreasing overbalance.

You have to grow your virtual world in an integrated way, or you risk shutting people out—with attendant problems for the players who remain[16].

We now come to the most important way that the player types model is misunderstood—most important because it has prompted surveys, data-mining endeavors, and (occasionally) bad design decisions.

Suppose you want to find out who the main socialisers in your virtual world are. You may wish to know this so that you can ask how you might improve your virtual world's provision for them, for example. So, what is it that sets socialisers apart from other player types? Well, they communicate. Therefore, if you check through your log files and find out who talks the most, those people will be your socialisers, right?

No, not right. Some socialisers are wonderful listeners but not enthusiastic speakers—"socialiser" does not mean extrovert. Yes, some socialisers do like to talk a lot, but a three-hour long conversation between two people could mean they're explorers exchanging notes, not socialisers gossiping. Sustained banter in guild chat could easily be driven by friendly and open

---

[16] Recall that because the player types are interdependent, the loss of one type will adversely affect the experience of another even for types that loathe each other.

socialisers, but it could also occur because achievers are getting bored grinding and if you don't give them something to do real soon they're going to get bored and leave.

The key point is that it's not what people *do* in a virtual world that defines their player type, it's *why they do it*.

Remember Dextrus? For over three months, Dextrus would have passed every field test for being a socialiser. She didn't try to rack up experience points, she didn't try to find out how esoteric parts of the game world worked, and she most certainly didn't try to kill people; no, she just helped them, because she liked being with them. Except, that wasn't why she was helping them at all. She was, the whole time, still a killer; everything she did was motivated by the desire to take down some extremely high-level character in spectacular fashion. Dextrus was, as she said, Dextrus. How could people ever have thought she was someone else?

There's a difference between "I chat" and "I like to chat"; between "I spoil people's play" and "I like to spoil people's play"; between "I find out how things work" and "I like to find out how things work"; between "I go up levels" and "I like to go up levels".

This is what is so often missed about the player types theory that I finally felt compelled to write about it here.

WHAT THE MODEL ACTUALLY SAYS

People play virtual worlds for different reasons. Watching what people do can help identify those reasons, but you can't map directly from observed behavior to the motivation that led to that behavior. To do so would be to mistake effect for cause. It's not what people do that's important; it's *why* they do it.

Sadly, it's very difficult to find out why people are doing things when your primary tool merely captures *what* they are doing. Only the players themselves can *truly* know why they're doing what they're doing, but rarely are they able to articulate their motivations beyond "because it's fun". This looks problematical: if you can't tell what type a random player is, how can you ever use the player type model *as* a model?

Fortunately, to apply the player type model's dynamics, you don't need to know what player type an individual might be—you just need to know roughly how many players there are in each group[17]. It may be

---

[17] You may also find it useful to relate their player type to their situation in the virtual world. If all the socialisers hang out in cities and all the achievers hang out in the wilderness, there isn't going to be as much interaction between them as you want, for example.

possible to do this using profiling techniques. How this works is that you identify the types of a few players independently, and then watch what they do in-world. You see how people identified to be the same type behave in ways that are measurably different to how other players behave. As long as you keep calibrating your system (because virtual worlds change over time, both in code and in culture), you should be able to get an estimate of player type numbers accurate enough to use. You will not be able to guarantee that any *individual* matching a particular profile will be of the type that the profile predicts, though; for that degree of detail, you need some other mechanism.

At this point, I should perhaps point out that as far as I know, the approach I've just outlined is not actually used by anyone. Here's why.

To calibrate your profiling system, you need some non-automated way of finding out a player's type. An example of how you might do this is simple observation. Suppose you were in a group instance in a game world such as *World of Warcraft*. The group consists of you (a researcher) plus four other people[18]. All of you are working towards the same game goal—to defeat the final boss and complete the instance—but what each of you is getting out of it could be completely different. Nevertheless, after a while the seasoned researcher should be able to form a reasonably good impression regarding which player is which type.

Sometimes it can be done with a fair degree of confidence quite quickly. The mage making imaginative use of arcane magic when every other mage you ever saw specializes in fire or frost magic is very probably going to be an explorer, for example. It's rarely that easy, though. Perhaps the tank would rather be elsewhere but came along to help a guildmate— that would be either socialiser or killer/politician behavior, and you could probably tell which by how they interacted with (socialiser) or bossed around (politician) the others in the group. However, if you didn't *know* they'd come along to help a friend, it would take you considerably longer to figure out why they were doing what they were doing.

It can take me up to an hour to get full measure of the players with whom I am grouped in a virtual world, and even then I could be wrong. Without knowledge of her history, I'd probably have thought Dextrus was a socialiser just like everyone else did, for example. Nevertheless, it doesn't take long to make a reasonably accurate appraisal as to why someone is playing—certainly good enough to be able to use the player types model.

You can do this multiple times, and will soon get a good idea as to what types a cross-section of the player base conform. This isn't all you have by then, though: you also have personal relationships with the individuals

---

[18] Because you yourself are in the group, this would make it (using a term from anthropology) *participant observation*.

concerned. This means that using them to calibrate a profiling mechanism is no longer necessary—you can simply ask them.

It's this, in fact, that is designers' preferred tactic for ascertaining how different player types are reacting to a virtual world. If you want to know what the generic socialiser thinks, you ask the particular socialisers with whom you are acquainted. Profiling is still the best tool for tracking overall balance, but the quality of feedback resulting from interviewing individuals gives that approach the edge for most other uses.

WHAT THIS MEANS FOR DESIGNERS

This is an integrated system: everything is in balance. You can't simply provide compelling content of a certain type to satisfy your players, because players need other players around them who will not be satisfied by that content.

Put another way, if you saturate a virtual world with content aimed at one type of player, as *GoPets* originally did, not only will it fail to attract players of other types (which you might have expected), but also it won't completely satisfy the type you did aim at. Player types don't exist in isolation; there's a balance to be maintained.

When designers create content, they need to consider *why* it's attractive, not merely *that* it's attractive. "Killing bosses satisfies achievers" may well be true, but it's not all that satisfies achievers, and achievers aren't the only people who are satisfied by it. Furthermore, there may be other player types who are dissatisfied by it—it might make a poor end to a narrative that was engaging an explorer or socialiser, for example.

Content is not made out of construction bricks that are labelled with those player types that find it attractive, yet believing it is makes for a common beginner's error. You can't say "we'll put in a PvP battleground system for the killers," because people can find player-versus-player combat fun for all kinds of reasons; the *ganking* of other players is only one of those reasons. However, if you read the forums of large-scale commercial game worlds, time and time again you will see people relating PvP directly to the killer player type as if the connection were a given. It isn't.

Likewise, it's often assumed that people who do crafting don't do combat, and must therefore be carebear socialisers who spend all their time gossiping when not baking virtual pies. Although this may well be true in some cases, nevertheless players can also find crafting rewarding for other reasons (as anyone who has grinded reputation in *World of Warcraft* just so they can brag about being the first in their guild to have the recipe for some über item will tell you).

Whenever you look at a gameplay mechanic in a virtual world, always remember that different player types will have different reasons for engaging with it. True, some features might indeed constitute "flagship" methods for particular types (such as chatting for socialisers), but this only makes them necessary, not sufficient. Sure, many socialisers will tend to chat a lot, but other types will chat to various degrees too, and the socialisers will themselves use content that is flagship for other types. If there is no such content, they'll feel they're missing something, and their enthusiasm will be damped until they get it (which is what *GoPets* discovered).

Remember, too, that individuals progress through different types over time[19]. If you don't cover all the types, you could well lose players sooner than you might otherwise.

WHAT USE IS A THEORY?

The player types theory explains why people play virtual worlds, but *not* what they do (in terms of identifiable actions) while playing. This may be alarming to people who plan on using it—especially designers, who actually have to write the "what they do while playing" part! Also rather scarily, it's not simply a check-box system that says "there are these categories of player and you need content for them all"—if that's what you want[20], go with a taxonomy such as [Yee07] instead. Rather, what the player types theory delivers is a full, working model, not a static categorization system.

So... what use is it?

Even if we ignore the mechanics of the model, the theory says something that had not been said until it said it: designers of virtual worlds must *understand their players*. People play virtual worlds for many reasons, and designers need to address them all—even the ones towards which they are antipathetic. The important thing is not that you *yourself* will enjoy playing the virtual world, but that you recognize the requirements of those who *will* be playing it. You have to give players the content they need, and this means you must know *why* they need it, not simply that it is needed.

If we do look at the mechanics, the theory helps give an understanding of the overall shape of a given virtual world in terms of the balance between the different player types (and therefore the content they consume). As a designer, you can add or remove content to widen or lessen its appeal to different types, but you must always remember

---

19 I don't discuss type drifting much in the original four-types paper, but it gets a full explanation in the eight-types extension [Bartle05].

20 This might be the case if you were more interested in causes than effects, for example.

that no virtual world is entirely for one kind of player—otherwise, it wouldn't be a virtual world. Even individual players aren't always one type all the time, because they transition through types as they grow in experience (the eight-types model explains why this is so). The dynamics part of the model can be used to figure out things such as why a virtual world that was well balanced before has suddenly lurched towards being over-dominated by achievers, say, or socialisers. This is something that developers need to know.

The theory also has meta-uses. For example, players will often complain that virtual world designers don't play virtual worlds with the same dedication that they, the players, do, and therefore it follows that they don't understand them to the same degree[21]. This can be a valid criticism, too, if the designer is inexperienced. After all, if a journalist is ridiculed for having written a scathing article about some MMO after only having played it for half an hour, why not slam a designer who does the same thing? Well, the answer is that accomplished designers have internalized virtual world design so much that they can pick up a great deal more intuitively from half an hour's play than can pretty well anyone else[22]. They're not playing the MMO for "player fun," they're playing for "designer fun"—enjoying the nuances of the design, not the play itself. They don't have to enjoy play *per se*, and in fact the player types theory suggests they *shouldn't* enjoy it. If they did, they'd be too blinded by their own experience to deliver on the needs of player types other than their own. Thus, what players regard as a weakness is revealed to be a strength[23].

Conclusion

My player types theory of virtual worlds says that players can be grouped together according to what they find is fun; it also explains how each of these groups needs the others. Its main thrust is that designers need to understand all such reasons if they are to create successful virtual worlds. Key to this is appreciating that *what* people do isn't as important as *why* they do it.

---

[21] This is a sign of an immature industry. In more established creative fields, it's not a problem: how many people have criticized Karl Lagerfeld for creating clothes for women by arguing that, as he himself won't be wearing any of them, he's disqualified as an expert?

[22] Actually, they'd probably need more than half an hour to get the main points straight in their minds, but things are usually pretty clear after two or three hours.

[23] Although some designers claim to be able to switch off their designer sensibilities, the condition of not being able to play for "player fun" remains a common one. It even has a name: designeritis [Koster05].

Yet even though this theory is well over a decade old, some people still seem to miss this point.

I've explained the issues here in terms of my own theory, but actually what I want to say applies to all of them: whatever theory you decide to use, you should make sure you *understand* that theory, not just the bullet-point takeaway. If you find holes in the theory but haven't made the effort to understand it, you can't be sure that they are indeed holes. If you do understand the theory and find it lacking, though, that puts you in a good position to propose changes to it, or to create a new theory entirely.

Designing virtual worlds is an art, but understanding them so that you *can* design them is a science. Treat their design as a science, and then the art will follow.

II

INCLUDE

In the second part of this book, you will learn about the diversity of players from some of the most vocal voices on diversity issues. But it would be wrong to assume these steps represent a merely perfunctory concern with social justice. When we fail to include *everyone* in the audience for videogames, and in the games industry itself, there is both money and intellectual capital at stake.

In Step Five, Sheri Graner Ray considers the impact of gender on videogames by examining what may have been the two greatest barriers to reaching out to a female audience.

In Step Six, Joseph Saulter laments the "closed door" policy of the games industry when it comes to cultural diversity, and compares it unfavorably to the music industry's investment in artist development.

In Step Seven, Michelle Hinn explores the topic of accessibility, and asks why multi-million-dollar development projects exclude disabled players who could so easily be accommodated.

In Step Eight, Chris Bateman looks at one model for the many differences in player skills, based upon the Temperament Theory.

Finally, in Step Nine, Noah Falstein brings everything together by considering the many ways in which a game can be structured to allow myriad different players to get what they want from their play.

5 INCLUDE BOTH GENDERS

by Sheri Graner Ray

Having learned about the diversity of videogame players from a theoretical standpoint, you are now ready to learn about the different audiences for games from a practical perspective. Each of the steps in Part II focus on the opportunities for including more players in the videogames market—some, like the female players discussed in this step, are becoming a very significant proportion of the marketplace. Making better games for everyone means including everyone in the audience for games, and that begins with including players of both genders.

GIRLS AND GAMES

It's not uncommon today to walk into a local retailer and find girls playing with the demo model of a Wii while their moms look over the nearby shelves of DS games. This hasn't always been the case. In fact, it wasn't that long ago—fewer than 15 years actually—when the mantra in the game industry was "girls don't play games." Although there were one or two small attempts at producing games for girls in the early 1990s, they went largely unnoticed as the industry focused squarely at their traditional market; males aged 12–18.

Although the industry could back their claim that girls didn't play computer games with numbers that seemed to support it, no one really bothered to ask the question of "why?" They were quite happy to leave it as a mystery of the female gender and continue producing titles that fed the male market's growing appetite for digital entertainment.

Then, in 1996, Mattel released *Barbie Fashion Designer* (Digital Domain, 1996). This little title in its pretty pink box became a juggernaut that racked up more than $500,000 in sales in its first three months. Unlike other "blockbuster" titles of the time, *Barbie Fashion Designer* continued to sell well for the rest of the year and the following year as well. This unprecedented success got the attention of game industry executives everywhere.

They saw the girls' market as an untapped audience just waiting for games. Although there were some developers who attempted to produce girls' games that were alternatives to Barbie, most publishers pushed their development teams to produce titles "just like Barbie" and soon boxes in varying shades of pastels filled the shelves.

Unfortunately it quickly became quite clear that these numbers wouldn't hold out for every game marketed in a pink box. The girls' games that weren't Barbie didn't sell near the numbers Barbie herself did. As the sales dropped, the quality of production dropped. This resulted in dissatisfied customers, which, in turn, resulted in lower sales. Pretty soon it became apparent that only Barbie could be Barbie and the interest in developing "girls' games" dropped off almost completely.

So, although Barbie had the unique ability to convince an industry that girls do, in fact, play games, it also had the dubious honor of becoming the model for what the game industry thought *all* females wanted in games. In other words, the industry redefined an entire market of women into a single genre of "fashion shopping and makeup for girls ages 6–10." What this led to was the industry returning to the original belief that "girls don't play computer games" and following this up with production of more games targeting the male market exclusively.

However, the game industry continued to grow and by the 2000s it was closing in on numbers rivaling the Hollywood movie industry. By this time, publishers had grown quite large and quite a bit more commercial.

They took a look at their audience and realized that it was still, after 15 years, primarily male ages 15–25. They understood that if they wanted to continue to grow at the rate they had been growing, they were going to have to expand their markets. In the mean time, girls had discovered IM chat, cell phones, MySpace, and other digital entertainment sources, so it was quite clear that they were technically savvy. The question became how could publishers reach that market without resorting to "pink" games? Was it possible to design games that reached a broad, inclusive market?

What Is Inclusivity?

The answer is: yes, it is possible to design games that are inclusive of the markets the developer wishes to reach. Although it is perfectly acceptable to produce a game for a specific market segment such as Asian men over the age of 30 or people living in urban areas over two million in population or women ages 15–25, if one wishes to develop a product that has the largest market appeal, one must look at how to include both the male *and* the female market. They must learn to be "inclusive" in their design.

Up to this point, the industry has continued to treat the female market as one monolithic audience, all with similar tastes in entertainment. Developers have responded to the call for gender inclusivity by producing titles or components within titles that are gender specific to the point of being stereotypical. Often it is said that to attract the female players, the game has to have a "shopping" aspect or a fashion aspect or a social aspect. If the game or genre doesn't lend itself to one of these gender-specific mechanics, the developer and publisher declare that it is not a game for females and they don't have to worry about attracting a female audience.

However, gender inclusivity does *not* mean putting a lipstick mini-game inside a first person shooter. What it does mean is taking a critical look at a title and identifying major barriers that could possibly be keeping the female market away from the title to begin with.

These barriers have nothing to do with genre or content. Too many times developers will say "women don't like war games" or "women don't like twitch games." However, if we don't identify and remove the barriers that are keeping women from trying these genres in the first place, saying women don't like them is a bit like saying "Women don't like food served at strip clubs." How can anyone say women don't like the food at strip clubs when the vast majority of women have never stepped foot *in* a strip club?

So where do these barriers exist? They exist in many places—within the game itself, in the marketing and advertising for the game, and even within the development environment itself. The list of places to look for barriers is long, so for brevity's sake we will focus on two major places that can stop a potential female customer right from the beginning; when she goes to buy the game and when she first attempts to play the game.

BARRIERS IN REPRESENTATION

When a potential female customer goes to purchase a game, she is faced with a rack of game boxes that are aimed at selling the game to the players the publishers see as their core market—white males ages 15–25. Unfortunately to reach this market, game industry marketing people continue to use images of exaggerated female characters: female characters dressed in armored bikinis, wielding improbable weapons above impossibly sized breasts. These exaggerated female figures are certainly not going to attract any female players. In fact, they will serve as just the opposite. They serve to tell the female customer that this game is not intended for her. Should the female customer get past the character art on the screen and into the game, she will likely be faced with female character choices that are strikingly similar to those represented on the cover: little to no clothing, exaggerated body proportions, and sexualized postures.

But many people will argue that male characters in games and in advertising are just as exaggerated as female characters and male customers aren't offended. They may go so far as to state they believe girls are just "too sensitive" and should "just get over it."

In some ways those people are right, but in many ways they are wrong.

An avatar is a representation of the user in the virtual environment. When players select something to represent themselves, they want that character to be a hero. In our culture today we expect our heroes to have certain characteristics. We expect them to be young, strong, and virile/fertile. To us, that's what a hero is. The way we know a person has these traits is through physical manifestation. The human body has distinct characteristics which indicate youth, strength, and virility/fertility.

For the male physique, youth, strength, and virility manifest in several traits. A young, virile male will have the traditional "V" shape with his shoulders broader than his hips, accented by a slender waist. His hair will be long and thick. Strength is indicated by large arms and legs and broad shoulders.

For the female physique, youth, strength, and fertility manifest in physical traits as well. A young, fertile female will have well-developed breasts which are high on her chest. She will have a slender waist and long, thick hair. Strength will be represented by a well-rounded derriere and well-developed legs.

So in order to draw attention to the heroic characteristics of the characters within a game, the game industry will exaggerate these "heroic" traits. Male characters will have exceptionally large shoulders and improbably huge arms. Females will have exceptionally large breasts placed nearly under their chins and hair that looks like a shampoo commercial as it swirls elegantly around her even in the middle of battle. These things are equally exaggerated on both genders because they say, "I am a hero."

But with the female characters, there is something else that is also exaggerated.

On the female characters there will also be an exaggeration of those physical signals that indicate sexual arousal and sexual receptivity. In other words, on the female characters, it is not only the heroic traits that are exaggerated but also those traits that say, "I'm ready for sex *right now*."

What are those traits? Any "Introduction to Human Sexuality 101" course teaches that the human body has several physical manifestations that indicate when we are sexually aroused and receptive.

When the human body is ready for sex, there is a blood rush to the face that causes the face to flush. This blood rush causes the lip tissue to engorge making the lips appear fuller and redder. It also causes a similar effect with the eyelid tissues, causing the eyelids to appear thicker and heavier, thus resulting in the look that is often referred to as "bedroom eyes." Respiration increases as sexual excitement increases, often causing people to breathe through their mouths. At this time the person's nipples will also become erect.

In female characters, not only are the "heroic" traits exaggerated, but these traits that show sexual arousal are also exaggerated. Female characters are pictured with a flushed face, half-closed eyes, erect nipples, and large red lips on an open mouth. Then she is dressed in a manner to emphasize and draw attention to these traits and she is posed in a sexually "receptive" posture such as standing with an arched back. And all of these traits are not just present, but they are present and exaggerated just as the heroic traits are exaggerated. These female characters are *hyper-sexualized*.

The most interesting point of all this is, the male body exhibits the *exact same traits* when ready for sex—the nipples, the lips, the eyes, the face flush. However, these traits are never present on male game characters, let alone exaggerated! And, of course, for the male body there is one additional indicator of sexual arousal as well—the erect phallus—and that is certainly something that would never be depicted in a game character!

So, essentially the game industry says to the female customers, "Here, girls, you get to be represented by this character who's ready for sex all the time" and yet they would never *think* of doing that to its male characters. In fact, if someone suggested to an industry marketing team that they put a male character indicating sexual arousal on a box cover they would think that person was insane. They would know an image like that would not help game sales and would probably actually hurt sales. Just consider how likely it would be for the average male gamer to pick up a copy of *World of Warcraft* (Blizzard, 2004) if it prominently featured a male stripper on the cover or in the Internet ad or in the in-game images during the download.

So, although the industry knows that putting a sexualized male character on the box cover would certainly be a barrier to its traditional customers, such companies do not hesitate to put hyper-sexualized females on the cover and in the advertising art. Yet they do not understand how this can keep a potential female customer from picking up the box. And she certainly can't buy it if she won't pick it up!

Why is this different from typical women's magazines? Those magazines are full of images of sexualized women. The difference is this. When a woman reads one of those magazines and looks at those sexualized women, she thinks "Wow... if I use that perfume... I can look just like her, *when I want to!*" In other words, she can look like that at her choice. She has options and has control over her sexuality.

Does this mean that the game industry should only use unattractive female figures? The answer is definitely no. Remember, the players want to be heroes. They want to be young, strong, and virile/fertile. This does not mean unattractive. It is possible to produce art of young, strong, attractive female characters without exaggerating the physical traits of sexual arousal. By removing this barrier, it becomes much more likely that the potential female customer will actually pick up the box—the first step to purchasing the title.

BARRIERS IN LEARNING

Once the female player has actually purchased the title, there comes the problem of how to teach her to play it. Traditionally the main *learning styles* are considered to be:

- **Visual:** Learning by acquiring and communicating information through visual means—reading, watching videos, using diagrams, charts, and maps, and taking notes to be read at a later time.
- **Aural:** Learning by acquiring and communicating information through audio means—listening to lectures, using memes and audio cues, and participating in group discussions.

- **Kinesthetic:** Learning by acquiring and communicating information through activity—hands-on activities and participating in small group discussions and activities.

There are other learning styles that are often mentioned in discussions of learning styles including solo, logical, and others, but visual, aural, and kinesthetic are the main three.

The learning styles define how a person learns, but there is another important aspect: the manner in which a person is most comfortable learning. These learning acquisition styles can be directly applied to how they learn technology, including how they learn to play games. The two learning acquisition styles are *explorative* or "risk taking" and *modeling* or "imitative."

Explorative or "risk taking" learning is an experiential style of acquiring learning. The explorative learner explores every option available and takes risks to learn. They are the ones who push every button and flip every lever. They are aggressive in their learning and may make mistakes while they attempt to acquire the knowledge. For a perfect example of explorative learning in action, simply take a typical 13-year-old boy to a video arcade and hand him a token. He will rush to the first machine that attracts his attention, throw his token in, and begin to beat on the controls while hollering "How does this work?" He will make mistakes, "lose the game," throw another token in, and try it again.

In contrast, modeling or "imitative" learners want to know how something works before they try it. They want a demonstration of what actions they will be expected to perform and what will happen when they do it. They want to understand the risks and repercussions of an action before they perform it.

An example of a modeling learner is the sister of the 13-year-old boy in the arcade. While her brother is pushing buttons and flipping levers trying to figure out how the game works, she is standing behind him, watching him play. She will likely stand there for a while, and then walk from machine to machine, stopping to watch the attract loops of each machine. The reason she is watching is she is trying to figure out how it works and how to play it before she drops her token in. But attract loops aren't designed to show the player how to play. They are designed to attract a player to the game with sounds, flashing lights, and exciting action. So after a while the boy's sister wanders away with her token still in her pocket—not because she is afraid or uninterested or unwilling to play, but because her learning acquisition needs were not met.

So explorative learning is predominantly experiential and involves taking risks to learn. Imitative learning is predictive and involves wanting to know what is going to happen before the new activity is tried [Gottfried86]. The most interesting thing about these two learning acquisition styles is they also tend to break along gender lines. Explorative learning is predominantly male and imitative learning is predominantly female.

 Note: It is important to note that, although each learning style mentioned here has a predominant population of one gender or another, they are not exclusive to that gender. Everything is a bell curve and there are certainly a number of male imitative learners and female explorative learners.

One of the consequences of imitative learning is that explorative learners will become frustrated when trying to get such learners to play a game. Often this means a male will attempt to get his wife or girlfriend to play but will expect her to also be explorative. Such an explorative learner will often get frustrated when she isn't willing to just jump right in and play, but would rather just watch him play.

People will often misconstrue this hesitancy as fear. How many times has a male gamer, in frustration, said, "I can't get my (mom/wife/girlfriend) to play because she's just afraid of the computer!" However, upon closer examination, although she may even describe herself as "afraid," what she actually may be is an imitative learner who simply is extremely uncomfortable being forced to learn in an explorative style.

Interestingly enough, this applies to technology even beyond games. Recently an IT supervisor who worked in a bank was tasked with teaching the tellers a new piece of accounting software. When the class broke for lunch the instructor returned to the IT department completely exhausted and frustrated. "Those women," she complained. "They are so stupid! They just do not want to learn anything new! They're afraid!"

A coworker overheard this and asked her how she was teaching the software. "Well," she said, "I explain how a basic functionality works and then I assign them a task that uses that functionality." The coworker, being aware of the different learning acquisition styles said, "Ah, well, maybe you should try a different approach. Try showing them a specific function on the overhead. Then have them try that particular functionality on their machines. Take the tasks one step at a time and let them imitate what you do on their machines. Don't move on to the next step until they are comfortable with the first step." The IT supervisor agreed to try it and returned to the class after the break.

At the end of the day the IT supervisor came back to the IT department. "Well," asked the coworker, "how did it go?" "It was amazing," said the supervisor. "It was like I was teaching a different class! They got it!" At that point the coworker explained the difference between explorative learning, which was how the IT supervisor preferred to learn, and imitative learning, which was how the students preferred to learn. By simply adapting the program to take into account modeling learning, the process of implementing the new accounting software went smoothly and much quicker than if the IT supervisor had continued to try to force the women to learn in a way that wasn't comfortable for them.

To understand how this applies to games, you only need to think back to the tutorial in your favorite game. Most developers expect the players to be explorative learners and design the tutorials accordingly. Typically a tutorial consists of a very brief explanation of the game after which the player is dropped either directly into the actual game or into a "safe" tutorial area. Either way, they are expected to explore to learn the details of how the game works.

If the player is not an explorative learner, this type of tutorial can be uncomfortable if not down-right intimidating. If the game isn't comfortable to learn, it is likely the player will choose *not* to learn it. If they don't learn it, they won't play it, and another customer is lost.

Because the imitative learning style is predominantly female, and the tutorials in the games are predominantly explorative, it stands to reason that it would not be a comfortable game for the potential female players to learn. Thus, actually learning to play the game is a barrier to the female audience.

Developers can overcome this barrier by paying attention to how the tutorial is constructed and making sure modeling learning is considered in the construction.

This is not as difficult as it might sound. There are several educational software products out there today that specifically target the imitative learning style. To do this they take each step of the subject and break it down into small steps that users can repeat as they wish. In other words, the software will give a demonstration of what is to be done and what the results of that action will be. For instance, it may show a mouse cursor move to a menu bar, click on a button to get a drop-down menu, and then select an item from the drop-down menu. It will then give the users an opportunity to try the same set of actions. The users may try these activities several times over until they are comfortable with the activity—meaning they understand the risks and the outcome—and then they can choose to move on to the next lesson.

Often when explorative learners are faced with this type of learning, they call it "boring" and dismiss it as "too simplistic." They will protest that they would "go crazy" if they had to try to learn something this way. This then clearly points out that as imitative learners are not comfortable learning in an explorative manner, explorative learners are not comfortable learning in imitative ways either. This simply draws more attention to the fact that both learning styles need to be accommodated when the developer wants to attract a diverse audience.

There are developers who believe that, although modeling learning styles are fine for productivity software such as accounting packages or word processing packages, they have no place in game tutorials because they require the designer to "break the fourth wall." This means they require the designer to address the users directly and not through the "world" of the game. The characters in the game would ostensibly have no knowledge of the keymapping for the game and would have no reason to be explaining "WASD for movement" or "R for autorun." Designers often feel that this diminishes the game and breaks the world fiction. If they are pushed to address it, they often simply provide large blocks of text explaining the technical aspects of the game that can be easily dismissed with one click. This is not an acceptable way to address modeling learning, or explorative learning for that matter.

Although "breaking the fourth wall" may not be comfortable for the developers, it is important to realize that the imitative learner will never even get to the game if they are not comfortable learning it. So if the developers intend to attract and maintain a larger female audience, they must address the imitative learning style.

There are a number of ways to do this both within and outside of the game environment. The modeling learning can be addressed in a separate tutorial before entering the game world. This way, imitative learners would be comfortable with the mechanics of the game before they are asked to immerse themselves within the game. Another method would be to provide a tutorial within the game but that utilizes different screens and art so that it appears to float "above" the game world and thus keeps the learning of the mechanics apart from the game world. If the developers are intent upon keeping the player within the game world at all times, a "guide" character within the world can address the player and explain the mechanics. However the developers choose to address it, it must be addressed if they intend to attract and keep a diverse audience.

CONCLUSION

Ultimately, the first steps in attracting and maintaining gender diversity in a game audience lie in the very first encounters potential female gamers have with a game. The representation of the female characters on the box cover and in the advertising art can either encourage her to pick up the game or cause her to pass it by without a second look.

Once she has the game in her hands, how she is taught to play the game can dictate whether she ever actually plays it and whether she enjoys learning it. By paying attention to these first two crucial steps, developers can substantially increase their odds of attracting the gender diversity that will help ensure their title's success—without even coming close to putting their game in a pink box!

INCLUDE CULTURAL DIVERSITY

by Joseph Saulter

After female players, the largest group of players that is often implicitly excluded from videogames are potential players from culturally diverse backgrounds, of which the most economically significant is probably black consumers in the United States. Many people in the videogames industry believe that taking into account the needs of different cultures and ethnicities is political correctness gone mad, but there are sound economic opportunities to be gained from incorporating diverse cultural voices in game development. The next step towards making better videogames for everyone is considering the opportunities gained from including new developers and new audiences.

NEW OPPORTUNITIES IN GAME DESIGN

There are great opportunities for a new developer to develop new games for a new audience. Why *new* developers? Because it is quite obvious the games industry is overlooking a financial opportunity because of a silent closed-door policy. *We suffer from a lack of diversity in our industry.*

When we look at our financial portfolio, we ask how we can diversify our finances for maximum returns. We never place all our assets into one financial instrument and pray for good returns; instead, we *diversify*. Although diversification is not the same as diversity, it does share with the latter the objective of investing in assets diverse enough so that the return on investment is maximized.

It can be argued that whereas diversification deals with financial assets, diversity deals with cultural and human capital assets. Thus the words will be used conterminously. The issue of diversity is such a pressing one. I view diversity as an opportunity to enhance creativity through people contributing their own unique experiences to humanity's culture.

The process of expertly using cultural differences to increase wealth, in the context of worldwide economic integration, is a hot topic for the new millennium. The videogame community, with its international appeal and its proven track record as a successful entity in the financial arena, would benefit economically, educationally, and ethically if it were to diversify (that is, be culturally diverse) for maximum returns.

Diversity involves creating an inclusive environment where a team of professionals creatively uses their differences and appreciates the opportunity to weave a multitude of new ideas into best practices. Creatively speaking, it's like composing a symphony in our organizations that utilizes the spirit of improvisational jazz.

Diversity touches the core of our existence because we all have deep-rooted cultural awareness. We continue to appreciate the richness of our own cultures, but the pure essence of diversity is to take the best of all cultures, give them a place and a voice, and create an atmosphere of creativity and inclusion.

An Increasingly Diverse Society

Demographic changes over the past decade predict that by the year 2050, racial/ethnic groups will make up 48% of the total United States population, and this percentage speaks volumes. Never before in the history of our country have our children been exposed and adapted to the information technology so readily available. They are far more advanced technically than earlier generations. Each generation changes our nation. As the impact of diversity moves through the gaming community, it must adapt to the changes.

A culturally diverse initiative on the part of the industry's leaders would create a new environment of creative entertainment. We all have a story to tell and the compelling stories of our diverse communities have not always been told with sensitivity. If the game business community were to explore the diverse community, it would find a grand opportunity to engage young minds and experience the rewards of its labor.

There is a whole generation that is changing the style, the music and marketing, and the complexion of our nation. They are the underground artists creating non-commercial styles. It's a sound so new and fresh with the spirit of jazz as its essence; an improvisation lyrically waving its new brush of creativity across the canvas of our lives. It is an invisible generation filled with diversity and a new vision. I await the day when the videogames industry lets them dance across the fingertips of a nation steeped in the all-consuming monitors, TV screens, and theaters of consumers, clamoring for more.

The bottom line is in the cultural statistics: AllHipHop.com receives 121 million audited impressions per month and growing. The average age of the AllHipHop.com users is 23 years old, with 63% of their audience falling between ages 19 and 31 [Creekmur08]. User demographics for the site are as follows:

- 58% Male
- 42% Female
- 32% African American
- 31% Caucasian
- 25% Latino
- 12% Asian

This is a huge market, and videogames are an active part of the community. The hip-hop market is one of the most coveted, elusive, and lucrative markets in the world. The 2008 Packaged Facts report, "The U.S. Urban Youth Market," conducted among 37 million young urban consumers between the ages of 12 and 34, analyzed the consumer choices of the tens of millions of people who connect with hip-hop music. Findings showed that young urban consumers enjoy an aggregate income of $600 billion, much of which is disposable income. These trendsetters and influencers who affiliate with hip-hop culture exercise a powerful impact on the direction of the fashion, media, entertainment, and other key consumer-focused industries [PackagedFacts08].

Over the past 20 years, hip-hop culture has permeated popular culture in an unprecedented fashion, and although it originated in the African-American sector, this study reveals that now more than 75% of the rap and hip-hop audience is non-black. From the street corner to the boardroom, hip-hop's potential to create unity across all ethnicities is substantial. Much in the same way that "beat culture" challenged the status quo in ways that unified liberals and prompted change in the 1950s and 1960s, the hip-hop culture has challenged the system in ways that have unified individuals across a rich ethnic spectrum.

The report includes information from other media outlets, too. *USA Today* reported that hip-hop is the fastest growing music genre in the US, and *The New York Times* reports that the preferences of youths in suburban America have shifted from the Rock-n-Roll sound of The Byrds, The Doors, The Eagles, Van Halen, and Guns `N' Roses, to hip-hop giants such as Jay-Z and OutKast. Similarly, according to the Recording Industry Association of America, rap music's share of sales began increasing by 150% in the 1990s and is still rising.

The evidence for the increasing influence of black culture in *music* is undeniable. In a few decades, hip-hop has exploded across the globe as a creative, cultural, and financial phenomenon. But where is the equivalent influence of black culture in *videogames*? Contemporary U.S. videogame development is the equivalent of The Eagles; where is our OutKast?

GAMES AS CULTURAL PRODUCT

Hirokazu Yasuhara, creator of *Sonic the Hedgehog* (Sonic Team, 1991), is one of the great heroes of game design. In the August 2008 edition of *Game Developer Magazine*, he discussed with Brandon Sheffield a question that brought a new sensibility to the cultural style of developers [Brandon08]. In terms of cultural output, they compared the U.S. development *Gears of War* (Epic Games, 2006) with Japanese development, *Pikmin* (Nintendo, 2001). Do these games represent the cultural differences of the people who made them?

Hirokazu Yasuhara said the following:

> *Yes, exactly and this process keeps repeating itself. You see some culture differences come to the surface with this, too. For example, a lot of Japanese people attain a feeling of security via creation, or making themselves look nice, or saving money. Not that Americans or Europeans aren't like that, but Americans may be more likely to take a more "destructive" process toward feeling safe. I think a lot of that is because the things that you "fear" can be very different between nations—not real, palpable fear, but more the lack of feeling at ease with yourself. Something you don't like very much; something that stresses you out—another word for "stress," really. And since sources of stress can be different between Americans and Japanese, it follows that the methods both populations take to relax would be different, too.*

To say that cultural difference creates development style is a perfect example of what is called *cultural sensibility* [Thompson95]. The basic idea is that people from different cultures approach the world with different ideas about how to think, feel, and interact—moral, emotional, and aesthetic assumptions. You can be aware of other cultures, and know that they are different than your own, but you cannot actually acquire the cultural sensibility without being from that culture.

If you have never had experience of a particular culture, game developers can vicariously give it to you. For instance, if you have never been to Hong Kong, you can play *Shenmue 2* (Sega AM2, 2001) and you can get something of the feel of living in this city. But what you get isn't really the cultural sensibility at all—it's a stereotypical experience that fools you into believing you've had some experience of Hong Kong culture.

Similarly, you can play *Grand Theft Auto: San Andreas* (Rockstar North, 2004) and *feel* that you now know what it is to be a young black man in a street gang. But in fact, what has been delivered is a valorized fantasy based around the idea of street gangs—you have acquired none of the cultural sensibility of this world from playing this game. Only someone who actually *was* in such a gang could have this sensibility. There's nothing wrong with creating these fantasies—it was encouraging to see a game with a black leading character sell so phenomenally well—but there is something amiss when the games industry isn't taking advantage of the variety of cultural sensibilities at work in the audience for videogames.

The games industry in North America is predominantly comprised of white males. 83.3% of the people who work at game developers are white, 7.5% Asian, 2.5% Hispanic, 2.0% black, and 4.7% other ethnicities, and 88.5% of these employees are male [IGDA05]. This inevitably means that those cultural sensibilities possessed by white males dominate the development of videogame titles. This can occasionally devolve into unintentional racism.

Let me give you a tangible example. I am the chairman of the International Game Developers Association's Diversity Advisory Board, and I have been holding a round table at the Game Developers Conference for the past four years. At the last summit there was a developer there who said: "I do fantasy online games; however, I do not have any black or brown people in my game because I don't want to offend anyone." There is a strange kind of logic behind this claim—a concern that people might be offended by the *inclusion* of ethnic diversity, whereas being oblivious to the idea that it could be tremendously offensive to *exclude* that diversity (particularly if you happen to be from the culture excluded)!

Similarly, at another round table at GDC one attendee told a story about a young, black girl who had been playing and enjoying *Guitar Hero* (Harmonix, 2005). She confessed that she had great difficulty choosing an avatar for herself. "Am I supposed to pick the black man, or the white woman?" she asked the developer in question, apparently genuinely confused by the options presented to her.

It may seem excessively politically correct to be thinking about supporting avatars for *every* conceivable combination of ethnicity and gender, but at the same time this is a game supporting seven basic avatar choices: four white males, two white females, and one black man. That actually matches the demographics of the people who *work* for game developers in the United States quite accurately, but it doesn't match the demographics of game players in the US quite as well!

The only way to get a new cultural sensibility into your company is to *hire* someone who has that sensibility. But perhaps even this is looking at the problem the wrong way around—perhaps what is needed is not to increase the diversity inside the existing game development companies (although this would be welcome), but rather to support new developers *who embody different cultural sensibilities*. The phenomenal success of hip-hop music demonstrates the real commercial benefits of doing so—there is a significant cultural difference in innovative creativity, and the only way to access this is to allow new voices to be heard.

I am excited to work at one of the first African-American game developers in the US, and I am captivated when I see a team like Nerjyzed Entertainment (an African-American Game Developer out of New Orleans led by CEO Jacqueline Beauchamp) making unique games like *Black College Football Xperience* (Nerjyzed, 2007). It says something about the state of the games industry that we can finally make games targeting a black audience [Gamespot07].

To found a game developer takes more than just money—to make a successful career in videogames, you need to have paid your dues. You need to have put in the time to learn the skills and build the industry relationships that are required for making publishing deals. The existence of companies like Nerjyzed shows that even though the employment statistics are still biased heavily towards white males, other cultures are making their way through the games industry and are finding a way to make their voices heard.

The Politics of Diversity

It's easy to dismiss concern for diversity issues as being mere political correctness, paying lip service to minorities out of a feigned sense of obligation. But diversity is not merely the concern of the minorities—as I mentioned earlier, in another 50 years or so *every* cultural background will become in effect a minority, as there will no longer be one ethnicity with a majority percentage!

Diversity is not a black thing, it is not a white thing, it is not a women thing or a disability thing, it is not a Latin thing, it is not a gay thing—it is the *right thing*. It is right for your company's bottom line and for the survival of the videogames industry (or any other industry). It has been written about by researchers from Harvard to MIT to Stanford and so on, across the planet [Alensina03]. The choice is simple, so why is it such a difficult challenge for the games industry?

Those of us dedicated to diversity issues represent a collective of people from across the planet, and together we believe we see the big picture. We know the issues and we have looked the dragon in the eye. We have felt his heated breath and we are confident and dedicated to change, and that a change is "gonna come."

What's more, I believe it will come swiftly for the games industry because there is really no one in the way. No one is trying to stop the movement with dogs or fire hoses—no one holding signs, no picket lines, no politicians telling lies. No bombs, no lynching, no opposition at all. The predominantly white males who the industry has employed thus far don't have time to be concerned about diversity issues one way or the other, because they are far more troubled by the poor quality of life they currently enjoy as a consequence of endless working hours and crunches [IGDA04a].

Almost every teenager, high school student, and college student across the world wants to get involved with creative technology. Universities throughout the United States have research development initiatives, curriculum development projects, and government contracts, all for interactive media [USAToday05]. The mobile interactive games industry is also exploding, as well as the international market.

Content, content, and more content, but whose will it be? There are so many videogames that could be made to express the diverse voices in the population, but right now we can only guess at what those games might be like. I want to know what a black man's *Final Fantasy* might be like, or a woman's *Half-Life*. I want to know what someone who is physically challenged would be able to show us about their life experience if only they were given the chance to make *that* game.

Mixing It Up

The challenge facing the videogames industry is accessing the wealth of untapped creativity that could be brought to bear if only the lack of diversity could be addressed. This involves not only hiring more people from diverse cultural backgrounds, but setting up developers who can develop their own unique development culture. All this will take organizing and education. It will not happen overnight, but it will happen.

For those of you who are African American, Latin American, Caribbean, or Asian, we have to rise to the occasion and become professionally visible. We need a legion of educated young people to pave the way for what has to come. I feel the pure essence of a nation in transition, an industry waiting to fuse creativity and technology for the next generation. And solving these problems in the United States is just the tip of the iceberg—there are so many cultures out in the world whose unique vision has yet to be explored in the new digital technologies.

Every once in a while it would be nice to change up the team just to get a bit of spice in the mix. If it works for the music industry and it is beginning to work for the film industry, why is it so hard to move the new developers into the videogames industry?

There are questions we can ask about whether our current business practices encourage innovation and creativity, or stifle it. In the music industry, money is made available for what is called *artist development*, which is to say, finding new talent and helping them bring their creativity into the marketplace. When I go to a corporate office in the music industry, I ask for the urban music department or the rap music department or the hip-hop department and someone directs me to an office. But there are no such departments in the videogames industry. No one has even considered that there might be a commercial niche worth pursuing in this vein (despite the phenomenal impact of diverse cultures in other media).

There are no finances made available for the exchange of ideas in the videogames industry. There are few if any mechanisms for newcomers to show a promising demo to industry leaders, so that the opportunities for new development ideas could be pursued and developed into finished products. The absence of this kind of artist development in videogames isn't just a failure to provide pathways for new voices from ethnic backgrounds, it effectively blocks *all* new voices from being heard, except in those rare and exceptional cases where a particular mod or student project manages to create a stir, as with *Counter-Strike* (Le and Cliffe, 1999) or *Narbacular Drop* (Nuclear Monkey, 2005), the student project that led to *Portal* (Valve, 2007). These games are certainly the exception and not the rule, and both achieved their success thanks to the efforts of just one company, Valve. Why can Valve see the benefits of this kind of artist development when no one else can?

Often when I speak for minority interests in the games industry, people seem to assume that what is needed is some kind of entitlement program, but that's as far away from the mark as it could be. We don't need developers from diverse cultural backgrounds because we need to pay lip service to some notion of political correctness or affirmative action, we need it because there are diverse *audiences* out there who want games they can play, and the most prudent way of satisfying the needs of those audiences is to create developers who share the same cultural background. I can put this idea more flippantly: to make a better game that reaches a new audience you don't just need a better mouse trap, you need a different kind of *cheese*.

I spoke earlier about the vast success of hip-hop music. The urban community is a huge arena; a lifestyle that was originally the black cultural lifestyle experience is now a global phenomenon in music, fashion, and entertainment. If the bottom line is financial, we have an opportunity to capitalize on a community that clamors for creative innovations. A community that uses technology to communicate beyond boundaries of race, creed, or color. A community that challenges social norms and expects more as a consumer. A consumer who you cannot fool, who is looking to identify with characters' lifestyles and stories not yet told. A community that wants to be included in the videogames they play and the interactive entertainment they consume. A youthful spirited community who is changing the very way we do business in all corners of entertainment and the world at large.

We are on the brink of an innovative technological surge of creativity and a convergence of interactive entertainment across all boundaries. The new developer brings a new audience; the new audience demands a sensibility that reflects the cultural and global experience. The new audiences bring billions of dollars of disposable finances, and represent a powerful collective of collaborators who experience creativity in a social community that reaches beyond the traditional.

New developers from diverse cultural backgrounds can offer new videogames with as much innovation as jazz gave to the music industry in the early twentieth century: they can give a new vision of what a game might be. There is a global improvisational movement in the arts that rivals art deco and the renaissance, but it still struggles to make a foothold in videogames. We need to provide these new developers direct access to finances that will assure an entry point into the industry, an area where they can comfortably create innovative stories and develop videogames for the next generation.

CONCLUSION

In November 2008, Barack Obama became the first black President of the United States, carried in on a message of change. When I look at the world of videogames I really don't see anything like the changes that I have been looking for in terms of new developers and new audiences. I would like to see in the games industry a reflection of what I can see in the political arena—*a movement of cultural change*.

That I have to say this at all should show you how the industry is struggling with this subject. Sometimes it is better left alone in a dark place where little demons hide, hidden behind the daily grind... there are a few people from unique cultural backgrounds who have managed to make it into games, and many of them don't want to talk about this subject. Perhaps they don't want to rock the boat. But I have to say it. When will there be a company who steps outside of the comfort zone and really looks at the possibility of a non-stereotypical movement in the videogames industry?

I am not talking about giving anybody funding in the name of diversity, and it would be absurd to expect to get something for nothing. But a chance to produce a console videogame as a creative work of art with a team of developers from a unique cultural background is *necessary* if we are serious about fulfilling the potential of this unique interactive medium.

The new developers and new audiences exist in an exciting arena of innovation and creativity. Herein lies an amazing opportunity for our industry to exchange ideas for products that can create new revenue streams. In the untapped potential of new cultural voices lies yet another resource to move the industry forward into the next generation, the chance of developing, discovering, or uncovering new genres for the videogames industry to explore. Cultural diversity is a challenge we cannot afford to overlook. As I said earlier, diversity is not a black thing, it is not a white thing, it's not a women thing, and it is not a gay thing— it is the *right thing* if we want to make better games for everyone.

INCLUDE PLAYERS WITH ACCESSIBILITY ISSUES

by Michelle Hinn

At the fringes of the audience for videogames are players who face physical barriers to playing games. In this step, Michelle Hinn discusses the nature of accessibility issues, and suggests a few simple changes that could accommodate players currently excluded from videogames.

INTRODUCTION

It's been a long day at work, but fortunately the sequel to your all-time favorite game, *Super Gears Saturn Attack 2: Ultimate Challenge!* came out today, you had the game pre-ordered, sent to work, and now all you have to do is get home and play it! Maybe you'll stay up all night trying to finish it... or at least call in sick tomorrow so you don't have to deal with *that* interruption to your gaming.

The traffic on the roads is insane today and you are now wishing you'd gotten one of those dashboard TVs and could be playing the game right now as you sit in traffic. You resist the temptation to beep your horn in frustration as the car in front moves forward exactly one inch, and decide to take advantage of the delay to examine your new game. You take out your game manual and look at the controller scheme to get an edge on your roommates.

That's strange. The booklet doesn't say anything about how to control the game. Well, it's probably the same as *Super Gears Saturn Attack 1*. But then, the early buzz on the game was that it's got a totally tricked out mode where, although you can use your regular controller as well, there's apparently some "special edition" controller that makes all the difference. Forget that—you're not laying out more cash on a game before you know if it's worth it. I mean, the special controller is $400—that's the price of the stupid console! Oh—and get this—they say that some of the moves are downright impossible to do even with the special edition controller. Come on!

Oh! Here's your exit—just five more minutes now! You are starting to get worried about the controls—what's so different about it? Somehow they managed to keep that whole thing a bit of a mystery. Before you know it, it's the moment you've been waiting for—you sink into your couch and put the game into the console.

Hmmm... what's this? "Please hook up cuff/belt combo to the USB hub, and then put belt on first followed by cuffs. Once cuffs are on, *do not attempt to touch controller with hands.*" You and your roommates look at the on-screen message in slack-jawed disbelief. Reluctantly, you follow the instructions, but nothing happens. You go to press the Start button on the controller...

ZAP!

"Ow... what the...?"

"Dude! Did it actually give you some kind of shock when you tried to touch the controller?"

"You aren't wearing the cuffs—you try starting it!" Your roommates try to work out what to do, but no matter what they try, it doesn't work.

"This is crazy!" you cry, "What is going on? Look it up online!"

Finally, the screen changes and a message appears telling you to attach the cuffs on your arms to either side of each belt.

"Okay, so how am I supposed to play this? I'm not a Jedi Knight!" you moan.

Your other roommate has found some information online: "I don't know what they are doing here, but it says that somehow it knows you are wearing that stupid belt/cuff thing. Duh! Okay, wait... you can use the controller with your feet, your face... just not your hands."

You're about to explode—you've been waiting for this game forever and now you can't play it?!

Your roommate reads some more: "Yeah, it says that if you had that special edition controller, it lets you access the controls by sipping in and puffing out air into these tubes and you have another thing that you control with your lips."

You completely blow a gasket when you hear this! "So if we want to play the game we have to shell out $400 for the special controller on top of the $80 it cost for the game and this belt/cuff piece of crap that won't let me use the controller with my hands? Who does this to their audience?" Disgusted, you decide to send the game back to the store.

This story seems completely ridiculous, but it mirrors in many ways the experience that gamers with mobility issues such as quadriplegia face with almost every game. In the story, the three roommates weren't actually disabled, but were *functionally* disabled by the game's quirky design. Gamers who are actually disabled are also often functionally disabled by the game's design (rather than being blocked by a lack of a suitable control device), often in ways that can be avoided—some of which we'll discuss throughout this step.

The "special edition" controller described is called a "Quad Controller" and runs around $400 depending on options chosen [QuadControl]. It really does have tubes to sip in and puff out air to "press" different buttons and it has multiple toggle switches that you use with your mouth to "press" and do other things. Unfortunately, it can be really hard to play a game with this controller when most games do not allow remapping the controls, forcing the disabled gamer into an awkward or even impossible control scheme—having to sip in and puff out air at the same time is not something that comes easily to humans, after all!

Just as the gamers in the story decided to return their game, many gamers with disabilities end up doing the same, having learned the hard way that they weren't going to get very far with a game even with expensive assistive technologies.

Throughout this step, I'll talk about a variety of disabilities and the challenges that gamers from those groups and subgroups of disabilities present for game designers, as well as a "top ten" list of easy ways to get started making games more accessible.

WHAT IS GAME ACCESSIBILITY?

For most of us, disability has impacted the life of someone we know and love—a family member, a friend, or at the very least some other person we've met such as a teacher, a student, a coworker, or even someone who rides the same commuter train with us every day. If we are lucky enough to grow old, disability will likely affect most of us personally—as we age, we all begin to lose our sight, hearing, mobility, and cognitive capacities. (And thanks to years of non-ergonomically ideal computer use and even repetitive button mashing games, many of us may have developed mobility issues such as carpal tunnel syndrome that limit the use of standard game controllers.) The term "disability" does not exclude, and is likely to include, most of us in some fashion sooner or later. For some, these physical limitations won't affect every aspect of our lives, whereas for others it will profoundly impact nearly every aspect of life, requiring those concerned to learn how to live and enjoy life in entirely different ways—gaming included.

I've served as the chairperson of the joint International Game Developers Association's (IGDA) and Entertainment Consumers Association's (ECA) Game Accessibility Special Interest Group (GA-SIG) for the past five years. During this time I have seen some amazing things. I've seen mods of popular commercial games designed by a single socially-conscious person for a disabled audience. I have played games written by visually impaired gamers for other visually impaired gamers. I have played the growing number of independent remakes of classic game titles that have been modified to resolve issues relating to just one disability type. I have seen and used some of the unconventional, hacked, and tricked out controllers that many gamers with disabilities rely on to play commercial games for both PCs and console systems.

There are many barriers faced by people with accessibility issues. Considering just the issue of specialized controllers, many of these controllers do not come cheap—certain custom models can cost over twice the amount of the console system it was designed to work with simply because they are complex electronic devices made by a single garage hacker hobbyist to fit the needs of the individual gamer.

For anyone who might think that there isn't an interest in gaming among people with disabilities, think again—some players with disabilities are among the most dedicated gamers both in respect of their financial contribution and also the sheer determination to play games using any means possible.

Accessibility enters the realm of social justice. Is gaming or any other leisure activity something that we all should have the right to enjoy? Of course, funding for games and other leisure activities should not take precedence over life support measures, but at the same time art, film, literature, sports, games, and so forth are just a few of the things that make our lives richer. Without them, we lose an essential part of being alive.

When I give talks to game developers, I often ask the audience to imagine that tomorrow—due to one false step, a few missed heartbeats, the onset of a delayed disability such as multiple sclerosis, or a terrible accident—they were faced with the prospect of no longer being able to work on games, let alone play them. Would they be willing to accept the loss of their life's passion? Wouldn't they be interested in learning how to engage with games as an active participant in a new way?

Although this may give us a pause for thought, talking about "what if" scenarios isn't often enough. Like many of life's unknowns, until you've experienced a disability that keeps you from participating in gaming (even if only temporarily), you may not be able to honestly consider the consequences of such a life-changing event. Over time, however, I have begun to learn that what can resonate with producers, development teams, and so forth are the stories of real gamers with disabilities. These stories can be powerfully moving, because they show the courage of those who face real physical limitations in their daily lives.

Gamers with Disabilities

As the chairperson of the gaming industry's lobbyist group to raise awareness and help designers find solutions to accessibility issues, I've worked with several companies to help them take the first steps toward making their games more accessible. But I've also been afforded the opportunity to learn exactly how important games are to people's lives.

I receive emails and phone calls every week asking about accessible games and controllers. Some come from the potential gamers themselves, which usually consist of vivid descriptions of a recent accident and a plea to help them find a one-handed controller because they've just lost a hand or an arm. Some come from doctors of veterans from Afghanistan and Iraq who contact me not just because of the potential games have for rehabilitation, but also because they have patients who are suffering from intense depression as a result of their injuries, for whom gaming used to be a big part of their civilian lives. Using assistive technology and accessible controllers, videogames can be brought back into the lives of such veterans—and learning to play games in a new way helps pave the way to wanting to learn how to do other things in a new way. It can be a first step towards returning to life for such people.

Perhaps the most emotional calls come from parents, who often start the conversation by telling me that before their child was in an accident they felt that videogames were a waste of time, at the very least, if not actually dangerous. Now, unfortunately, their child cannot play with his or her friends and they want to know if there is any way to get them into a multiplayer game of some kind. They want their child (and their friends) to understand that even though one of them has a disability, life goes on—they are still friends, and they can still play together.

It's hard to get these calls and emails and know that the gaming industry as a whole has not done much to respond to the call for increasing the accessibility of their games. Fortunately, there are a lot of garage hackers and hobbyists who have taken up the cause to make sure that there are at least plenty of controller options for all the latest systems—Microsoft's Xbox 360, Nintendo's Wii, and Sony's PS3 all have specialist devices available.

This is only a part of the battle. Even with an accessible controller, many—too many—games do not allow keys/buttons/control sticks to be remapped so that players with accessibility issues might be able to play them. Although smaller companies may struggle to develop on the funding available, many high-profile games are now developed on budgets in excess of $20 million and could easily afford to support such a feature (which many players without disabilities might also benefit from).

Other issues include lack of closed captioning, poor audio cues, inability to change colors, font sizes that are too small to be read, and many more. Before discussing these kinds of issues in more detail, however, I want to leave you with a few quotes that nicely capture what it is that gamers with disabilities want in a videogame experience. These are taken from a 2006 survey that asked blind gamers what they are looking for in commercial videogames [VanTol06]:

- "...Making a game accessible won't just convince blind players to buy it—many of us have [non-blind] friends who play games and [we] would love the chance to play against them in multiplayer modes."
- "I've liked to play like sighted people, play with sighted people, and be like 'my score was this!' I mean [I'd] have something to say, you know? But I never get this chance... but I'm hopeful I will."

Games are often social experiences. Although these are just two opinions from blind gamers, the desire to play with non-visually impaired friends as well as being able to have bragging rights (just as their sighted counterparts have) resonate with gamers who have other kinds of disabilities. In an article on CNN about a game called *AudioOdyssey* (Gambit, 2007) that was designed to be played by both the blind and sighted together, one blind gamer was quoted as saying "It's important that games be mainstream and inclusive—rather than "special" and [only] for blind players." [Mollman07]

FORMS OF DISABILITY

Each kind of disability presents different game design issues, but there are a few things to keep in mind throughout.

The first is that having decreased ability in one area generally means increased ability in other areas. The most famous example of this is the popular conception that a blind person has a more keen sense of hearing. This is substantially true, and indeed their sense of touch and smell may also be heightened. Although it's beyond the scope of this chapter to discuss theories as to why this may happen, the brain is a versatile organ which (as you learned in Step 3 with the research on London taxi drivers) changes according to the circumstances it faces. So people who don't use their sense of sight develop their other sensory cortices more completely. As a result, some designers of accessible games have highlighted sound and touch in versions of games for those with severe visual impairments, such as blindness.

The second issue to keep in mind is crossover. Some people with disabilities will have, say, both a cognitive and a mobility disability or some other combination of disabilities. This is fairly common and may result in the need for a combination of solutions. Sometimes one of the disabilities is more pronounced than the other(s), which can ease the solution combination.

A third issue is that within every disability category is a wide range of different issues. For example, visual disabilities can include partial vision, color blindness, and at the extreme end, total blindness (complete loss of vision). Just these three examples of visual disabilities require entirely different considerations by game designers.

Finally, some design solutions for one group will alienate another group entirely. For instance, a game that relies solely on audio cues (with no visuals whatsoever) will be completely inaccessible to those with significant hearing impairments. In fact, audio-only games have been a genre that game designers for the visually impaired have been making for many years. More recently, designers of alternate reality games (ARGs) have been experimenting with this form.

Improving Accessibility

There's a term in the computer and web accessibility worlds called *universal accessibility*—meaning that all computer programs and web pages should be able to be accessed in some way by all people. Here the emphasis is on education and productivity applications, operating systems, and getting information from websites, usually in areas where it is required by law for a company, school, or government agency to do so (these laws vary by country, but most countries in North America and Europe have adopted some variation of these laws). However, the laws are not as clear when referring to games.

Ideally, we might want to make all games accessible for everyone, but the reality is that there are some game experiences that cannot be transformed to be accessible and, more importantly, to be fun, for every type of gamer—with and without disabilities. As a result of this, I don't stress the idea of all games being accessible to all, but rather push to have as many games as possible accessible to *more* people—aiming not for universal accessibility, but simply for improved accessibility.

I've been at industry shows and have been asked why a one-button version of a first person shooter would be fun for anyone since it takes the "aiming" away from the gamer (by using a utility that performs an auto-sweep of screen). You just press the button over and over—how can that be fun? This sort of comment represents a fundamental misunderstanding about the nature of fun. Yes, playing with an auto-sweep or auto-aim may not be fun for an FPS expert deeply immersed in the challenge of these games, but these games deliver many other experiences that can be fun (something Chris explored in Step 3). For a gamer with a profound disability, being able to play these kinds of games *at all* can be fun, and although simply clicking a button to fire may seem like a limited form of play, it's not wholly unlike the earliest of videogames in its simplicity.

We show work like this at conventions not to show designers that all games should be made this simplistically but rather to demonstrate that they can be modified—whether it's by the game company or the modding community—to make them more accessible. Taking things to extremes can be useful and fun for some players, even if it doesn't seem fun for those who prefer to play the game the way the designers intended. This naturally creates some confusion and may make some designers wary about implementing changes in their designs. Game designers should trust that players will not use an option that will remove what's fun about a particular game for them—but adding a simplified form of the game can support many different kinds of disabled gamers at very little development cost (not to mention those players who are not disabled, but simply not competent at the game!).

Before I move on to the descriptions of disability types, I want to bring up a question that I'm often asked. What game genres are most popular for gamers with hearing impairments or gamers who only have one arm? As is the case with all gamers—with and without disabilities—everyone has different preferences with regard to game genre. Gamers with disabilities have just as varied opinions about which game types are fun for them as do gamers without disabilities. Having a disability doesn't mean that your preferences are exactly like every other person with a similar disability.

As a result, you can't assume that including closed captioning in a FPS title is going to mean that everyone with an auditory disability is immediately going to buy a copy. However, it does mean that having it there and letting that potential audience base know it's there *will* result in increased purchases from those with auditory disabilities. This will happen firstly because you've made your game accessible to gamers with an auditory disability who *already* enjoy FPS games—as happened with *Half-Life 2* (Valve, 2004), which contained closed captioning after a large lobbying effort by deaf gamers. And it will happen secondly because you've opened up another opportunity for gamers with auditory disabilities to consider a genre they might previously have ignored because it wasn't accessible to them.

Visual Disabilities

Visual disabilities relate to problems of sight. Three types of disability exist: blindness, low vision, and color blindness.

Blindness refers to the complete loss of vision that is not correctable even with lenses. Some lights and shadows may be seen, but most experience "total blindness" and in all cases the sense of vision is not enough to rely on even in the most limited situation. It makes all forms of visual feedback in games impossible to use and a blind gamer relies on feedback delivered through other senses; for example, via sound cues or force feedback cues [IGDA04b].

A gamer with low vision may be able to detect motion and may be able to differentiate between images given sufficient magnification. Such players need ways to raise the font sizes (which may then overlap with the game's other visuals), and may have parts of their visual field occluded such that they can see fairly clearly in spots but not at all in other places.

I'll talk about "official" statistics later, but one disability that developers rarely think about is one of the largest subtypes—color blindness. This is estimated to affect at least 10% of men (it is much rarer in women) [Saunders07]. Color blindness leads to confusion with regard to certain color schemes. The severity of the condition ranges from total color blindness, meaning the person sees in grayscale, to specific color differentiation problems, where the person may be unable to tell the difference between red and green (the most common variety) or blue and yellow. Depending upon the severity, the user may have difficulty with specific color use in a game, or may be rendered effectively blind. Games that rely upon color differentiation, such as color-matching puzzle games, may become unplayable [Bierre05].

Auditory Disabilities

Hearing problems vary between mild hearing difficulty and total deafness. Deafness naturally causes problems with picking up audio cues, and any non-subtitled dialogue will be missed. Music and atmospheric sound design will also be lost, potentially changing the feel of the game [Bierre05].

Hearing difficulties (separate from total hearing loss) may lead to problems too. Although people with hearing difficulties may be able to hear dialogue, they may lose the sounds if music plays while characters are talking. Any given audio cue may be missed due to similar issues, and the increased cognitive demands of having to read on-screen text while looking for signs representing specific audio clues can cause players with hearing difficulties to miss important information that would normally be apparent.

Mobility Disabilities

Mobility disabilities include paralysis (via accident, disease, or a birth defect), neurological disorders, repetitive stress injury, and age-related issues. These factors lead to a loss of mobility and steadiness, which may result in the players being unable to press a button rapidly enough, unable to react quickly enough to events on-screen, or unable to use commercial game controllers because of lack of movement in their hands or arms [Bierre05].

In the introduction to this chapter, I described an unbelievable gaming scenario that three roommates without disabilities encounter. However, swap out some of the text and you have the "real-life" scenario of gamers with little or no movement in at least their hands and arms. This could be a person who is quadriplegic or has a disorder that limits arm or hand movement, such as muscular dystrophy. Alternatively, it could be someone who has the use of only one hand and thus cannot use all of the dozens of buttons on a typical videogame controller.

Custom interface devices may be required, ranging from ergonomically designed controllers to ease steadiness problems, to single-switch mechanisms allowing paralyzed users to exert control with, say, small head movements.

Fast action games are unlikely to be enjoyable for users with mobility issues. Other styles of game, such as turn-based games, may be more suitable. Strategy games and classic adventure games (text or point-and-click) effectively wait for the players to instruct them, reducing or eliminating the need for rapid response on the part of the players.

Commercial custom peripherals (such as dance mats, light guns, guitar controllers, and the like) may aid or hinder users with mobility problems. For games of this nature, controller design is a core aspect of the game's design, and should include the same considerations regarding accessibility as any game.

Cognitive Disabilities

Problems with cognition are wide in scope, taking into account memory loss, attention deficit disorder (and other learning disabilities), and dyslexia [IGDA04b].

Games can better support users with cognition problems by offering support tools. For instance, weak memory can be countered via in-game automatic note-taking devices (such as journals, self-updating maps, and so on). The effects of dyslexia may be reduced by minimizing the need for reading, by recording dialogue, or by offering symbolic/iconic representations of actions in addition to text. Learning disabilities can be countered via free-access tutorial systems, save-anywhere features, and by the presentation of game material in tight, controlled bursts.

DISABILITY STATISTICS

Because videogames are a commercial industry, I often get asked questions about the numbers of a disability type—such as "Well, what's better for our bottom line? Do we go with gamers with hearing disabilities or mobility disabilities?"

According to the latest information from the U.S. Census data, shown in Table 7.1, there were 43.1 million people with some sort of disability living in the United States in 2006 [USCensus06a]. The survey measured persons aged five and over who were not living in an institution such as a prison, a nursing home, or long-term hospital rehabilitation such as Veterans Administration hospitals. Even without the data from those in institutionalized living situations, this represented *nearly one person in six*. If that data were included, the proportion would be even greater.

Although it is important to know that number when we speak about disabilities—especially, in this case, for products intended for the U.S. market—it's more important to understand what goes into categorizing someone with a disability and even more importantly, how many of the disabled population are blind or quadriplegic or have a hearing impairment. If a disability, such as a learning disability, is not "visible," does the person being surveyed mention it? Whether or not people self-identify as having a disability is just one way that census results can become skewed.

And, as mentioned earlier, there is often crossover into other disability "categories" because a person can have more than one disability, whether you use the IGDA Game Accessibility Special Interest Group's categories or the US (or another country's) census categories. As you will discover, the number of people affected by the three subtypes—Sensory, Physical, and Mental—adds up to a higher number than the 43.1 million people with a disability in general. This adds to the confusion concerning the scale of the problem.

But the breakdown of disability subtypes has not been very helpful for those who want to include accessibility features that will include the widest possible audience that their studio can afford. For those of us working in the accessibility world, it can be really difficult to tweeze out what the "largest" disability gaming groups are with regard to visual, auditory, mobility, and cognitive disabilities and even within those subtypes when one of the world's largest surveys do not break down their categories with more specific questions. (They have in the past, but changes were made to the data collection schema that effectively prevent data comparison from post-1999 to earlier data, when the subtypes were broken down further.)

Regardless, surveys such as the U.S. Census do provide a more general picture of the disabled in the United States.

Table 7.1 2006 U.S. Census Population with One or More Disabilities (Non-Specific)

	Male	Female	Total
Total U.S. Population by Gender	133,533,893	140,301,572	273,835,465
5 to 15 Years	22,862,328	21,834,461	44,696,789
No Disabilities	21,042,647	20,824,520	41,967,167
One Disability	1,451,152	783,234	2,234,386
Two or More Disabilities	368,529	226,707	595,236
Disability Total	**1,819,681**	**1,009,941**	**2,829,622**
16 to 20 Years	10,939,399	10,552,739	21,492,138
No Disabilities	10,073,807	9,917,147	19,990,954
One Disability	542,096	398,258	940,354
Two or More Disabilities	323,496	237,334	560,830
Disability Total	**865,592**	**635,592**	**1,501,184**
21 to 64 Years	84,582,607	87,493,471	172,076,078
No Disabilities	73,697,888	76,016,277	149,714,165
One Disability	4,548,812	4,621,189	9,170,001
Two or More Disabilities	6,335,907	6,856,005	13,191,912
Disability Total	**10,884,719**	**11,477,194**	**22,361,913**

continued

Total U.S. Population by Gender	Male	Female	Total
65 to 74 Years	8,556,268	10,129,880	18,686,148
No Disabilities	6,027,290	7,034,679	13,061,969
One Disability	1,396,114	1,572,061	2,968,175
Two or More Disabilities	1,132,864	1,523,140	2,656,00
Disability Total	**2,528,978**	**3,095,201**	**5,624,179**
75 Years and Over	6,593,291	10,291,021	16,884,312
No Disabilities	3,330,015	4,611,386	7,941,401
One Disability	1,355,103	1,924,657	3,279,760
Two or More Disabilities	1,908,173	3,754,978	5,663,151
Disability Total	**3,263,276**	**5,679,635**	**8,942,911**
One or More Disabilities Totals	**19,362,246**	**23,717,244**	**43,079,490**

The U.S. Census combines the category of auditory and visual disabilities, which already have subcategories of their own that require independent solutions. A "sensory disability" includes difficulty in seeing and hearing, including the blind and the deaf in the same category. The Census asks a yes/no question, which reads "Do you have any of the following long-lasting conditions: Blindness, deafness, severe vision, or hearing impairment?" [USCensus06b].

This is perhaps the most frustrating category with regard to game accessibility, because the solutions for the blind are often barriers for the deaf and vice versa. According to the census data, as shown in Table 7.2, some 11.8 million people in the United States have a sensory disability. That's 27.3% of the disabled population or 4.3% of the overall population [USCensus06a].

Table 7.2 2006 U.S. Census Population with Sensory Disabilities

	Male	Female	Total
Total U.S. Population by Gender	133,533,893	140,301,572	273,835,465
5 to 15 Years	22,862,328	21,834,461	44,696,789
With a Sensory Disability	292,440	229,490	521,930
No Sensory Disability	22,569,888	21,604,971	44,174,859
16 to 20 Years	10,939,399	10,552,739	21,462,138
With a Sensory Disability	155,199	125,690	280,889
No Sensory Disability	10,784,200	10,427,049	21,211,249
21 to 64 Years	84,582,607	87,493,471	172,076,078
With a Sensory Disability	2,926,225	2,215,759	5,141,984
No Sensory Disability	81,656,382	85,277,712	166,934,094
65 to 74 Years	8,556,268	10,129,880	18,686,148
With a Sensory Disability	1,028,473	835,121	1,863,594
No Sensory Disability	7,527,795	9,294,759	16,822,554
75 Years and Over	6,593,291	10,291,021	16,884,312
With a Sensory Disability	1,674,445	2,347,116	4,021,561
No Sensory Disability	4,918,846	7,943,905	12,862,751
Sensory Disability Totals	6,076,782	5,753,176	11,829,958

The U.S. Census term of "physical disability" corresponds with what I have termed here "mobility disability"—and this category is extremely diverse internally, with different individuals requiring radically different assistance in order to play an off-the-shelf game title.

The Census asks respondents a yes/no question, which reads "Do you have any of the following long-lasting conditions: A condition that substantially limits one or more basic physical activities such as walking, climbing stairs, reaching, lifting, or carrying?" [USCensus06b]. And according to further explanation from the Census Bureau, this includes having one or more of the following:

- The person may use a wheelchair, cane, crutches, or walker to get around.
- The person may have difficulty with one or more functional activities, ranging from "walking a fourth of a mile, climbing a flight of stairs, lifting something as heavy as a 10-pound bag of groceries, grasping objects, and/or getting in or out of bed".
- The person may have one or more conditions that is the cause of activity limitation, including but not limited to "arthritis or rheumatism; back or spine problems; broken bone or fracture; cancer; cerebral palsy; diabetes; epilepsy; head or spinal cord injury; heart trouble or hardening of arteries; hernia or rupture; high blood pressure; kidney problems; lung or respiratory problems; missing legs, arms, feet, hands, or fingers; paralysis; stiffness or deformity of legs, arms, feet, or hands; stomach/digestive problems; stroke; thyroid problems; or tumor, cyst, or growth".

So 25.7 million people (59.6% of the disabled population and 9.3% of the population in general) have some kind of physical disability, as shown in Table 7.3. But when referring to videogames, as mentioned in the mobility section earlier, we are primarily talking about gamers who have, for one reason or another, something that limits, or prevents altogether, movement in the hands and arms. To a lesser degree—at least until "exergaming," as exemplified by *Wii Fit* (Nintendo, 2007) becomes even more prevalent—this includes gamers who have limited mobility in the feet and legs. So the census category of "physical" disabilities is a bit more encompassing than the IGDA Game Accessibility SIG's category of "mobility" disabilities. However, it gives us a general sense of the scope of these types of disabilities that gamers may have.

Table 7.3 2006 U.S. Census Population with Physical Disabilities

	Male	Female	Total
Total U.S. Population by Gender	133,533,893	140,301,572	273,835,465
5 to 15 Years	22,862,328	21,834,461	44,696,789
With a Physical Disability	289,115	218,376	507,491
No Physical Disability	22,573,213	21,616,085	44,189,298
16 to 20 Years	10,939,399	10,552,739	21,492,138
With a Physical Disability	172,555	179,284	351,839
No Physical Disability	10,766,844	10,373,455	21,140,299
21 to 64 Years	84,582,607	87,493,471	172,076,078
With a Physical Disability	6,345,913	7,432,706	13,778,619
No Physical Disability	78,236,694	80,060,765	158,297,459
65 to 74 Years	8,556,268	10,129,880	18,686,148
With a Physical Disability	1,828,244	2,515,297	4,343,541
No Physical Disability	6,728,024	7,614,583	14,342,607
75 Years and Over	6,593,291	10,291,021	16,884,312
With a Physical Disability	2,346,047	4,453,039	6,799,086
No Physical Disability	4,247,244	5,837,982	10,085,226
Physical Disability Totals	**10,981,874**	**14,798,702**	**25,780,576**

The census category of "mental" disabilities is a very tricky term to use. In game accessibility, concern is usually focused upon cognitive issues such as learning disabilities and conditions that cause memory or attention loss. However, this does not mean that other conditions such as autism, post-traumatic stress disorder, psychiatric disorders, and profound cognitive limitations are not relevant, especially in the realm of educational or serious games. This latter grouping is also of interest in the realm of games for health and therapy. According to the U.S. Census data, 15.9 million people (36.8% of the disabled population and 5.8% of the overall population) have a "mental" disability, as shown in Table 7.4.

However, the "mental" disability category is probably the most broad and vague of all of these groupings. The census also takes the yes/no question approach to respondents about having a disability in a mental domain, which reads "Do you have a physical, mental, or emotional condition lasting six months or more that made it difficult learning, remembering, or concentrating?" [USCensus06b].

Further explanation of this category by the Census Bureau does little to clear up any confusion. In essence, this category is intended to mean that in the past six months or more, one or more of the following conditions apply [USCensus06b]:

- The person may have "one or more specified conditions (a learning disability, mental retardation, or another developmental disability, Alzheimer's disease, or some other type of mental or emotional condition)."
- The person may have any other mental or emotional condition that seriously interferes with everyday activities. For example, such a person may be "frequently depressed or anxious, [have] trouble getting along with others, [have] trouble concentrating, or [have] trouble coping with day-to-day stress."
- The person may have difficulty managing money/bills.
- They may have one or more conditions that often result in activity limitations such as attention deficit hyperactivity disorder, autism, learning disability, mental or emotional problems, mental retardation, or senility, dementia, or Alzheimer's.

Although some of this definitely overlaps into the category of cognitive disabilities, this grouping has the most severe influence in the context of non-mainstream games and games for health and education. So although the commercial game industry may not yet be able to do much beyond helping with certain cognitive disabilities, this category is of keen interest to people developing educational games and games for therapeutic purposes.

Table 7.4 2006 U.S. Census Population with Mental Disabilities

	Male	Female	Total
Total U.S. Population	133,533,893	140,301,572	273,835,465
5 to 15 Years	22,862,328	21,834,461	44,696,789
With a Mental Disability	1,529,025	758,485	2,287,510
No Mental Disability	21,333,303	21,075,976	42,409,279
16 to 20 Years	10,939,399	10,552,739	21,492,138
With a Mental Disability	626,261	388,599	1,014,860
No Mental Disability	10,313,138	10,164,140	20,477,278
21 to 64 Years	84,582,607	87,493,471	172,076,078
With a Mental Disability	4,033,109	4,186,154	8,219,263
No Mental Disability	80,549,498	83,307,317	163,856,815
65 to 74 Years	8,556,268	10,129,880	18,686,148
With a Mental Disability	654,610	782,893	1,437,503
No Mental Disability	7,901,658	9,346,987	17,248,645
75 Years and Over	6,593,291	10,291,021	16,884,312
With a Mental Disability	1,053,199	1,915,125	2,968,324
No Mental Disability	5,540,092	8,375,896	13,915,988
Mental Disability Totals	7,896,204	8,031,256	15,927,460

As I mentioned, at least one person in six is personally affected by an "official" disability, and since we're all aging, we'll all eventually find it harder to see, to hear, and to move around at the same clip we might have in our younger years—or even just the year before. Companies such as Nintendo are putting out titles like *Brain Age* (Nintendo, 2005) to help "train your brain" because people are becoming increasingly concerned when news services report that conditions such as Alzheimer's appear to be striking earlier than expected. Concern about disabilities is increasing, and as *Brain Age* demonstrates, some of these situations present commercial opportunities.

I still haven't answered all the questions that those of us working in the game accessibility realm get asked all the time, such as which disability group should we support to get the most additional sales? The blind? The deaf? And how many of them would be gamers if they could be? How many more units of my product am I going to sell if I make sure I have included X, Y, and Z into my game design?

These are difficult questions to answer. Roughly 1 in 10 people are affected by physical disabilities and about 1 in 20 people are affected by either a mental or a sensory disability. But as I mentioned earlier, there's significant crossover that results in a combined total of 53.4 million people representing the three disability categories out of the 43.1 million people with a disability in general—either that or there's been a serious mathematical error. To be frank, no one knows how many of *any* group of people would be a gamer if a game were made accessible for that group—this is true both for disabilities and for other issues such as culture and language.

Waiting for some sort of "exact number" only keeps us from making any changes to increase the accessibility of our games. This isn't a subject that lends itself to this kind of approach, so rather than trying to work out how to maximize returns by identifying a single group of disabilities to target I'd like to issue a call to arms for the industry to just *start working on accessibility*. There are many easy changes that could be implemented right now at very little cost, any one of which will result in significant improvements for the disabled and non-disabled gamer alike.

DESIGNING FOR ACCESSIBILITY

What can designers do to begin their journey towards making games more accessible to gamers with disabilities? I realize it probably seems quite daunting to "just get started" with regards to improving the accessibility of your game designs without any guidance as to how! In order to address this hurdle, the IGDA Game Accessibility SIG has been working on an ever-evolving list of ways that game designers can make games more accessible. This "top ten" list, summarized in the following sidebar, details practical steps that developers can take with a minimum of effort, and without greatly hampering or intruding upon gameplay in general. [IGDA06].

In other words, this list includes ten "low-hanging fruits" with regards to accessibility issues. All you have to do is pick which ones to implement and then go for it!

TOP TEN WAYS TO GET STARTED IN GAME ACCESSIBILITY

1. Allow all controls (mouse, keyboard, gamepad) to be remapped.
2. Add closed captioning for all dialogue and important sound effects.
3. Provide documentation in an accessible format (HTML or plain-text).
4. Provide assist modes (auto-targeting, training options, and so on).
5. Provide a broad range of difficulty settings, from incredibly simple to highly challenging.
6. Make interface fonts scalable.
7. Allow for high-contrast color schemes.
8. Add audio tags to all significant elements (actors, doors, items, resulting actions, and so on) in true spatial 3D.
9. Allow for a varied range of control over play-speed.
10. Announce accessibility features on packaging, websites, and forums.

In the sections that follow, I will give a short explanation of each of these solutions. Some of these solutions are more applicable to a particular type of videogame, but the underlying ideas behind them should be applicable to most games.

In the meantime, copy this top ten list and tack it somewhere on a visible portion of your desk. Make another copy and tack it to your design books and carry it with you. If you are a project manager who wants to lead your team to take just one of these items and go for it, make a copy of the chart for everyone and talk about which item is the most feasible (and logical!) for the game you are making.

Even if what you and your team decide on is an accessibility feature that will help mainly those with auditory disabilities, you are doing something—you are taking one step toward expanding your audience and inviting players with disabilities to play. And until this accessibility movement catches on, even just that small step might help in inspiring others to actively foster positive social change within the industry!

So read on and get ready to take one or maybe two of these (if you are feeling bold) and commit to it! Commit to making games playable by more people. You are no doubt proud of your games—why not add to that pride by giving more people the gift of play?

Remappable Controls

Allow all controls (mouse, keyboard, gamepad) to be remapped to better suit accessible controllers.

Alan, who is quadriplegic, uses a special game controller called a "Quad Controller," which was introduced at the beginning of this chapter. It allows Alan to play his favorite game titles entirely with his mouth via a series of tubes that he breathes in and out of, depending on the buttons he's trying to press. There are also levers to move up or down and buttons to press, and movement is controlled via a mouthpiece. He can get through a fair number of games with it, but he is hugely frustrated that hardly any of the videogames he bought let you remap any of the controls. There are times when he'll start up a game only to find out very quickly that he's not going to be able to get anywhere in it because he has to press a two-button sequence constantly—requiring him to puff air in one tube and sip air out of another tube at the exact same time—which is entirely impossible...

Remappable controls are still common in PC gaming, but are extremely rare in the world of console gaming. It is not unheard of for a console game to allow full remapping of controls, but it is far more common for games to offer a finite set of predefined control schemes, presumably because this is easier for the Quality Assurance process.

Fully remappable controls allow users to define the game inputs irrespective of the hardware they are using to control the game. Predefined control schemes may not suit specialist interface hardware, of the sort required by users with significant mobility problems, and are thus a barrier to accessibility.

It may be that developers are avoiding remappable controls on consoles because of the problems they produce in QA. This is understandable, but this problem isn't going to disappear if developers don't start tackling it. If necessary, we can petition the console manufacturers to provide support for this kind of feature in the tools they supply for development, but this would be easier to achieve if developers joined in the crusade to establish remappable controls as an industry standard.

Closed Captioning

Add closed captioning for all dialogue and important sound effects.

Maureen, a deaf gamer, can play games in which the sound and dialogue aren't important to gameplay. But often—far too often—she picks up one of the latest titles to discover that there is an audio cue that she has to hear—otherwise her avatar is going to keep on dying over and over and over until she decides to write the company in disgust. She doesn't know what's more annoying—games that have subtitles for some things but not for everything, or games that just don't even bother.

The vast majority of contemporary games offer subtitles for in-game dialogue, but make no attempt to provide full captioning for other important sound cues. Sound effects, which are vital to a full understanding of the gamespace (as opposed to the representational space of the game), are needed in order to alert deaf players—or even players who choose to play with the sound off, such as commuters playing on a handheld device without headphones.

Note that closed captioning might not be the best solution for certain audio cues, specifically vital cues that occur very regularly. Visual effects that represent the audio cues in question obviously provide the same support for deaf players as well as players of standard hearing, and are usually inexpensive to implement.

Half-Life 2 includes full closed captioning, and is considered a pioneer case. *Doom 3* (iD, 2004) has been modded by its technical community to provide a closed captioning function. The mod is called *Doom[CC]* (Games[CC], 2006) and the project was led by Reid Kimball, a hearing-impaired gamer and game developer (and an IGDA Game Accessibility SIG member!).

Accessible Documentation

Provide documentation in an accessible format (HTML or plain-text).

James, a blind gamer who is an avid player of first person shooters, uses sound cues in the games not only to play the game but also to beat everyone in the neighborhood. He uses a screen-reader—software that "reads aloud" the text on-screen—to read through the game forums on the web for tips, new mods, and so on (some gamers with cognitive disabilities that make reading quickly a nearly impossible task also make use of screen-readers). Unfortunately, it doesn't work with his console system so he can't have it read the game text.

He's often annoyed that he can't access the game manuals from the company's website. Sometimes companies will put them online in PDF form, but manuals are so graphics-heavy that his screen-reader fails. He wonders why they just don't put up a text-only HTML document, or even just a plain-text file so he can listen to them. Half the time he wants to know more about a game directly from the game manual before he considers buying the game so he has a better idea if he'll be able to play it. Most of the time the manual is inside the game's DVD box, which he has to break the seal on and then he has a hard, if not impossible, time returning the game. If developers had accessible versions of their manuals available online, it'd probably save him, the game store, and even the company a lot of grief.

Outside of the game itself, documentation needs to be more accessible. The use of screen-readers or even Braille-output devices (an assistive technology solution that produces Braille on a special hardware device so that gamers can read rather than listen to the documentation) by some visually impaired gamers requires some sort of "meeting place" between developers and gamers.

Accessible documentation is especially needed when it comes to "manual heavy" games such as role-playing games and strategy games. A player that cannot use paper manuals needs to be able to refer to the game documentation in easily useable formats. So in addition to paper manuals, documentation supplied as HTML or plain-text allows for a great deal of flexibility.

Assist Modes

Provide assist modes (auto-targeting, training options, and so on).

Platform games have always been Mary's favorite genre but in almost all of the titles she tries, there are several points in the game that will stop her gameplay cold unless she can find someone to take the controller and, say, get past a very tricky series of jumps that require more fine motor skills than her muscular dystrophy allows. This is a pain because it means once she finds someone who agrees to try to help her move past the point where she is stuck (and more often than not she finds a lot of well-meaning but not very skilled volunteers), she has to swap out her accessible controller because, even though she can use it doesn't mean anyone else is going to have an easy time of it when used to a standard controller!

Mary uses a hacked controller that used to be a fighting stick controller from Japan but is now connected to several "switches" (large single-button pads, not unlike the buttons on the walls at school that open the wheelchair accessible doors, only more colorful). She has an arcade-style playstick on it, and someone has also drilled into the controller and rewired it so that the four main buttons that she uses are each connected to their own switch. It's cumbersome but it is "function over form" when it comes to gameplay, she always says.

The thing is, it would be nice if some of these companies knew about these specialist controllers because if they did, maybe they would understand why she doesn't care if it's "cheating" to call upon some kind of assist mode that would allow her to make the jumps a little more easily. For Mary, she just wants to play and enjoy the game—she has no desire to enter some videogame competition where that would make a difference.

Game design in the 1980s was necessarily challenge-oriented. The zenith of twitch gameplay was to be found in the arcades, an environment that made money by tempting the player to pay to play. Design elements like bosses evolved to provide reward (visually, and in terms of a signifi-cant post-boss score boost) while killing the player as often as possible. If a game were easy, skilled players would hog the machine on a single credit, and profits would be impacted.

The role of challenge in mainstream action games began to change when games became playable at home. Although home systems were available throughout the '80s, the games released for them were heavily inspired by arcade games. As the '90s progressed from SNES to Play-Station, elements other than challenge became part of the game designer's remit—for instance, game environments post-1996, the year of *Mario 64* (Nintendo), *Resident Evil* (Capcom), and *Tomb Raider* (Core Design), attempt to mimic the logic of real-world environments, as opposed to merely providing a game experience. Compare these kinds of games with classic side-scrolling games such as *Sonic the Hedgehog* (Sonic Team, 1991), which features completely surreal worlds, for instance.

The 2000s brought a new spin, in the idea of games for non-gamers. Players who refer to themselves as gamers (the "hardcore") generally require a certain degree of challenge, as they are adept at certain game forms—they are game literate and pick up new games very rapidly. New players—those who never played a *Mario* or a *Sonic*, let alone *Strider* (Cap-com, 1989) or *Cannon Dancer* (Mitchell, 1996)—aren't seeking challenge. Much of this book discusses this broadening of the role of videogames from challenge-oriented Hard Fun games to a multiplicity of roles suit-able for different audience types.

Although it is natural to design games of a different style for new audi-ences, it also makes sense to maximize audience potential for existing game genres by the inclusion of player assistance. It should be noted that, although play-aids may allow players to enjoy games of a given form, they do actually alter the nature of the gameplay—using aids actually changes the game. But as I pointed out in Mary's scenario—she doesn't care, she just wants to play and enjoy the game even if she doesn't play it in the exact same way others do. Should she be prevented from doing so because a small number of gamers are offended by providing the option to "cheat"?

The trend is fortunately in favor of more support for players, as it is becoming undeniable that reaching into the mass market requires these kinds of changes. Driving games, for instance, began to feature braking aids and steering assistance, a trend that led to the active racing line repre-sentation of *Forza Motorsport* (Turn 10 Studios, 2005). This aid can be turned off, but does generate gameplay (playing with the line is effectively a different game experience than playing without the line).

Halo: Combat Evolved (Bungie, 2001) demonstrates a similar principle. It's a console-based FPS game that employs an auto-aim system to make up for a lack of accuracy in a console twin-stick controller when compared to using a mouse to aim (as with PC-based FPS games, the standard of the form precisely for this reason). The aid works by snapping the player's aiming reticule to a live target when the reticule nears that target; this stops the players from getting into a feedback loop in fine aiming. This aid is not optional, and forms a crucial component of *Halo's* play design: its core play becomes biased against fine aiming, and instead becomes more positional in nature (the relative positions of the players and enemies become more important than the speed of aim).

The trend continues in this direction with each passing year. *Alone in the Dark* (Eden Games, 2008), although suffering from some flaws in its gameplay design, features an innovative system that allows players to skip any challenge and move onto the next one. The developers were motivated by a desire to make the game more like a DVD experience, with an eye to reaching a wider audience. Although many gamers confessed that it "felt like cheating," this kind of mechanism is a boon to the many millions of players who struggle with some of the tougher challenges in videogames, effectively allowing them to get past any obstacle.

But the industry can be extremely resistant to these kinds of changes, because of objections like "it's cheating" or "why would anyone want to play like that?" Chris informs me that just a few years ago a publisher stopped him from including a feature that would allow players to continue to the next challenge after failing because of the objection that, with such a feature, "it wouldn't even be a game anymore".

Player aids such as *Forza's* racing line and *Halo's* auto-aim naturally allow less-skilled players to participate in play, as well as allowing gamers who are using assistive technologies/accessible controllers to play. *Alone in the Dark's* "skip" feature allows anyone to see the whole of the game, without any risk of being stuck. But features such as these also change the nature of play: the game might be realized in different ways than those the designers idealized. It takes a certain amount of courage to accept this kind of transformation, especially because the people who make games sometimes feel that the game is theirs. But designers are being paid to make the game, while others are paying to play it. Don't the people who buy games deserve some influence over what they are buying?

In theory, there is no limit to the amount of aid a player can be given without diminishing the sensation of play, and it is necessary for games designers to continue to develop such mechanisms in order to expand the accessibility of games in general to the widest possible audience (everyone). Problems only emerge in the space of competition. Simulating the same level of competition using different degrees of aid is impossible—as noted— and the use of aids fundamentally alters gameplay. So players in direct competition using different levels of play aid are in fact playing different games against each other. Naturally, this is a problem only if the players have extremely "hardcore" sensibilities, and not for the many gamers who are just enjoying the game experience in their own way.

Easier Difficulty Settings

Provide a broad range of difficulty settings, from incredibly simple to highly challenging.

Troy's son, Brent, has autism but often enjoys playing a variety of games when the mood strikes. But Brent, who is 10 years old, will often get stuck in spots and will want to move to the next level *now*. So he screams in what feels like some kind of panic until Frank comes into the room to disarm the situation. Because Brent is only allowed to play games rated "E," Frank gets frustrated, because even though he's showed Brent how to set up the game to "easy" mode (it's part of Brent's "script" he follows when he plays his games—a script that must be repeated "just so" or there will be trouble), "easy" mode is often far from it for Brent! And Brent won't allow his dad to take over the controls and help him past the stuck point, so usually the game ends in frustration and tears until Brent can be soothed by something else. Frank wishes that some of these designers would realize that children with disabilities play these games, and that there needs to be some mode that lets them just play through without much difficulty.

The thing is, Troy also likes to play videogames on his new PS3 (Brent has his old PS2), even though he doesn't have much time to play. He knows that if his friends knew what a "newbie" gamer he was that they would give him complete crap about it. But it's his system and there are times when he's exhausted and just wants to blow off some steam. So he wants to just be able to set his games to "amazingly easy" and kill everything on-screen with lightning speed (definitely not an "E" rated game!), except that option rarely exists.

Broadly, there are two aspects to challenge in games, one that may be related to interface, and one that may be related to parametric design. The former, involving the difficulty of mastering the interface of the game (that is, the mechanisms that allow the player and game to communicate, which include the game controls, HUD data, vision modes, audio cues, and so on) can be made easier via player aids, as discussed previously.

Parametric difficulty is based around the qualities of the contents of the world. Games are made up of numbers, such as the health points of an enemy, that enemy's distance from the player's gun, and the damage levels inflicted by a direct hit from that gun. These numbers—parametric values—can create difficulty. If the enemy has a million hit points and the gun does one hit point damage per hit, the enemy will take one million hits to kill. If the enemy fights back at all, setting the damage so low will naturally make such a fight rather difficult.

Both types of difficulty must be addressable by players. This is true of all players—they have paid for the game, and so they should expect to be able to play it. Games of Hard Fun, however, thrive on being just slightly harder than players can deal with on their first play; if players can decrease the difficulty, this can be seen as a "cop-out" or "cheating".

This doesn't cause problems with a classic difficulty selection system (which involves a player choice before the game begins, usually between easy, normal, and hard modes—although even here players are at the mercy of the developer's interpretation of these terms). But there is a general assumption within the games industry, possibly still a holdover from challenge-oriented twitch arcade games, that because interface difficulty seems to decrease as the game progresses (because the player gets better at using the game), parametric difficulty must increase. Not only that, but it is often assumed that the overall difficulty at the end of a game should be significantly higher than at the start.

Although part of this fits the idea of Flow you learned about in Step 1, these assumptions can become highly dubious in practice: no one can know in advance how much better an individual player will become from continued play, and without access to this kind of information, it is impossible to know if it is appropriate to increase difficulty.

To maintain full accessibility, game difficulty should be manageable by the players on the fly, at any point in the game. This suggestion may immediately incense any player who is primarily concerned with Hard Fun. If a reasonable strategy to bypass a bottleneck in parametric difficulty is to choose an option from a menu, surely the point of the game is completely diminished! But since such players consider these kinds of changes to be "cheating," doesn't this problem become self-limiting? And of course, players who play for any of the many other reasons players play games need not fear this at all.

Videogames that have allowed for flexible difficulty settings throughout the game include *Magic and Mayhem* (Mythos Games, 1998), *Disgaea: Hour of Darkness* (Nippon Ichi, 2003), and *Oblivion* (Bethesda, 2006). Since *Oblivion* has sold more than 3 million units, as well as scooping up several Game of the Year awards, it can safely be assumed that allowing players to change the difficulty setting at will isn't a significant barrier to commercial success anymore.

The fact of the matter is that people who work in videogame development routinely misjudge just how difficult their game might be for someone with considerably less game literacy, let alone someone with accessibility issues. There is no need to shy away from making supremely easy difficulty settings, because players seeking a challenge will not choose a setting called "ridiculously easy" or anything of the kind (such players often balk at playing on Normal!). Making the easiest difficulty setting in a game as simple and easy as it could possibly be will benefit a vast number of players, and not just those with disabilities.

Scalable Fonts

Make interface fonts scalable.

Mike can see, technically, but not without special glasses and even then he still needs things to be enlarged. He'd like to play more games—sometimes he does okay with simple games like solitaire where he can take his time—but he hears such great stories about some of the videogame titles on the market. He'd like to try them, but so many of them have so much on the screen and the text is so small that he doesn't know what's going on. And he knows he can't change the font size even though he thinks by this day and age he should be able to. He wonders if he'll ever be able to try them out so he knows what his friends are talking about.

With the advent of HDTV, it seems to be assumed that tiny text is acceptable in console games, because the quality of the display will make up for it. This is clearly not the case, and many users with impaired vision are unable to comfortably read text from their screen, irrespective of its size and resolution. PC games suffer less from this problem, having a more standard visual display, but text size is still an issue. Where in-game help functions are incorporated, it is imperative that they are easy to use.

According to some game design professionals, having large readable text is even more important in games than in productivity software because of the lack of a standard visual display and the need to read text quickly in order not to interfere with gameplay [Saunders07]. Magnification options would solve this problem. Note that spoken dialogue does not diminish the requirement for legible text; deaf players cannot hear it, and many players prefer not to listen to the spoken dialogue, since reading is generally much faster.

This may be another area where QA concerns are the substantial barrier. Since getting text to display properly on-screen is a problem for most game titles, having scalable fonts represents an even bigger problem—especially when localizing into languages such as German, which often produces incredibly long menu names. This may be another instance where the console manufacturers need to be lobbied to provide supporting tools to developers before any significant progress will be made.

High-Contrast Colors

Allow for high-contrast color schemes.

JoAnne's husband loves a good puzzle, so she is confused as to why he won't even try to play the games she likes to play. JoAnne is a casual gamer but is obsessed with a wide variety of puzzle games, and she'll lose track of hours in what seems like no time at all when she's playing them. But her husband just becomes annoyed when he sees JoAnne playing her games, and tries to distract her by asking her to play board games with him instead. Conversely, she just cannot understand why he finds those games so much more fun than the computer games. She likes both, but right now she's really into the puzzle games on her computer and she wants to be able to play some of them against him, and compete with him for higher scores.

Seemingly out of nowhere, he agrees to play one game she's been raving about and she's thrilled! But what she doesn't quite understand is why he can't seem to "get" the game. It's simple—just match up the different colored boxes. And then it dawns on her... oh... my husband is color blind! It all looks the same to him!

Alternate vision modes could potentially enable a large audience of new players. Color blindness and low vision are not rare conditions—the former affects roughly one in ten men, whereas low vision is harder to quantify (but consider the number of people who wear glasses or contact lenses...). Settings that allow for high-contrast visuals or alternative color schemes can give these players access to a game that would otherwise be impossible for them to play.

One guideline that has been suggested is never to use color contrast as the only way to convey information—so if something has to be red and green, make sure it's shaped differently or has a distinctly different look to it as well. Games that use power bars often use "green" for full health and "red" for poor health, which can be problematic—but color blind gamers can at least use the length of the power bar as a cue in these instances [Saunders07].

Audio Tags

Add audio tags to all significant elements (actors, doors, items, resulting actions, and so on) in true spatial 3D.

According to Jim, who is blind, there are very few audio games out there that are any good. He'd like to play adventure games he hears about on TV but there's no way for him to know in what direction he's going. In the "real world," he can navigate pretty well thanks to his companion dog, but he doesn't have one that can help him in the virtual world.

Significant elements include doors, items, resulting actions, and so on. Blind players should not be assumed to be experiencing the same game as sighted players, but this does not necessarily mean they are unable to enjoy the game. Non-time-dependent games such as point-and-click adventures (especially those with a significant amount of dialogue) may be enjoyed irrespective of their graphical displays, if audible navigational tools are included. 3D sounds representing directional points—North, Northwest, and so on—can be used, for example.

Chris tells an anecdote that illustrates this point nicely. He worked on several point-and-click adventures while he was with Perfect Entertainment, who made the popular *Discworld* series (1995 onwards) of point-and-click games. At a convention, he met with a blind girl who was a huge fan of the games. Chris was surprised and amazed that she could play a game that depended to a great degree upon seeing what was on-screen, but she assured him that although it took her a long, long time to make any progress, she could at least play these games, because when you clicked on a tag the game spoke.

Players with visual disabilities are much more patient with videogames than many typical gamers. Because such players are inherently limited as to which games they can play, they are much more likely to tolerate what might, to a sighted player (or game designer), seem intolerable. By providing reasonable audio feedback—and especially if this feedback can be provided in full 3D so such players can orient themselves properly—the door can be opened for many players with visual disabilities to enjoy games that otherwise would be impossible for them to play.

Play-Speed

Allow for a varied range of control over play-speed.

Mary has a friend who also uses a similar accessible controller to hers (a larger flight stick and buttons rewired and hooked up to separate larger buttons, or switches). Her friend, who was born with cerebral palsy, finds that most of the time games move too fast for him to enjoy them. He likes to play games but there's no way he can keep up with what she would consider a reasonable speed (and remember, Mary is the platform game lover with muscular dystrophy) but that's the lowest speed that the game allows for.

Another aspect of parametric difficulty, the speed at which a game moves (and the relative speeds of entities within that world) is defined by the numerical values that make up that world (as well as the technological limits of the hardware). Users with mobility or cognitive difficulties may wish to experience gameplay at a different pace. Slowing the entire game helps compensate for slow reaction times, difficulty with rapid controller manipulation, cognitive difficulties regarding the processing of visual information, and so forth. Once again, this may feel like "cheating" to some gamers, but access to these kinds of options makes the world of difference for certain players with disabilities.

Some games use relative speed changes as part of their core play design—bullet time, for instance, typically slows both player and enemy movement speed within the game world, but slows enemy speed more greatly. It might be a more difficult proposition for developers to allow players to perform fine-tuning of this nature, if only from an interface perspective.

The exact needs of users can be determined only by testing, however, and the games industry has only scratched the surface of user-solicited difficulty features. At the very least, developers should not assume that the speed they comfortably play at is the only speed at which the game can be enjoyable, or even challenging.

Announce Accessibility Features

Announce accessibility features on packaging, websites, and forums.

Finally, once you've included your first accessibility features—and of course you've tested these new changes with gamers who have the disability you are trying to address in your efforts—you need to advertise this fact!

Game packaging is slowly evolving; it is currently normal to include information on boxes regarding suitable age range, number of players, save game requirements, required PC specifications, and so forth. In order for accessibility features (player aids, alternate color schemes, closed captioning, and so on) to be of value to the players who require those features in order to play, it is necessary to inform the players of the existence of those features before they buy the game. This creates a necessity for clear information on the game packaging regarding accessibility options. A useful side effect of such a measure is that it helps legitimize the features themselves, in the minds of players and also in the minds of developers.

A word of caution is perhaps required: don't just put subtitles into your game (because localization made you do that anyway...) and announce that your game is now 100% accessible to the deaf. Without subtitled cut scenes or having ambient sounds addressed visually or in some other appropriate manner, you may be able to claim your game "contains subtitles," but you cannot call this closed captioning. Subtitles are only part of the problem—without the rest of the follow-through, you haven't made your game accessible to deaf players. Too many times a company has made this particular announcement only for it to result in disappointment and a lot of complaints by deaf gamers [Hight08]. It's okay, you have to start somewhere—I just wanted to remind you that there are always additions to make along the journey to being a more accessible game company.

I recommend you read game forums thoroughly, because gamers with disabilities will often post a specific problem they are having (that's how Valve got into the closed captioning game!). You can also visit disabled gamer communities such as AbleGamers to read about issues that members of the community may feel more comfortable posting at that site [AbleGamers]. And don't shy away from using accessibility to promote your own projects! If you learn about any accessibility solutions, say a mod that makes a part of your game more accessible, post it on your own website! It's good publicity for your game.

Accessibility features are worthwhile only if people find out about them, and it's up to you to make sure this happens.

Conclusion

There is an undeniable need, both from the perspective of social justice and also from a financial perspective, to enable the widest possible audience for games. Videogames themselves, as interactive entertainment, already bear an implied responsibility to reach out to as wide an audience as possible, which means that accessibility issues are, in effect, already core to the general philosophy of game design.

Even a person with no disabilities of any normally recognized kind can still be blocked from enjoying videogames by the conventions and normal standards of the industry. Consider both the number of new players reached by Nintendo's mass-market-friendly Wii and DS consoles, and also the tendency for game developers to gear the difficulty of play based on the assumption that its audience consists entirely of highly game-literate players who are seeking a challenge (not coincidentally, the kind of players who work for game developers). These kinds of assumptions create a "digital ceiling" that blocks inexperienced players from a medium they are perfectly capable of enjoying.

Beyond the necessity of accessibility measures, there is an ongoing need for improved understanding of the play needs of the broadest possible audience. The commercial games market is an inexact laboratory for such delicate study; testing is required, and it should include as many different players as possible. This is a genuine opportunity for game developers and academia to fruitfully collaborate, but at the moment the possibilities are far from fully utilized.

Ultimately, investigating accessibility issues will lead not only to a broader range of satisfied players, but also to new ways of gaming, which may in turn broaden the range of the gaming audience. Consider, as one final example, gaming with a biofeedback device such as Emotiv's Epoc controller (Emotiv Systems, 2008), which offers to all players the realization of the dream of doing the Jedi Mind Trick, even if for now it is possible only in virtual worlds.

8

INCLUDE PLAYERS WITH DIFFERENT SKILLS

by Chris Bateman

So far in this part you have learned about including both genders, different cultures, and people with accessibility issues, thus expanding the audience for videogames. In this step, you will learn about another way that you can include more players—namely taking into account the different skills that players have. Not everyone can enjoy a first person shooter, or a strategy game, and to make better videogames means including players whose skills might be very different than how we usually think about videogames.

INTRODUCTION

People are absurdly diverse—things that I can do very easily might present a great challenge to someone else, and there is no end of things that I can do only with great struggle that other people consider to be trivial (such as catch a ball!). Accepting that people have more fun employing skills with which they are competent (as suggested by Csíkszentmihályi's theory of Flow), an analysis of skills pertinent to videogame playing has obvious value.

Because of the great diversity of human capacities, it can be very difficult to provide a high-level examination of human skills in general, or player skills in the specific. To make this process simpler, I have used an existing psychological model known as *Temperament Theory* that groups skills into four general patterns.

In this step, you will learn about the skill sets suggested by Temperament Theory as I apply them to the context of videogames. I will call each of these applications of the relevant skill sets a *play style*, but this is not to suggest that this is the only way that play styles might be characterized. I will also discuss patterns in the history of the development of particular videogame designs capable of connecting with the relevant skill sets.

The material developed here draws heavily from the work of two psychologists, Dr. David Keirsey [Keirsey78] and his student Dr. Linda Berens [Berens00], who have been the most prominent figures in the development of modern Temperament Theory.

Temperament Theory

Temperament Theory is a scientific model constructed at a statistical level: the model is based upon observations made across a wide population of case studies, and collects the common elements in these observations to form its four patterns. It is closely related to the famous Myers-Briggs type system, and indeed can be seen as a partial projection of this. Everyone expresses all four of the temperament patterns to different degrees and in different situations, so it is not that such-and-such a person "is an Artisan" so much that he or she might express Artisan more obviously than the other three temperaments.

The four patterns, and the skill sets associated with them, are as follows:

- **Rational,** which is characterized by a desire for knowledge, competence, and achievement. People who strongly express Rational tend to be theory-oriented, and want to find a rationale for everything, desiring precision in thought and language. The accompanying skill set is known as *Strategic*.

- **Guardian,** which is characterized as a desire to fit in and have membership in a group, with a desire for responsibility, reliability, and predictability. People who strongly express Guardian tend to be focused on the past and tradition, and seek to protect and preserve. The accompanying skill set is known as *Logistical*.
- **Artisan,** which is characterized by a desire for the freedom to choose the next action, and to have an impact and get results. People who strongly express Artisan tend to be focused upon the present, and seek adventure, stimulation, and spontaneity. The accompanying skill set is known as *Tactical*.
- **Idealist,** which is characterized by a desire for authenticity, benevolence, and empathy. People who strongly express Idealist are relationship oriented, and tend to look to the future, focusing on developing potential and fostering growth through teaching, counseling, and communicating. The accompanying skill set is known as *Diplomatic*.

In the sections that follow, I will discuss each of the four skill sets that accompany these four temperament patterns in terms of the *talents* associated with the particular play style (skill set), and the main sources of *friction* that are likely to frustrate players who prefer a given play style. This is followed by a review of the history of games from the perspective of the relevant skills.

Statistical Disclaimer

Remember that Temperament Theory, and the skill sets related to it, is a statistical model. When dealing with statistical science, it is important to remember that reasoning in the general does not allow us to make firm statements about the specific. For instance, most university students drink alcohol, but knowing that this is a statistically valid observation does not allow me to know whether an individual university student drinks alcohol—they might be teetotal for religious or for health reasons, or they might not like alcohol.

STRATEGIC PLAY

Strategic play relates to mastering complex game systems and problem solving, with a drive towards perfectionism. It is arguably the oldest play style in videogames, and its commercial importance peaked in the 1980s and 1990s. Now in decline, there nonetheless exist great numbers of hobbyist players whose play needs are best met by the Strategic play style.

The Strategic skill set is associated with the Rational temperament, which is related to a need for the mastery of concepts, a desire for understanding, and a drive for competence. Those who strongly express this pattern of emotional response strive to discover the underlying principles of the universe, and may go on to develop theories by which to encapsulate their understanding. It is arguably the driving-pattern behind science, philosophy, venture capitalism, science fiction, and the process of game design.

The Rational temperament is defined as abstract pragmatism with a focus on systems. It drives those affected by it to seek mastery and competence, and often to avoid those areas where they cannot be capable. The strategic intellect associated with this pattern is capable of analyzing complex situations and devising models or processes in order to reach goals.

Stressed by feelings of powerlessness, the Rational temperament is also associated with paranoia and depression when it is out of balance. Caught between a skeptical desire to examine all doubts carefully and a self-confidence born from resolute will, the powerful strategic skills of those who express this pattern strongly should be tempered by an understanding that their way is not the only way one might think or act. Nonetheless, when people have complex problems that need solving, people who express Rational are most likely to be able to help.

Possible Neurological Basis

Although I can currently only speculate, it seems quite likely that the Rational temperament relates to high levels of dopamine in the decision center of the brain (the orbito-frontal cortex). This part of the brain, which lies above the eyes, is involved in making decisions of all kinds, and is closely tied to the pleasure center (nucleus accumbens)—making good decisions is especially rewarding. I hypothesize that the expression of the Rational temperament, and the accompanying Strategic skills, relates to high levels of dopamine in the decision center, and this could easily be tested with the new brain imaging technology.

Talents

Complex systems are the focus of most, but not all, Strategic play—with examples including the majority of simulation and turn-based strategy games, as well as many computer RPG games (cRPGs). Players who favor this play style show greater than usual tolerance for *complexity*, and indeed will generally persevere with games they feel that they do not yet understand, provided they believe their tenacity will eventually be rewarded. This allows them to tolerate far longer learning curves than players favoring other play styles—but note that every player can be frustrated by any game for a variety of reasons. The Strategic play style only gives players the *capacity* to learn how to use complex game systems. It does not guarantee that they will persist with any given game.

Coupled with this tolerance of complexity comes an ability to perceive ways to optimize the complex systems in question. This gift for optimization is expressed as a tendency to evaluate every situation in order to determine how to get the maximum benefit for minimum cost. So pronounced is this tendency to *min-max* game situations that it is even mentioned in Keirsey's description of the Rational temperament, even though play is not a focus of his work. There is a relationship between complexity and min-maxing, since in simple systems there is limited scope for this kind of optimization. The love of turn-based strategy games associated with Strategic play is partly related to the capacity for these games to afford multiple optimal routes, and thus to allow for both min-maxing and choice.

A third talent associated with the Strategic play style is *problem solving*, and the related ability to think ahead. In many respects, this is simply an extension of tolerance for complexity, since every problem represents a situation of incomplete information (which represents a more convoluted arrangement than the equivalent situation where the solution is known, but must be implemented by skill). Given the relationship between science and the Rational temperament, the gift for problem solving associated with Strategic play is unsurprising, and the games that leverage this talent are often solved by what might be considered a scientific approach—hypothesizing possible solutions, exploring the outcome of those solutions, and using this data to produce new hypotheses until a solution has been found. All classic adventure games—text adventures, point-and-clicks, and modern descendents based on this form—find their most loyal fans among people whose play needs lean towards the Strategic.

The driving force behind Strategic play is the Rational temperament's desire for knowledge and mastery, and as a result Strategic play can seem more focused on *perfectionism* than "fun"—although it must be understood that by making perfection the goal, players expressing this play style achieve fiero and personal satisfaction by achieving mastery. The greater trials they endure en route to this goal, the more it enhances the ultimate reward in fiero.

When this theme is expressed purely in Strategic terms, the focus of the perfectionism will tend to be a desire for complete game knowledge. An examination of the FAQs available online for complex games, for example the *Pokémon* games (Game Freak/Creatures Inc., 1996 onwards), shows the output of this drive for complete understanding. When this theme is tempered by Logistical skills (which I will discuss shortly), the focus will tend more towards complete acquisition—a drive to collect everything that can be found in the game space. Finally, when this theme is tempered by

Tactical skills, the focus will tend more towards mastery of skills; the ability to finesse a situation, and not just to win.

Keirsey does not often mention play in his temperament description, so it is noteworthy that he includes the following comment in respect to Strategic skills:

> [People who are strong in Strategic skills] play not so much to have fun but to exercise their ingenuity in acquiring game skills. Fun for [them] means figuring out how to get better at some skill, not merely exercising the skills they already have, and so for [such people] the field of play is invariably a laboratory for increasing their proficiency... When [they] play sports, or even cards and board games, there must be continuous improvement, with no backsliding. [Kiersey78]

When playing with other people, those preferring the Strategic play style often seem to be highly competitive (which is mentioned in passing in Berens' account of the Rational temperament). But for those players expressing this style who are introverted by nature, this competitiveness is the product of their personal drive towards a high degree of proficiency. The other players are simply part of the complex system they are trying to master. Such players often prefer to play alone.

Friction

Players favoring specific play styles are also prone to different frustrations. Different elements of play cause varying degrees of friction for players, according to their preferred way to play.

The principle source of friction associated with Strategic play is *limitation*, specifically limitation of choice, and the consequent disempowerment this can lead to. The Rational temperament that drives this style of play is associated with a need for autonomy, and players who prefer the Strategic play style have a strong need to feel completely in control of their play—to have the freedom to make choices about how that play will proceed. When insufficient choices are provided, this creates a state of powerless limitation.

For example, a typical first person shooter game consists primarily of a linear sequence of fights. This structure is generally sufficient for players expressing other play needs, but for Strategic play it is unacceptably limited. The player faces no meaningful (Strategic) choices in this situation, and as such, this limitation becomes a source of frustration if the game does not engage the player by other means.

Deus Ex (Ion Storm, 2000) is a good example of a game that sets out to minimize this source of friction for players favoring Strategic play, by adding choice at every level of the design. The player is afforded virtually unlimited choices for proceeding through the game space. But in the process of providing these choices, the game develops such a degree of complexity that *only* players favoring Strategic play can manage to enjoy it. This is the likely reason for the eventual commercial failure of this franchise, as Strategic players have become a minority among videogame players.

This problem with *limitation* should not be confused with the Tactical play style's issue with *constraint*—constraint is intended to refer to immediate barriers to action or movement, whereas limitation is intended to reflect a lack of meaningful options for affecting the game situation. Players favoring Strategic play may tolerate being temporarily constrained provided they have a sufficient choice of actions with which to figure out a way to remove the constraint, whereas players favoring Tactical play will generally be frustrated by the constraint itself.

A Brief History of Strategic Play

Because the Rational temperament is associated with programmers and game designers, early videogames were extremely influenced by Strategic play. Consider, for instance, early mainframe games in the 1970s, such as *Star Trek* (Mike Mayfield, 1971), *Adventure/Colossal Cave* (Will Crowther, 1975), and *Dungeon* (Don Daglow, 1975) and its spiritual descendent *Rogue* (Toy, Wichman and Arnold, 1980). Many early games were influenced by the tabletop wargames (and role-playing games) of the 1970s, which were also great examples of Strategic play—providing complex play resulting from many different rules and options.

In the 1980s, new computers allowed Strategic play to flourish further. *Elite* (Braben and Bell, 1984) appealed to a number of different play styles, but the apparent lack of limitations (go anywhere, do anything) had particular Strategic appeal. But the real focus of Strategic play in videogames from the 1980s were adventure games, typified by *Zork* (Infocom, circa 1980) and its many sequels, and at the latter end of the decade, graphical adventures such as *The Pawn* (Magnetic Scrolls, 1986) and *Guild of Thieves* (Magnetic Scrolls, 1987). These games seemed to provide few limitations, since players could enter any command in plain-text, although in practice this was a somewhat illusory state of affairs. Near the end of the decade, simulations drawing from Strategic play, such as *SimCity* (Maxis, 1989) started to emerge.

In the 1990s, turn-based strategy games raised Strategic play to a new level with games such as *Civilization* (Microprose, 1991), *Master of Orion* (Simtex, 1993), and the *X-COM* series (Mythos Games et al, 1994 onwards). Additionally, strategic role-playing games such as the *Heroes of Might and Magic* series (New World Computing et al, 1990 onwards), and point-and-click adventures such as *The Secret of Monkey Island* (LucasArts,

1990) made this decade the golden age of Strategic play for many people preferring this play style.

Sadly for players preferring Strategic play, the arrival of the PlayStation in the mid-90s marked a change in the focus of the videogame market. Until this point, players favoring Strategic play were (arguably) in the majority, and the bulk of the games being made appealed to these players in some way. But a new era was arriving in which effortless 3D graphics opened the door to a wider market. The Strategic player was about to go from being the key audience for videogames, to being a strong but diminished niche market.

This change was to mark the end of the commercial importance of adventure games, and a gradual narrowing of the importance of turn-based strategy games that today support very few viable franchises, and *maximum* audiences of no more than 2 million units (whereas other types of games were able to pull in maximum audiences of 8 million units during this time). Today, Strategic play in isolation is a commercial backwater, although many successful games support Strategic play along with other play styles.

Summary of Strategic Play

Strategic play was the force behind adventure games, strategy games, and simulations, as well as an influencing factor in the development of computer RPGs. Once the most important play style in the videogames industry, it has since been eclipsed by the more popular Tactical and Logistical play styles, and now represents something of a niche market.

With talents for dealing with complexity and problem solving, and a partiality for min-maxing, the Strategic player is something of an expert in figuring out games. Strategic players avoid play that in their eyes is limited, and, armed with their strong drive for perfectionism, they generally master the games they adopt as their own. In many ways, they are the very model of the gamer hobbyist.

LOGISTICAL PLAY

Logistical play relates to following rules and pursuing acquisition, with a drive towards completing stated goals and hoarding. It may be the most basic, and hence most widely distributed, play style, and most games have some Logistical element in their structure. It underlies several of the most successful game structures, arguably provides the most addictive responses in the gaming audience, and its commercial importance may not yet have reached its peak.

The expression of the Guardian temperament is related to a need to belong to organizations, a desire for order, and a drive to be dutiful. Those who strongly express this pattern of emotional response make up roughly half of the populace and collectively provide the dependable backbone of our societies. It is arguably the driving pattern behind commerce, shop keeping, libraries, and museums, as well as law and law enforcement.

The Guardian temperament is defined as concrete affiliation with a focus on organization. It drives those affected by it to seek membership and responsibility, and to trust in the authority of those institutions they have allied themselves with. The logistical intellect associated with this pattern is capable of establishing and maintaining procedures, as well as supplying support and protection.

Stressed by feelings of exclusion, or by the insubordination of others, the Guardian temperament is associated with pessimism and when it is out of balance, depression. Caught between a genuine desire to do what is good, and a need to be a dutiful and responsible member of the institutions and cultures they belong to, there is a danger that people expressing Guardian will do what they are told without question. Nonetheless, the very fabric of society depends upon the assistance, protection, and support of those who express the Guardian pattern, without whom none of the daily comforts we take for granted would be possible.

Possible Neurological Basis

The psychological pattern associated with the Guardian temperament and Logistical skills seems to be intimately tied to that part of our neurology which concerns habit formation—namely the pleasure center (nucleus accumbens). Because one of the things associated with Logistical skills is the ability to form and maintain habits, this hypothesis does not seem farfetched. Additionally, there is likely to be some involvement of the association areas (regions surrounding the hippocampus) since a good memory is another trait linked to the Guardian temperament.

Talents

Goals are the primary focus of all Logistical play, and players preferring this play style are considerably more *goal-oriented* than those who do not. Play for the sake of play is all very well, but there must be a goal to focus upon. Rewards are valued, but to some extent the completion of the goal can be a prize in its own right—success is its own reward. There appears to be an accompanying assumption of "fairness"—which is to say, that the difficulty of a goal will be matched by the degree of reward to be gained. However, since players preferring this style of play are generally content with linear stories punctuated with goals that must be completed for the story to continue, the most basic game story structure (effectively an animated film interspersed with play that purports to relate to the next narrative step) is sufficient justification for play—provided the story itself is appealing.

Players who express this play style show great tolerance for repetition, and hence a natural talent for *persistence*. Such players will persevere with almost any game task provided both the goal and the rules governing play are clear. Their tenacious desire to avoid failure (that is, to complete any goal that has been set) creates an effective split depending upon the individual's attitude towards the emotion fiero. Those fiero-seekers who thrive on more challenging play will throw themselves repeatedly at difficult tasks, failing over and over again in some cases before eventually completing the task and therefore receiving the reward in fiero (the eventual reward heightened by the frustrations endured along the way). Players who are less fiero-motivated but still engaged by Logistical play instead seek game actions where gain can be acquired through repeating the same tasks without the need to fail to repeat the task—failure and the sense of re-doing a failed task are unpleasant for these players. Both tendencies are well served by the repetitive task structure of computer role-playing games, especially those built upon a linear structure such as the *Final Fantasy* series (Square, 1987 onwards).

A common recurring theme of Logistical play is the process of *acquisition*. Whether it is the simulation of an economic model and hence the acquisition of wealth, finding and collecting tokens in order to pursue goals—as in the classic 3D platform game structure, established by *Super Mario 64* (Nintendo, 1996)—or the scavenger hunt play of a "stamp collection," the theme of acquiring is as intimately associated with Logistical play as rules and goals.

The focus on acquiring can be seen clearly in almost all real-time strategy (RTS) games, such as *Command & Conquer* (Westwood, 1994), which center upon the Logistical play of developing a resource-producing infrastructure, and ironically support very little Strategic play.

Furthermore, the nature of most Logistical play tends to be both thorough and cautious. There is a tendency towards meticulousness— "collect everything, search everywhere" is a motto that many players favoring this approach dutifully execute. For this reason, it is possible to create additional opportunities for Logistical play quite easily in most games—stamp collections of all kinds can become motivating, as exemplified by the museum in *Animal Crossing* (Nintendo, 2001), where players are encouraged to collect all the insects, fish, and fossils in the game simply by virtue of the implicit goals of these collections. Even when this kind of play is not intended by the developer, some players who express Logistical play (often when expressed alongside a tendency for Strategic play) may pursue this implicit goal anyway, proceeding to collect all things of a kind in a game, and lists of collectibles from all manner of games can be found in great numbers on the Internet.

Friction

The principle source of friction associated with Logistical play is *bewilderment*, especially the perplexity of insufficient instructions. The goal-orientation associated with Logistical play thrives on clear instructions: goals should be spelled out, and completing one goal should lead to the next goal without any uncertainty as to what is expected. Imagine that the relationship between player and game is that of master and servant (or general and captain): players may be in charge of their avatars, but their assignments are being provided by the game. When these tasks are not specified, it is as if the player has been abandoned, and this causes the stress.

An ironic alternative cause of bewilderment is an overabundance of rules. When there are too many rules, the problem is simple confusion: "but what am I supposed to do?" the player in this predicament asks. Again, the game is expected to provide clear directions, and when the complexity of play is too great the player becomes lost. There is no clear goal, and in the absence of a goal, the player feels perplexed and abandoned.

With players who also favor Strategic play, both of these problems can be significantly mitigated, since players expressing both forms of play are usually willing to apply their problem solving skills to the issue of working out what is expected of them. However, when this additional skill is absent, players expressing Logistical play need to have their instructions clearly stated, and generally will not tolerate ambiguous or incomplete directions. Similarly, Strategic play offsets the problem of excessive rules, since a high tolerance for complexity is associated with Strategic play.

Another source of friction that must be considered in connection with Logistical play is fixation. The fiendishly addictive properties of certain games to certain players almost always relate to the goals of play (implicit or explicit), and when Logistical play is expressed, tasks can be pursued compulsively. Players involved in Logistical play may become obsessive about overcoming a specific challenge. Every failure increases the motivation to return and tackle the same problem again. The tolerance to repetition associated with Logistical play sustains this process—players will keep going until either they achieve victory (in which case the emotional reward of fiero usually drowns out the memories of frustration), or until they are so agitated they angrily stop playing—or, not uncommonly, throw the game controller across the room in frustration.

Another aspect of this fixation is a willingness to carry out repetitive tasks in order to drive forward a Logistical acquisition process. The clearest example of this kind of play is found in computer role-playing games, which provide players with rewards (in terms of improved avatar power or abilities) in return for overall progress through a repetitive progress structure. The exponential level structure typical to cRPGs provides a powerful motivating force for the acquisition of the central resource, namely experience points.

Here, frustration is not usually the issue—rather, players become so absorbed in the repetition of play, so fixated upon the improvements they are earning for their character, that stopping play is difficult, and even when players do break, they will likely return to play at the earliest available opportunity. Note that in this case, the fixation is only a source of friction if players find conflict between their desire to play the game, and the demands of their everyday lives (as is notorious in the play of MMORPG games).

It is this pattern of behavior, allegedly associated with Logistical play, which is probably the underlying reason that many people say (when interviewed) that they do not like videogames because they are "too addictive".

A Brief History of Logistical Play

In board games, Logistical play has always been a significant factor—one cannot help but notice that *Monopoly* (Parker Brothers, 1933) bears key marks of this flavor of play—specifically its repetitive goal-oriented structure, and the focus on acquisition. However, it did not take long for Logistical play to find its way into videogames.

As early as the 1970s, Logistical play makes an appearance in early computer role-playing games such as *Dungeon* (Don Daglow, 1975). The form did not achieve popularity however, until the 1980s with the hugely influential *Ultima* series (Origin Systems, 1980 onwards). Another side of Logistical play that emerges in the 1980s is the platform game (itself an advance of earlier collection games), as epitomized by the most successful game of all time, *Super Mario Bros.* (Nintendo, 1987), which sold a staggering 40 million units (albeit as a result of being bundled with the NES). However, it is worth remembering that platform games and cRPGs also meet the requirements of other play styles—without exception, successful games support the play needs of many different people.

In terms of sales, the cRPG finally reached the mass market with *Final Fantasy VII* (Square, 1997), which sold 8.6 million units. Undoubtedly, the popularity of the new PlayStation console, and the shortage of other interesting titles in 1997, contributed to the success of the game, but it also featured a design that favored Logistical play over Strategic play (which was present, but less significant), thus appealing to a wider audience. The same decade saw the arrival of the world's most popular cRPG franchise, *Pokémon* with *Pokémon Red, Blue,* and *Yellow* (Gamefreak/Creatures Inc, 1996), ultimately selling some 30 million units on the back of the same mix of primarily Logistical play supplemented with some Strategic play.

In the same decade, developers were experimenting with applying the usual cRPG structure (that is, progress by exponential acquisition) to other game genres. The most notable franchise is perhaps *Gran Turismo* (Polyphony Digital, 1997 onwards). These games meet many different play styles, but stand out from other car games by their underlying structure of acquisition: earn money to buy new cars in order to progress. The first game in the series sold some 10 million units, and although the largest part of its success was undoubtedly a result of its illusion of realism, its success may have been enhanced by building some Logistical play into the structure.

The '90s also advanced the platform game, with Nintendo once again leading the charge with its seminal *Super Mario 64* (Nintendo, 1996), which specified the form and structure of almost all commercially significant 3D platform games until their eventual near-demise in the 2000s. These games served a number of play needs as well as Logistical, but their overall structure of collection and acquisition was unmistakably in this style. The collapse of the commercial importance of this genre can perhaps be traced to the decision by key players Naughty Dog and Insomniac (who shared a common engine technology) to push away from the established 3D platform structure and towards run-and-gun games with *Ratchet and Clank* (Insomniac, 2002) and *Jak II* (Naughty Dog, 2003), thus leaving the genre subscribed to by no major players except Nintendo.

Another key development in the history of Logistical play was also focused in the '90s, namely the advent of the infrastructure-focused real-time strategy genre, which can be traced to *Dune II* (Westwood, 1992). This led directly to two significant franchises, *Warcraft* (Blizzard, 1994 onwards) and *Command & Conquer* (Westwood, 1995 onwards). Despite the name, these games have very little to do with Strategic play, and in fact are a model of acquisition-focused Logistical play. Success in almost all such games is about building an infrastructure that acquires available resources faster than the opposition, thus allowing a larger army to be built, which then overwhelms the enemy. It is the logistics of building and maintaining the player's economy that is the focus of play, and these games might better be termed real-time logistical games.

But arguably the most significant development in the history of Logistical play was the release of *The Sims* (Maxis, 2000), which went on to sell 16 million units of its basic game, and a staggering 54 million units across the franchise. For the first time, the Logistical cRPG structure was divorced from its traditional fantasy and science fiction context and instead attached to an apparently mundane domestic context. The result was a virtual dollhouse game whose play was expressly Logistical—much of the play is guiding the characters through repetitive tasks in order to earn rewards such as promotions—and which enjoyed unprecedented success with female players (between 60 and 70% of its audience). That the game was set in the familiar and ordinary world of people's homes only added to its appeal with a non-traditional game audience.

In the same decade, the success of the MMORPG at acquiring loyal players with its extremely well established Logistical structure (unmistakably the same as in most cRPGs) is also notable. This genre has hit its current peak with *World of Warcraft* (Blizzard, 2004), which enjoys some 8 million subscribers globally. Although this is considerably smaller than the maximum sales figures that can be achieved by single player games, the subscription model at its heart means that in commercial terms it is at least as significant as the most successful game sold through a traditional retail model, if not more so.

MMORPG games, including *World of Warcraft*, offer only one feature in addition to the traditional Logistical play of the cRPG: the capacity to play with other people. Since Logistical play is presumed to correlate with the Guardian temperament, and a core need of this pattern is membership, the ability to engage in Logistical play as part of a group (a guild, for instance, or a party on a smaller scale) provides an intoxicatingly powerful combination for players favoring this play style. Furthermore, because Guardian correlates with some 50% of the population as its primary temperament, it is perhaps to be expected that the commercial importance of this form of play will necessarily dominate the mass market.

Summary of Logistical Play

Logistical play is present to some degree in almost all games, but especially in those games with a focus on acquisition such as most platform games and almost all computer RPGs and RTS games. Indeed, the conventional cRPG structure (acquire some resource in exponential increments to progress) finds its way into many different genres, bringing with it elements of Logistical play. Although not proven, it may be that Logistical play is the most commercially important play style, since it correlates with the Guardian temperament, which is dominant in about 50% of people.

With a natural goal-orientation, talents for persistence and meticulousness, and a taste for unfettered acquisition, Logistical players will tackle their chosen challenges tenaciously, even to the point of becoming fixated upon victory. Such players generally desire clear instructions to avoid bewilderment, but provided they are given comprehensible goals and straightforward rules, they will patiently work their way along the spine of any game, collecting what they can, and generally enjoying what other players might dismiss as a grind.

TACTICAL PLAY

Tactical play relates to improvisation, and competence with all manner of tools. To other people, those preferring this style of play can appear to be both reckless and lucky. Second only to Logistical play in terms of its apparent distribution, it is a key commercial force in the modern games industry, and it may be an influencing factor in the success of the many games that focus their play upon the most popular tools in modern games—cars and guns.

The Artisan temperament is defined as concrete pragmatism with a focus on the immediate benefits that can be won. Driven by a desire to have impact through freedom of action, those affected by this temperament tend to be hedonistic free spirits who don't wish to become tied down. The Tactical intellect associated with this pattern is capable of tremendous spontaneous creativity—an enormous capacity to achieve immediate goals through inventive action. This intellect appears to be the force behind arts and crafts, as well as high-risk professions such as fire fighting, and challenging machine control professions such as piloting. Furthermore, most of the modern cultural heroes—singers, musicians, professional sports players, and actors—express the Artisan temperament to a tangible degree, making this perhaps the most celebrated temperament pattern.

Stressed by feelings of constraint, ineffectiveness, or the boredom that results from a lack of stimulation, the Artisan temperament is associated with recklessness and compulsive behavior when it is out of balance. Procrastination can be a problem for people expressing the Artisan pattern, as such people would rather be doing something exciting and stimulating than attending to the mundane. Always requiring their own freedom, and needing to have an impact on the people and world around them, the expression of the Artisan pattern can be filled with a joy of life, and a reckless abandonment that can be intoxicatingly rewarding for those who share in the life of everyday adventure and excitement that this pattern inspires.

Possible Neurological Basis

It is possible that the Artisan temperament and the associated Tactical skills may relate to the cerebellum, since this is associated with motor skills, and these are associated with this pattern. It is possible that the association areas are also involved, however.

Talents

Whereas Logistical play is focused on goals and Strategic play on systems, the focus of Tactical play is *improvisation*. Every game grants players a number of possible actions they can take, and players gifted in Tactical play will naturally conceive of immediate and effective ways of combining these actions to have an effect. For any situation, they will naturally have ideas as to what they can do, and proceed rapidly to trying these ideas out. Sometimes, they will even chance upon novel and unexpected solutions to problems, which can be a particular source of satisfaction for such a player.

The effect produced may advance the game by meeting a goal, but it is the capacity to have an impact that is important to players favoring Tactical play, not the goal itself. Indeed, such a player may have just as much fun making something happen that has nothing to do with advancing in the game—with a sufficiently interesting game world, such players can entertain themselves for some time just by exploring what they can make happen as a consequence of their own actions. (The playground worlds of the *GTA* games in particular lend themselves to this approach.)

Another key talent associated with Tactical play is a natural proficiency with *machines* and *tools*. Players who prefer Tactical play seem to possess an immediate degree of competence with any tool or vehicle the game provides them—provided they are in control of it. A device that does everything without player input is not an interesting source of Tactical play; a device that allows players to demonstrate their natural skills is what is desired. The most obvious example is with driving games of all kinds—these base their play around the player's capacity to control a vehicle, and generally have immediate appeal to players who enjoy this play style. (Note that players preferring Logistical play may also enjoy a driving game, but in such instances competence is learned through repetition, rather than being immediately present.)

What seems to be desired for Tactical play are tools (weapons, vehicles, and such) with a degree of analogue control, such as the analogue control of a car through both its steering and acceleration, or the analogue control of a gun through a free aiming mechanism. Given the games industry's obsession with the commercial appeal of guns and cars, these are by far the most common examples of analogue control found in modern videogames, although environmental negotiation abilities (jumping, climbing, and so forth) occasionally afford opportunities for Tactical play—especially with secondary jumping abilities, such as a double jump or gliding ability.

Other examples can also be found. When *The Legend of Zelda* franchise moved into a 3D world with *Ocarina of Time* (Nintendo, 1998), it centered its play on a diverse collection of tools, most of which are essentially analogue in nature. (The roots of the toolset lie in earlier 2D games in the franchise, but these earlier tools were not analogue in nature.) The sling-shot, boomerang, and bow are effectively variations on the gun theme but each still allows for skillful free aiming. The hookshot (a type of grapple) has more of the nature of an analogue tool, cuccos (chickens) can be used for gliding, bombs have a variety of uses, and the ocarina of the game's title provides all manner of additional abilities to its players. Although the *Zelda* games meet a variety of play needs, they are notable examples of the tool-focus associated with Tactical play.

Players who favor Tactical play sometimes seem to be naturally *lucky*. This is not to suggest any supernatural element, however—rather, this capacity for serendipity seems borne of simple psychological roots. Players who express this play style often show an exceptional tolerance for adapting to random variation—what might be considered compensating for noise (again, this may relate to a preference for analogue controls). Furthermore, Tactical play can be associated with openness to risk, sometimes expressed as impulsive recklessness. It is this combination of a willingness to take chances and capacity to adapt quickly and effectively to random events that creates the impression that players with strong Tactical skills are naturally lucky—the more chances one is willing to take, the more opportunities one has to fluke success. On analysis, then, this is simply a further expression of the spirit of improvisation that lies at the heart of Tactical play.

Friction

The chief source of friction associated with Tactical play is *constraint*. The player favoring this style seeks to improvise and overcome, and anything that gets in the way of this approach is an annoyance. Tactical play thrives on the freedom of the player to act, and to have an impact in the game world, and thus anything that constrains the player's freedom will frustrate a player preferring this play style. If a game prevents players from using one of their tools in an arbitrary manner, this is an unacceptable constraint—"why can't I use that here?" is the natural question. If Tactical players cannot act freely in a game, they would often prefer not to play at all—"I'm not putting up with that!" is the natural response to excessive constraint.

This should not be confused with the Strategic player's problem with limitation, which is concerned with insufficient choice of actions—the Tactical player is annoyed by *immediate* constraints to action, rather than too narrow a set of choices. For instance, in a typical FPS the player often only has the capacity to move, and a choice of weapons—limited from a Strategic perspective, but more than sufficient for Tactical play. Conversely, if a game's story imprisons the players and takes away their weapons and tools this can be an engaging puzzle from a Strategic perspective, but it is pure irritation for solely Tactical players.

Another source of friction associated with Tactical play is *boredom*. This may seem a strange suggestion—don't all players have a problem with boredom? But players favoring Logistical play have tremendous tolerance for repetition provided they are progressing towards a goal, and players favoring Strategic play can be willing to spend considerable time trying to solve a tough puzzle or beat a difficult foe. Neither situation will suit a player whose preferences lie firmly in Tactical play; such players will quickly lose interest if what they are doing becomes routine, or takes too long to achieve. The opportunity to have an impact must always be present, and when it is not, boredom is the natural result. Often it will cause such a player to give up entirely and play something else instead, and players favoring this play style start many more games than they ever finish.

A Brief History of Tactical Play

The early arcade games of the 1970s were too abstract to have wide appeal for players favoring Tactical play, although such players probably did enjoy early videogames such as *Space Invaders* (Taito/Bally Midway, 1978), *Pac-Man* (Namco/Midway, 1980), and so forth, for the novelty if for nothing else. The players who persisted at these games, however, were more likely to prefer Logistical play, as the capacity to have an impact was limited.

The 1980s moved arcade games into a more accessible place, and driving games such as *Out Run* (Sega, 1986) and *Hard Drivin'* (Atari, 1989) could be found alongside shooting games such as *Operation Wolf* (Taito, 1987), all of which provided opportunities for solid Tactical play. Additionally, it is likely that fighting games such as *Street Fighter* (Capcom, 1987) attracted Tactical players. On the home computers and consoles, the most Tactical games were probably the early platform games, such as *Manic Miner* (Mathew Smith, 1983) or *Super Mario Bros.* (Nintendo, 1985), although inevitably these also supported Logistical play through their structures.

The move to polygonal 3D in the 1990s was to see an explosion of interest in Tactical play. *Wolfenstein 3D* (id Software, 1992) and *Doom* (id Software, 1993) laid down the first person shooter (FPS) template, which has always been distinctly Tactical. Although the only tools provided are guns, the properties of the weapons are sufficiently different that Tactical play can emerge in the capacity to choose the right weapon for the right situation, as well as the spatial play elements key to FPS games, which also suit players favoring this play style.

The superior graphics of *Quake* (id Software, 1996) gave it notoriety in game fandom, but the title sold only a few million copies (*Doom* is estimated to have sold 4 million copies, and to have been downloaded and played by some 10 million players). The most commercially successful FPS games of this decade were *GoldenEye 007* (Rare, 1997), which combined solid game design with a hugely popular license, and *Half-Life* (Valve, 1998), which combined the technology of *Quake* with an inventive story implementation. Both sold 8 million units, the highest sales figures achieved by FPS games to date.

Driving games were similarly invigorated by the move to 3D, with games such as *Virtua Racing* (Sega, 1992), *Ridge Racer* (Namco, 1993), and the seminal kart racer, *Mario Kart* (Nintendo, 1992). All of these games afforded the Tactical play of driving (although most driving games also supported Logistical play, in that courses could be learned by repetition). Other racing games to provide opportunities for Tactical play included skiing games such as *Alpine Racer* (Namco, 1995) and the more successful genre of snowboarding games such as *1080* (Nintendo, 1998). However, cars remained the commercial center of racing games, and *Gran Turismo* (Polyphony Digital, 1997) sold 10.5 million units on the PlayStation, with each of its sequels selling roughly the same numbers, to total 44 million units across the franchise.

The next decade was to see cars and guns combined in the same titles, thus concentrating the Tactical focus of certain games. A notable title is *Halo: Combat Evolved* (Bungie, 2001), which featured a greater focus on the shooting element than the vehicular element, and which provided excellent opportunities for Tactical play—players enjoyed being able to make an impact with weaponry, explosives, and vehicles. Commercially, the game enjoyed reasonable success, selling some 5 million units; sufficient to mark it as a hit, and certainly nothing else on the Microsoft Xbox console enjoyed greater commercial success.

But it was the advent of the playground world structure in games such as *Grand Theft Auto III* (DMA Design, 2001) and its sequels that served to take Tactical play further. For a start, these games combined both driving and shooting elements (thus combining the most popular sources of Tactical play into one game), but additionally the capacity to wreak free-roaming mischief allowed players the opportunity to have an impact in a more direct way than ever before. (Although the playground world structure has earlier roots, it was only when it was used in 3D and in the context of cars and guns that it achieved the full measure of its success.) Such games also included an effectively linear sequence of missions, and thus supported Logistical play as well; by strongly appealing to the two most significant play styles—and doing so with the added appeal of cars and guns—commercial success was all but guaranteed, and the games have sold up to 14 million units in their recent iterations.

Note: The use of the term "Tactical" may cause some confusion as to why games that are characterized as being "tactics" games are not mentioned. Although some real-time tactical games do indeed correlate with what is being discussed here as the Tactical play style, most tactics games—such as Final Fantasy Tactics (Square, 1997)—are turn-based and thus represent a form of Strategic play in the terms discussed here.

Assuming the distributions of players preferring the Tactical play style correlate with the Artisan temperament, I would expect some 25% of the population to greatly enjoy this style of play—second only to the Logistical play style in hypothetical popularity (50% of the population, if it correlates directly with the Guardian temperament). As a result, games that meet the needs of both Logistical and Tactical play could appeal to as much as 75% of the population, and thus supporting both play styles is increasingly essential to mass market success.

Summary of Tactical Play

Tactical play is a key factor behind the success of driving games and shooting games—especially the ever-popular first person shooter—although it can be found to some degree in a wide variety of different game genres that focus on a single avatar, and provide the capacity to have an impact. Although not proven, it is hypothetically the case that Tactical play is second in commercial importance only to Logistical play, and comparisons of sales figures for the most popular games support this claim.

With an irrepressible capacity for improvisation, and a reckless experimentation that can result in them seeming to be naturally lucky, players favoring Tactical play seek immediate freedom in their game worlds. Constraints are a particular annoyance, and such players can become bored easily when they lose the ability to have an impact. Naturally proficient with machines and tools with analogue controls, Tactical players seem to have an immediate competence with almost any game that attracts their interest.

OTHER PLAY STYLES

You have already seen how applying Temperament Theory to the field of play reveals three distinct play styles—Strategic play, Logistical play, and Tactical play. In this section, I will look at the fourth hypothetical play style relating to this theory, and also other kinds of play style, such as those that relate to specific emotions.

Diplomatic Play

The expression of the Idealist temperament is related to a need for meaning and significance, a desire for authenticity, and a drive to seek the unique identity of all things. Those who strongly express this pattern of emotional response are empathic, cooperative, and altruistic, and it is arguably the driving pattern behind the humanities—especially literature, poetry, and fine art—counseling, journalism, mysticism, and humanitarianism.

The Idealist temperament is defined as abstract affiliation with a focus on the motivations that allow people to be themselves. Those affected by it seek meaning and significance in all aspects of their lives, and strive for authenticity. The Diplomatic intellect associated with this pattern unifies through abstraction, and can use this to see how different perspectives are similar, as well as expressing this similarity in symbolic terms, such as metaphors. Empathy and cooperation are recurring themes.

Stressed by conflict, insincerity, and all things impersonal, people expressing the Idealist temperament often find themselves in extremely conflicted states as they try to balance their need for authenticity with their desire to be benevolent, or at least positive. Trapped between the demands of society and their own need for unique identity, those who express Idealist can ensnare themselves in a terrible emotional oubliette. Yet the Idealist temperament seems to express all that is good and valuable about humanity—fine art, poetry, literature, altruism, and spirituality all seem to spring from this pattern of emotional response, which enriches both our lives and our cultures.

Given the link to empathy, it is possible that mirror neurons are involved in the underlying neurology associated with this pattern, but since research on these is still in its infancy, it would be premature to draw a conclusion.

Although a discernible Diplomatic play style might be expected, the research is currently not sufficiently developed for anyone to have much confidence as to what constitutes this play style. It may be that Diplomatic play can be identified, but that it does not relate well to videogames, or it may be that there is no form of play that relates to the Diplomatic skill set (although this seems highly unlikely).

I will hypothesize as to what Diplomatic play might involve by looking at the skills that have been related to the Idealist temperament. Thus, I expect Diplomatic play to be involved in a process of unifying or *harmonizing* through an abstractive process, and also to be rooted in *communication* and *empathy*. This relationship with communication (either the private communication of writing and art, or the public communication that takes place directly between people) suggests that Diplomatic play might be found more easily by examining multiplayer games, but it may also be difficult to separate from *extroverted play* (see the next section).

It is also possible, given the Idealist temperament's relationship to narrative and metaphor, that certain forms of story play might be opportunities for Diplomatic play to be expressed. But since our current videogames are not especially good at supporting story play, this may be difficult to ascertain. An examination of tabletop roleplay might be the best place to search for such a play style. I would expect a player expressing this play style in such a game to be enjoying resolving disputes and conflicts; given the general bias in most tabletop RPG play towards combat, an empirical study should easily show if there was a contrary form of play taking place in such games.

Extroverted Play

I mentioned earlier that Temperament Theory was related to Myers-Briggs typology. One aspect of the latter which is not expressed in the former is the notion of introversion and extraversion. When this is taken into account, there is another side to play to be considered: extroverted play. This relates to the People Fun discussed in Step 1, and the social play discussed in Step 2.

According to Linda Berens' extension to Temperament Theory, there are four distinct Interaction Styles that, when combined with the four temperaments, yield the same inventory of 16 general "types" as the Myers-Briggs typological system (although since individuals express many different "types," it is perhaps better to think of these as roles they are capable of adopting). Two of these Interaction Styles, which Berens calls *Get Things Going* and *In Charge*, relate to extroversion (the remaining two—*Chart the Course* and *Behind the Scenes*—relate to introversion) [Berens01].

There are, therefore, two hypothetical extroverted play styles that accompany the four temperament-derived play styles you have already learned about:

- **Participant play** (which I have named after one of four player types named in the DGD1 model [Bateman05]) relates to Berens' *Get Things Going* Interaction Style. Its concern is *involvement*—making something happen or keeping things moving. To some extent, when this kind of play is in effect, it doesn't matter what is happening as long as *something* is happening. It is much easier for this side of play to express itself in a group playing in the same room (where emotional contagion can take effect) than online, although it is all but certain that this style of play can be found in either situation.
- **Leadership play** relates to Berens' *In Charge* Interaction Style. Its concern is, unsurprisingly, executing the role of a leader—that is, *directing* a group of players. The satisfaction relating to this play is in having a group execute skillfully under the leader-player's command

(which may be equally satisfying to the rest of the group—especially if they strongly express Logistical or Participant play). It probably does not greatly relate to team-oriented single player games (which tend towards Strategic play) so much as it does to the multiplayer space, and I would anticipate online games with voice communication to attract players who enjoy this kind of play. Nick Yee's research shows that Leadership is indeed one of five key motivating factors for players to join virtual worlds [Yee02].

It is possible that the two introverted Interaction Styles also have a corresponding play style. More research is needed to investigate this.

Emotional Play Styles

Finally, I want to suggest some play styles relate to the key emotions of play, as exemplified by the Four Fun Keys model you learned about in the first step. It is possible that the play styles already identified have specific relationships to the key emotions of play—for instance, the DGD1 model that I developed with Richard Boon [Bateman04][Bateman05] suggests that the emotion *fiero* is more intimately connected to Strategic and Logistical play than to other forms, and that the emotion of curiosity might be more intimately connected to Diplomatic or Tactical play. However, the DGD1 research is by no means robust enough to postulate anything more than hypothetical connections. As ever, further research is required.

One of the Four Fun Keys—People Fun—relates to extroverted play, described previously. The emotions associated with this key, namely amusement, *schadenfreude* (delight in other's misfortune) and *naches* (the mentor's delight in her student's successes) should all be considered to contribute to extroverted play in general. You will see now how the other emotions of play can be considered possible play styles in their own right:

- **Conqueror play** (which I have named after another of the player types from DGD1) relates to Lazzaro's Hard Fun, that is, to the emotion of *fiero*—triumph over adversity. I have related this feeling specifically to Caillois' pattern of agon (which I talked about in Step 3), that is, to games of competition. Conqueror play values fiero above all else, and is almost inevitably angry (one could justifiably call it *angry play*). The games that provide the greatest payoffs in fiero (including most first person shooters) almost invariably frustrate players (anger them), thus pushing a Conqueror's buttons and making them play on until they can achieve victory, and hence the eventual payoff in fiero, which is heightened by prior hardships.

- **Wanderer play** (which once again I have named after another DGD1 player type) relates to Lazzaro's Easy Fun, that is, to the emotions of *curiosity* and *wonder*. The experience of players preferring this approach to play is one of exploration, although not necessarily spatial exploration (the Wanderer play style does not appear to correlate with navigation skills!). Enjoyment is gained from purely experiential elements, and therefore this play style appears to relate to Caillois' pattern of mimicry (which I talked about in Step 3). Game worlds must contain rich detail or strange oddities to excite the interest of players favoring this play style.

- **Serious play** is the last of Lazzaro's Four Fun Keys—Serious Fun—and relates to the emotions of *excitement* and *relief*. It may be that there is another play style focused upon these emotions, and hence I include it here. However, I suspect that while these feelings contribute to the enjoyment of many different players, they do not represent an identifiable play style in and of themselves. For instance, Conqueror play almost always features elements of excitement and relief, but is notably focused on the fiero. These emotions do relate noticeably to Caillois' alea and ilinx patterns (as I talked about in Step 3). The unanswered question is whether there are players who seek out games that focus on these emotions, in the same way that players preferring other play styles seek out games that will fulfill their play needs. And as ever, further research is needed to resolve this question.

Future Research

The nine play styles you have been introduced to here represent an early attempt at an inventory of the different ways people approach the play of games, with a particular focus on videogames. There are many unanswered questions at this point, and of particular interest is whether or not the emotional play styles correlate in any measurable way with the temperament-based play styles—and indeed, whether the combination of factors associated with the temperament-based styles really constitute measurable patterns. In order to investigate this question, it would be necessary to devise instrumentation that could identify elements of the play style definitions without building the assumptions of the underlying model into this instrument.

There can be little doubt, however, that the play of games is a diverse activity, and that attempts to understand it in terms of a sole underlying factor (a purely reductionist approach) will deliver an incomplete picture. Different people approach play with radically different play needs, and the way they meet those needs can be highly varied, but beyond this it is hard to reach any firm conclusions. More research is needed on player skills. In the meantime, the models we have give us an incomplete but intriguing picture of the diverse ways people play games.

INCLUDE STRUCTURES THAT ADAPT TO PLAYER NEEDS

by Noah Falstein

In this final step, you will learn to bring together all the techniques and approaches studied in the previous steps. The essential question to be answered is: Knowing the diversity of players who may be coming to any given videogame, how do you structure the game to allow players to get what they want from the play?

INTRODUCTION

Men and women, from different races and cultures, with different skills, abilities, or physical and mental challenges... how do you choose the structure and content to satisfy such diversity? With interactivity, you can eat your cake and have it too[1].

The previous steps have provided a variety of views on game design. Some are clearly compatible with each other; some have elements that may seem contradictory, as befits the still-coalescing art form that is game design. Of course there is no edict that a single game must reflect all the points of view expressed in this book, and indeed game design is like any other creative endeavor, with room for many different approaches. But all games do have a key component that makes it possible (at least in theory) for them to include a wider range of integral elements than their linear counterparts like novels, film, or paintings. Games are interactive.

Interactivity itself is a very important quality, perhaps the defining quality of a game. By their very nature, games adapt to the individuals—or groups—who play them. Even going back to some of the simplest origins of videogames this has been true. *Pong*, arguably the first videogame successful as mass entertainment and certainly one of the simplest, was different every time it was played, and responded fundamentally and constantly to the input of its players. In this, videogames are not distinct from their non-electronic game counterparts, but having a computer at the heart of a game adds another strong element of adaptability. Interactivity is key, and in particular the ability for a game to adapt and change in response to choices of individual players provides a tool for us to integrate and reconcile the diverse design approaches described in this book and elsewhere.

It is this technique of adaptive game design that is the core topic of this final chapter, a technique that has great power and potential for its own merits, distinct from the others covered in this book. I will delve into some of the methods game designers have learned to infuse games with adaptive qualities, placing greater control of the play experience into the hands of the players. I have been a professional game designer since 1980 and have often incorporated these adaptive techniques in my work. I'll draw on my own anecdotal experience of games I've worked on myself, as well as other notable examples from the early days of videogames to the present.

---

[1] I am indebted to Patricia Pizer who enlightened me (in true game designer fashion) of how this phrase was corrupted into "have your cake and eat it too" which of course is not extraordinary at all!

Money Matters

Game design is all about tradeoffs. Arguably the most important factor is cost. Often a decision to include or exclude a feature is made on a basis of whether it will result in increased popularity and hence sales. Of course, there are myriad other factors in play, but even a designer who aspires to create a game as a work of art with no commercial aspirations has limited resources in which to do so, and so he must pay attention to relative costs, and certainly most of the games referenced in this book were created with the hopes of financial success as a major consideration, at the very least in the minds of the people who funded them.

Consequently, game designers have learned to be extremely careful about adding a feature meant to attract one player that may repel another. Many of the adaptive design techniques I will describe were conceived of in order to make the games reach the widest audience at the lowest cost possible. In fact this desire to be as economical as possible is at the heart of at least some of the non-inclusive nature of videogames to date. It can be difficult and expensive to break out of a rut and create a game that will reach a wider audience, and easy to keep going after the same proven one. I believe that much of the lack of games' focus on women, on non-white characters, and on people with disabilities can be attributed to mere greed or simple lack of imagination, and not a will to exclude others.

Game developers learn early on that they must "put the money on the screen," not spend valuable resources creating game elements that will only be viewed by a subset of the players, or will appeal specifically to a demographic not known for buying games. That is happily changing as the games industry matures. Now that games have become such a universal form of mass market entertainment, it is no longer a matter of reaching people who don't play games, but rather reaching *more* of the diverse types of people who do.

Coin-Op and Early Adaptive Design

Over the years, designers have sought and discovered countless ways to adapt the game to fit its players. One of the first hurdles was adapting difficulty levels of games to fit different player skills. Current designers have access to the kind of sophisticated psychological analysis you saw in Steps 1 through 4 to help them craft games to fit specific player needs, but in the late '70s and early '80s, there was little focus on subtleties. The most popular games were coin-operated arcade games (called coin-op in the business) and since they were physically accessible to anyone who frequented the arcades, bars, and convenience stores in which they were placed, they needed to appeal to the widest possible audience to be profitable.

Because it was all about profit—specifically, "coin drop," new arcade machines were coming out all the time, and new models frequently replaced low-earning ones. If a specific machine was a consistently low earner, it was sold off. Profit was based on three factors: people had to be attracted to the game in the first place, they had to be motivated to keep paying as frequently as possible, and they had to keep coming back to the game over and over. Elaine Ditton of Incredible Technologies has summed up these three key points as "the 1st quarter, the 2nd quarter, and the 1000th quarter" [Ditton95].

This meant that there were multiple ways to fail and make an unprofitable game. The worst thing was to simply have a theme or initial impression that held so little appeal that few people even tried the game—that was the challenge of the first quarter. Then the players had to have a good enough experience that first time—exciting and fun, not too difficult, satisfying—to reach into their pocket and put in another quarter to keep going. That was the second quarter hurdle, to tap into a source of fun (often the Hard Fun of fiero and challenge that Nicole introduced in Step 1) and keep players interested. Finally, although as with all other entertainment the popularity would drop off over time, if a game had "legs" and brought in decent coin-drop over the course of a month or two, it could be quite profitable. Some games from nearly 30 years ago, like *Ms. Pac-Man* (Namco/Midway, 1981) or *Galaga* (Namco, 1981), are still managing to bring in respectable earnings as the children or grandchildren of the original players enjoy them—the 1000th quarter and beyond.

But having a popular game was no guarantee of profitability. If someone put in a single quarter (the standard cost of a single play in the US during that early time) and was able to play for 20 minutes, it wouldn't much matter if there was a long line of people waiting to play, at best it would bring in 75 cents an hour, and as the games cost the arcade owners as much as a few thousand dollars at the time, that was insufficient. There had to be ways to get players off the machines quickly, so they could pay another quarter for their next try (or let someone else step up to do that). Of course, if players finished *too* quickly, for example playing for only 30 seconds before losing their last life, they would quit in frustration and not put in another quarter. The optimum time settled in fairly quickly at an average of about 2 1/2 minutes. A popular game that had a constant flow of customers with that average time (and presuming a short break between them) could bring in about five dollars an hour, and could earn back the money it cost to buy the machine in as little as a few months at a busy site.

So what does this have to do with adaptive game structures? Early coin-op game makers had a tough paradox. In order to get that second quarter, the game had to be perceived as fairly easy, at least easy enough that it could be mastered over time. But if it was too easy, it would quickly be perceived as boring, or (just as bad from a financial standpoint) be played for many minutes, even hours, on a single quarter. The simplest answer was to ramp up the difficulty of the game over time, a game design rule so old and ingrained as to be second nature to designers. In Step 1, Nicole talks about the Flow Channel—even before videogames, Mihály Csíkszentmihályi was aware of the necessity of increasing challenge over time. His first mention of the Flow Channel in his 1975 work "Beyond Boredom and Anxiety" used the example of tennis games, neatly foreshadowing *Pong* (Atari, 1972) and the rise of videogames [Csíkszentmihályi75].

And yet simply increasing difficulty over time has its own limitations. If a coin-op game begins at an easy difficulty and gradually increases in difficulty over time, it will work well for someone new to the game. But someone coming back to an arcade after having played enough to gain a good level of mastery will still have to go through those early levels. This has a double penalty—the Flow theory shows us that these players are going to find those easy levels boring and "just something to get through" before the challenge of the higher levels, and may stop coming to play the game over time because of the burden of having to spend long minutes getting up to the point at which they are challenged. It is as if you had a long book to read over multiple sittings, but had to re-read it from the beginning each time. And of course those "long minutes" cut into the profitability of the game. Something had to be done.

One of the first adaptations was to allow players to continue play at the point where they left off. They would typically have a number of "lives" for each quarter, and when they lost their last life and were at an advanced, challenging level of the game, they could insert another quarter and continue from that point. This was a decent partial solution, because it kept players from having to always start over at the beginning, but only when they chose to continue immediately after losing a game. *Atari Football* (Atari, 1979) was likely the first game to use this sort of continue function.

Another early solution was adopted by my old employer, Williams Electronics, famed for games like *Defender* (1980), *Stargate* (1981), and *Robotron: 2084* (1982). They incorporated special operator settings in the games so that the difficulty of the games could be adjusted by the people who owned and ran the machines. This meant that over time as a game was out in the arcade it could be gradually tweaked to be more difficult and the gradual increase in average play time as players gained skill could be counterbalanced.

But of course this only really worked in places where a consistent group of players came regularly. If an operator had increased the difficulty of a game and a novice player approached it, this new player would likely experience the "dead in 30 seconds" syndrome and not put in that second quarter. Something needed to be done to let players have greater control.

Millipede (Atari, 1982), a sequel to *Centipede* (Atari, 1980), was one of the first games to employ an elegant solution of adaptive design that other companies quickly followed. The game allowed the players to choose their initial difficulty from a set of several levels with an initial point total commensurate with the level chosen, and also kept the innovation of letting players continue from their last level achieved when they finally lost their last life. This was an eminently practical and clever solution for several reasons. It addressed the issue of variable player skill level directly, so that experienced players could walk up to the game and dive into the play at a higher difficulty level, avoiding the boring process of starting from scratch, but still feel that they were getting the points due them. And of course these players were now playing against faster and tougher computer-controlled enemies, which meant their games lasted for less time for each quarter, which pleased the operator.

Paradoxically, because of the intensity of emotion and excitement at the higher levels of the game, subjectively players experienced a more exhilarating and satisfying experience by starting at a higher level, even though their actual time playing the game was shorter than if they started from the first level. There was also a bravado trap involved. Because playing arcade games tended to be a social activity, and was often limited to young males, there was a testosterone-fueled competition involved and players who did not skip the easier levels were sometimes heckled by their friends.

It is also important to note that the innovation of allowing players to start the game at a higher difficulty level and awarding them corresponding points was an extremely cheap and easy innovation. Because it was already standard to allow players to continue games where they left off by inserting another coin, the internal structure and coding to support an advanced start was already part of the design, and adding a handful of preset starting points was quite easy and cheap to do. Not all adaptive design techniques are this cost-effective, as I will cover later, and the leverage gained from such a simple change is part of why *Millipede's* solution was so elegant.

Millipede was also intriguing in that, as a high-action game of the sort Chris refers to in Step 3 as rushgames, it was very popular with young males. As such, it was an early success in reaching a large audience in part by employing a variety of adaptive design techniques at quite low cost. It is also intriguing that it was partially developed by Dona Bailey, the sole female engineer at Atari at the time, and her choice of color palette is among the features rumored to have made it more popular to women than most of the contemporary arcade games.

MEN, WOMEN, AND THE TOOL ROOM

In Step 5, Sheri talks about including both genders in game design. It is certainly true that even now, the vast majority of game designers are male, topping 90% by the latest *Game Developer* survey, and undoubtedly higher in the early days of the industry [GameDeveloper08]. So it is not surprising that many male play patterns have crept into the lexicon of designers' favorite techniques. I have to admit to perpetuating a few myself.

In 2003, I heard Sheri lecture on gender differences. One of the things that quite surprised me was when she identified a particular design pattern as catering strongly to males. This particular pattern was to include, early in a game, an opportunity to try many of the basic elements of the game interface in a sort of open playground. In an action game this might be done by providing a small, safe area that is designated as a training area—if it is a fighting game, perhaps players are shown a rack of weapons and has several "practice dummies" to attack, or if it is a strategy game players can be given several different military units to use to capture a "simulated" enemy base, where the enemies don't shoot back. I recognized this as a classic pattern that we had incorporated consciously into many of our early adventure games at LucasArts.

LucasArts in the late '80s was a very collaborative studio, with only a few dozen employees in one building, with lots of opportunities for informal discussions. We talked it over and agreed that it was best to start by giving the players some simple tasks to perform in one small geographic area—a "room" in the parlance of our game engine, although it could in fact be an outdoor setting, and sometimes two or three connected ones were used. In this area were at least one of each basic type of puzzle and the items and characters necessary to solve them.

We thought of this as similar to having a tool room with boxes of tools open and mechanisms to fix in varying states of disrepair, although that was more of a metaphor than reality. Then the players would be able to experiment, tinker, and explore on their own, at their own pace. I rankled when Sheri described this as "typically male" explorative learning behavior. Surely a desire to explore and try things out was just human, not male! And then I thought about the group at LucasArts avidly debating game design and how to structure our games. We were all men. It wasn't until years later that we had female designers.

But I still felt that Sheri must be overlooking something, so I approached her after the talk and asked her what an equivalent pattern would be for women, to encourage them to learn to use an interface. She described to me how males like to explore on their own and not have others around to see them mastering unfamiliar situations. Females, on the other hand, in general would prefer having an imitative approach, with someone showing them how to use the interface rather than being left to figure it out on their own. This means that for typical women it would be preferable to design a game where there was a guided introduction, with a character or narrator or other mechanism to take you through the process step by step.

As soon as she said this, I thought of my own daughter, who was about 13 at the time. There had been many instances where I had started her on a new game, often one that had a tool room or equivalent, and told her to give it a try. "No Daddy, you show me," she usually protested. I would sometimes persist, expecting it would be more fun for her to discover it on her own, but usually when I gave in and showed her how to get started, she really appreciated it. Later she would play with her female friends, and they would always play in a group, with an experienced person controlling the mouse at first, and later the newcomers gradually taking over when they felt they understood how to do it, precisely the imitative behavior Sheri cited. I remember staring at Sheri dumbfounded, realizing that the truth of her premise had been staring me in the face for years, and yet I just hadn't seen it.

Since then, I've tried to compensate for that difference in typical male and female play styles, and have also paid attention to how other games do it. There is value in both explorative and imitative methods. As I suggested in my description of adaptive design, there is no need to pick one or the other—you can do both, and with a bit more effort (and sometimes expense) you can do them seamlessly. Imagine a situation where a guide or mentor character brings the players into a tool room or equivalent, and asks the players if they'd like to be shown how to begin. If the player says yes, the guide demonstrates the necessary actions (perhaps even breaking the fourth wall and telling the players, not the character or avatar, what to do; for example, "use the mouse to point the cursor at the trampoline and click twice to perform a double-high jump"). If the player says no, the guide can go into an adjoining room and close the door, which has a prominent "knock for assistance" sign on it. Then the players have the benefit of either method, or of a blend of the two. This also can be a good mechanism to compensate for players of different ages or skill levels who may be sharing the same game, or even the same character in a game. Players with less experience can call on help as necessary, but more confident or self-motivated players can explore on their own.

Lara Croft's Bum

There is one relatively basic design option intended to make games appeal more to women that has recurred frequently throughout my career, going back to some of the earliest games that depicted a human character as the player's avatar[2]. This is simply to allow the player to choose a male or female avatar to represent them throughout the game. The popularity of customizing one's avatar in current MMORPGs like *World of Warcraft* (Blizzard, 2004), or in sports games like those employing Electronic Arts' "Gameface" technology makes it seem like an obvious option, but in fact being able to choose the gender of your avatar is still a relatively rare option in games now as then, for one basic reason—it is difficult to justify on the basis of cost.

At first glance, allowing players to choose whether they will control a male or female character seems like an obvious way to widen a game's appeal to both genders. Even early titles like the text adventure *Leather Goddesses of Phobos* (Steve Meretzky, 1986) or the ZX Spectrum game *3D Ant Attack* (Sandy White, 1983) provided a gender choice, and the latter may have been the first to offer this. But as realistic graphics became increasingly important at the end of the 1980s, a financial barrier to gender choice emerged. Often the main character in a game is shown with the widest range of animations and in more detail than any other character. Creating a second version of that character so players can choose the gender of their avatars can be quite costly, adding as much as 20% to the cost of a game, primarily adding to artwork but also to voiceover, coding, and testing costs.

This always brings up the question of whether having that choice will actually increase sales by more than that amount. For many years, conventional wisdom said no. Games were played mostly by males, and "everyone knew" a boy wouldn't play the part of a girl in a game. Conversely, the females playing games were by definition used to controlling male avatars, and it was expected that even if they appreciated the choice of a female avatar, it would not be enough of a boon to attract many women who were not already gamers. Another argument I heard several times was that if we were going to add 10 to 20% to the cost of a game, wasn't it better spent on features that both sexes would enjoy and see, instead of setting up a choice at the beginning that would effectively toss away all the extra work done for the avatar the player did not choose. This emphasis on putting the money "on the screen" is a common concern in

---

[2]   Although now common as a term for an animated character in a game controlled by a player and serving as their agent in the game, this term was to my knowledge first used in this sense by Chip Morningstar in working on *Habitat* (Lucasfilm Games, 1986). Chip and I shared an office at the time.

game development and recurs in the following section regarding multiple-path games like *Indiana Jones and the Fate of Atlantis* (LucasArts, 1992) and *Blade Runner* (Westwood Studios, 1997).

The situation is even more complicated than that, for the argument that the game will broaden its appeal by allowing a choice of the avatar's gender may be superficial if the only difference between playing a male character and a female one is the character's appearance. In real life, people rarely respond to men and women—or boys and girls—identically. Games, being primarily about interaction, must focus on the character's choices, abilities, and interactions in the game world—a merely visual difference in avatars, although potentially costly in itself, will not go far to satisfy a player's desire for a true choice between avatars. And if one has to change not only the depiction of the character but that character's interactions with the environment and with other characters, the cost objection becomes even stronger.

But then the original *Tomb Raider* (Core Design, 1996) took a bold step in breaking gender barriers. With its iconic creation of Lara Croft as the main character, it was far from the first game to offer a female protagonist, as there were female characters in ensemble cast games like *Street Fighter 2* (Capcom, 1991), and the adventure game *King's Quest IV: The Perils of Rosella* (Sierra, 1988) featured a Disneyesque Princess as the main character. But *Tomb Raider* was daring in that it cast its female protagonist as a gun-toting athletic explorer, often described by reviewers as a "female Indiana Jones". *Tomb Raider's* success showed that the gaming world was ready for a female action hero in their games, even if it was the only choice available to the player—just as Angelina Jolie's success in the movie version of the game showed that this readiness applied to films as well.

In many ways *Tomb Raider* was a validation of the principle of just creating one character but doing it with grand style and high quality, instead of trying to please everyone with a choice of male or female protagonists. Intriguingly, I believe that also opened the door to other non-traditional choices of game protagonist, as in *Grand Theft Auto: San Andreas* (Rockstar North, 2004), as mentioned by Joe in Step 6, and discussed later in this step.

But it raises a fascinating question—what prompted the people at Core Design to take this step? I had the chance some years ago to ask Toby Gard, the creator of the character Lara Croft. As I had worked on several *Indiana Jones* games in my tenure at LucasArts, one of my favorite pet theories was that a male character in that game would come too close to Indiana Jones himself, and the choice of a female character was influenced by a desire to protect against Lucasfilm's dreaded legal team. But I was also curious about the possible feminist angle, wondering if it had been an idealistic attempt to reach a larger female audience, despite the hypersexualized nature of Lara's physique. Toby told me that in fact the decision had been much more pragmatic and not a legal concern or feminist statement at all (which explains Lara's improbable measurements), inspired by fighting games like *Street Fighter 2* and *Virtua Fighter* (SEGA-AM2, 1993). He'd noticed that the male players of the game enjoyed the sexy female characters. Because the particular third-person 3D view of *Tomb Raider* meant the player's view of the action was typically behind the main player, Toby said he'd concluded that male players at least would rather "watch her bum than some bloke's bum". From such humble beginnings are great social strides made!

DIVERSITY ISSUES AND INSULTS, REAL AND PERCEIVED

The Lara Croft story illustrates an aspect of the games industry (and entertainment in general) that deserves some scrutiny. In the course of my career there have been many times where I've been introduced as a game designer to people whose only experience with games is through their children's passion for them, and often I am asked to explain—or even fix—the parent's perceived problems with the games in particular and the industry in general. Perhaps the most common question is, "Why are so many games so violent?" Occasionally there is an implied accusation that it is the game industry that is the cause of all problems among kids today. I usually answer the latter implication with a reminder that before videogames the culprit blamed for misleading youth was comic books, or rock music, or heavy metal, or depending how far back you go, actors like James Dean in *Rebel Without a Cause* and Marlon Brando in *The Wild Ones*.

The question of the role of violence in games is a serious one. The reality is that some games that feature realistic violent acts are popular, and the controversial ones like the *Grand Theft Auto* series (DMA Design et al, 1997 onwards) get a lot of media attention. But they still are outnumbered and outplayed by non-violent casual titles, sports games, cute platform titles, and more. *The Sims* series (Maxis, 2000 onwards) has sold 100 million units over the course of its lifetime, for example. *World of Warcraft* boasts only 10 million subscribers worldwide—and that game, although certainly featuring violence, is also full of non-violent social interaction and other play styles.

And yet games like *Grand Theft Auto* or *Halo: Combat Evolved* (Bungie, 2001) do sell well, even as Hollywood blockbusters feature violence (and sex) do well, as do TV shows, books, and plays about cops, detectives, doctors, soldiers, and spies. It's a simple principle that people are hardwired to care about basic matters of life and death. You can create drama about a stamp collector, but it's easier to reach a wide audience if your main character is brought into daily contact with life and death issues.

Sexuality has been less prevalent in games, but as both the visual fidelity of CG humans and the online social aspects of games improve, there is a notable increase in sex and romance in games as well. It's not a matter of all games focusing on violence any more than all movies or books do, but it is an easy if not very creative direction to resort to. So I explain to concerned parents that it is truly not a matter of evil game executives plotting to subvert children, but rather just greed or even lack of imagination. If you examine questions of the lack of diversity in games—why don't they include more female characters, or Blacks or Latinos, or are designed so they can be played by the blind or by paraplegics—the answer tends to be similar. The lack of game features catering to disabled people, as Michelle discusses in Step 7, is certainly primarily a case of neglect due to financial costs of those features compared to the revenue they would bring in.

As I mentioned earlier, sometimes it's a matter of the predominantly white, male, and young block of game developers just making games about people like themselves, and if conscious thought is applied, it is not a plot to perpetuate stereotypes or repress minorities, but merely a desire to reach the largest number of players—who for much of the early years of the videogame industry were in fact fairly close to the demographics of the developers themselves. This situation has changed significantly in recent years as the audience for games has dramatically diversified, although the developers (as Joe has noted in Step 6) are still lagging significantly behind this trend. Entertainment tends to reflect culture, not drive it. In games, as in books, TV, and film before them, cultural stereotypes are often repeated without conscious intent.

Personally I believe it is a good thing to take some risks and break stereotypes, but the games industry is a business and as such tends to have the same inertia that can be seen in other entertainment media.

I have myself seen the forces at work against diversity, sometimes with the best of intentions. At LucasArts I had a small creative role on the first two games in the *Monkey Island* series. We had an aggressive program of international distribution, and our adventure games in particular, of which the *Monkey Island* series (Lucasfilm Games et al, 1990 onwards) was a popular example, eventually sold very well around the world. But we were having trouble translating the first game, *The Secret of Monkey Island*, into Japanese. The main difficulty involved an aspect of the game that I'd contributed called insult swordfighting. The game featured a comic storyline about pirates and a hapless protagonist named Guybrush Threepwood[3]. Guybrush learns early in the game that the key to swordfighting is not

---

[3] Guybrush Threepwood got his last name from a P.G. Wodehouse character, and his first name from the project's lead artist, whose first incarnation of the template or "brush" for this unnamed guy was accordingly called Guybrush.

possessing prowess with a blade, but rather in having a quick wit and a sharp tongue. In swordfights in the game you are repeatedly insulted by your opponent, and need to make an appropriate rejoinder to win an exchange—and do so repeatedly to win a fight. At first Guybrush (and the player) knows no good insults or rejoinders, but gradually he can learn them from opponents. A few insult/rejoinder pairs include:

Insult: "I've heard you were a contemptible sneak."
Rejoinder: "Too bad no one's ever heard of YOU at all."
Insult: "You fight like a dairy farmer."
Rejoinder: "How appropriate, you fight like a cow."
Insult: "I once owned a dog that was smarter than you."
Rejoinder: "He must have taught you everything you know."
Insult: "You make me want to puke."
Rejoinder: "You make me think someone already did."

The problem was twofold—we didn't want the insults to be too controversial in a different culture (Japan, in this case), and we weren't sure the humor would come across. We were working with two Japanese men who were visiting Lucasfilm to learn about creativity, and during their time with our group (which at that point was the games division of Lucasfilm), we thought we could work with them on our translation problem.

The first aspect was fairly straightforward, although surprising. Most of the insults were not perceived as problems, but the one about dairy farmers was immediately squelched, as we were told that farmers in general were held in very high regard and this would be too controversial. But the question of humor was much more difficult. Our guests were politely incredulous that the idea of insulting each other was perceived as funny. Trying to explain that this was fairly common in the US at least made me feel quite the *gaijin*—Japanese for "outsider" with overtones of "barbarian". But when they just didn't understand the last insult and I had to explain what "You make me think someone already did" was meant to imply, my discomfort was so evident they tried to backpedal.

They suggested that in Japan they just didn't have humor—an obvious stretch, as even in those pre-YouTube days I'd seen some outrageous video of Japanese game shows—but I realized they were trying to mutually save face. Eventually we agreed that the best approach was to remove the few particularly offensive insults and just allow the rest to stand as they were. The theory was that Japanese who bought American games (then, as now, a fairly small percentage) did so because they wanted an American perspective, not a Japanese one.

I experienced a similar culture clash from the other direction more recently. Several years ago I was in discussions with a Pakistani game development company. They had a preliminary design for a game that they wanted me to review, and possibly work with them on the game that they hoped to release in the U.S. market. Their concept had a very Hollywood-inspired feel to it, with an international team of heroic stereotypical characters setting off to fight evil.

Most of the team in their fiction would fit into any summer blockbuster film, but they had also included one Pakistani character they were quite proud of, a scientist named G. A. Kahn. I was shocked, as the papers had recently been full of stories about A. Q. Kahn, a Pakistani scientist who was the father of their nuclear weapons program, and was being reviled in the U.S. press as having helped the nuclear programs in Libya, Iran, and North Korea. Their character was very clearly modeled closely after him, and the name of course made the connection inevitable. In Pakistan he was a national hero, and I found myself in the position of our Japanese visitors at LucasArts, having to somehow politely explain that this choice would be insulting at the least to his intended audience. We were not able to find an effective compromise, and I did not end up working with them on the game.

These incidents have raised my own awareness of the problems of trying to achieve cultural diversity. In these cases it was an overt clash between two distinct cultures from different countries with little shared tradition. But as you can ascertain from what you have learned in Steps 5 through 7, even if the slight is unintended or the result of young, white, male game designers simply perpetuating their own cultural assumptions, the insult can be quite real.

ADAPTING TO PLAYER SKILLS

Another adaptive design technique I learned during my tenure at LucasArts involved pleasing different players who come to a game with different expectations about the experience they will have. Sometimes this is based on player skills. In Step 8, you learned from Chris about a model for player skills based upon the Temperament Theory psychological model. Game designers often also try to create games that will appeal to a wide range of player skill in a more concrete sense, as can be measured by how quickly players can get through a game to the end.

This was a primary consideration at LucasArts in part because of our early success and dependence on adventure games. In many other types of games, it is possible to adjust the level of difficulty, either explicitly by the players as mentioned earlier in the case of *Millipede* and with the many games that allow the players to select a difficulty level, or more subtly with dynamic difficulty adjustment and other techniques I will mention later in this chapter. But adventure games do not lend themselves easily to adjustment in difficulty. Players progress through the game primarily by solving a series of puzzles. One can add more puzzles to make the game harder, or make the existing puzzles more complicated, but that makes the game harder for all players.

Providing more puzzles for some players and not for others is not very cost effective, as the additional scenes, characters, and puzzles that are present for the more difficult levels of the game are not seen by people who play the game at an easier difficulty level, leaving money off the screen. Contrast that for example with a first person shooter game, where a higher difficulty level can often be created simply by replicating more enemies, or having them move faster, or attack more often—all easy and inexpensive changes to make. This problem was exacerbated by adventure games being largely designed to be played through only once, with much of the enjoyment coming from the story-intensive nature of the play. Although some stories bear repeating, there is much less motivation to see how it all comes out a second, much less third time around.

The game where this issue came to a head was *Indiana Jones and the Last Crusade: The Graphical Adventure* (Lucasfilm Games, 1989). It was the first time our group had taken on a popular franchise from our parent film company, and we knew we would have a large potential audience because of the popularity of Indiana Jones. We wanted to reach both novice and expert players. We had learned that people who played a lot of adventure games could fly through a game, finishing it in a matter of three or four hours, whereas a beginner might take 10 times that long. And unfortunately those avid players included many of the influential reviewers in magazines of the time.

Our solution was to harness the very passion and avidity of the hard-core expert players. They might finish the game in three hours—but if so, we gave them a reason to play it again. These hardcore players took pride in their ability to zip through the game, and so we hit upon an idea that we called "IQ Points"—in this case IQ stood for "Indy Quotient" and was a deliberate attempt to hook into the pride of the hardcore players who were driven to feel they were smarter than other casual players.

The idea was that accomplishments that players could make in the course of the game had point values associated with them—in this, they presaged the Achievements popular on the Xbox 360 today. As you played through the game, you were given a running score of your IQ points so you could see what you had earned, and it was compared against a perfect total of 800 points, as in "327 out of 800 IQ Points". This dovetailed with another technique we had learned to employ, providing alternate solutions to puzzles in order to prevent frustrating bottlenecks where a player was unable to solve a given puzzle and couldn't move forward.

In the case of *Indiana Jones and the Last Crusade*, we did this in part to capture the different qualities that attracted people to Indiana Jones himself. He was a rough-and-tumble adventurer, using his whip and gun and fists to fight his way through trouble. But he was also a Professor, with a Ph.D. and a position teaching at a university. He used his intelligence to solve puzzles too. So in many parts of the game we let the player progress by either means—fighting his way past Nazis in an Austrian castle, or solving a puzzle to get a Nazi uniform that let him walk right past them. Or later, fighting his way through checkpoints, or producing a pass signed by Hitler himself, harking to a scene in the film that the game was based on where Hitler meets Indy and assumes he is asking for an autograph.

But the catch is that if you use one solution, it precludes the other. For example, if you use a pass you cannot fight as you are allowed to pass. And we awarded IQ points for both options. This meant that in order to get every point of the 800, one had to replay the game several times, trying new things, and eventually seeing every scene and puzzle and battle we'd created.

This rather neatly solved several problems at once. It meant that hardcore players now had reason to play through the game multiple times, and even at their lightning pace, this took time. It let the Strategic players Chris describes in Step 8 feel smart for having eventually gotten every one of the 800 points. And it spells out each task that must be accomplished to do so, hooking the Logistical players. And it meant that these players, typically the most critical and exacting ones and also some of the most loyal purchasers, got to see every bit of the money spent on the game on the screen. But just as important, it did so without compromising the experience for the novice or the story-oriented players. Novices who barely managed to get through to the end after 40 hours of play still got a satisfying resolution to their efforts, and in our experience barely noticed the IQ points, because they were so glad to reach the end.

The success of *Indiana Jones and the Last Crusade* led us to create a second Indiana Jones Adventure Game, called *Indiana Jones and the Fate of Atlantis*. I was a co-designer on both games, and took the opportunity to explore more techniques for adaptive design. We preserved the notion of IQ points and of having alternate solutions to puzzles, but we also added a third mode of play that we felt was lacking in the previous game. In addition to being an adventurer and a professor, Indiana Jones was known for being a lover. Adventure games were one of the few game genres in the '80s and early '90s that had significant numbers of women players, and at LucasArts we wanted to reach that audience (although as I've described, our male design staff made a few mistakes along the way).

So for *Fate of Atlantis*, I proposed that we enlarge on the trend from the previous game, and actually have a section of the middle of the game separate out into three separate tracks based on the facets of Indy's personality and the archetypes of the players that we thought would enjoy them. The Fists path emphasized action and fighting, the Wits path emphasized puzzle solving, and a new Team path emphasized dialogue and allowed the player to control Indy's cohort for the game,

Sophia Hapgood. Sophia was a confident and self-sufficient counterpart to Indy, based in part on our appreciation of Marion Ravenswood in *Raiders of the Lost Ark*, and largely the creation of Hal Barwood, the Project Leader and other co-designer of the game. Hal was new to our group, having been a successful screenwriter and film producer before walking away from that to make videogames. He brought an understanding of character, dialogue, and setting that was a revelation to me, and in turn I tried to rise to the occasion with innovative game design.

The multiple path solution was yet another attempt to balance the cost of production with the expected benefits. We did our best to re-use game assets, but despite that, our best guess was that the game cost about 50% more than if it had had a single path like most games. Of course there is no way to know for sure if it was an effective choice, but several interesting statistics suggest it was probably a good thing to do. For one thing, people reported fairly even adoption of the three different pathways through the game, and our IQ system meant that quite a few people played it through more than once, trying two or all three. Virtually every review of the game cited the path system as innovative and interesting, yet another reason why it can be worthwhile to cater a bit to the jaded tastes of hardcore reviewers.

We also had one of the highest percentages of women playing the game of any we had released to date, based on our feedback cards—I believe it was around 30%, which in the early '90s was quite unusual. And the final test was money—the game was the best-selling adventure game that LucasArts ever created, selling over 1 million copies.

This approach to adaptive design through multiple pathways has also been slowly gaining acceptance. The Westwood title *Blade Runner*, based on the movie of the same name, took what we had done a step further, creating different pathways with profoundly different outcomes, and even different love interests for the hero of the game. True to the film, when you begin the *Blade Runner* game you do not know if you are an artificial human (a replicant) with an ersatz set of childhood memories, or a real human tasked with killing replicants. Your actions in the game determine your destiny. If you save replicants, it's a good thing, because it turns out you are one. If you kill them, *that* is a good thing because you're a human and they are a menace...

Like most people who played the game, when I tried it I didn't even realize there were other options, as the game simply and cleanly assessed my choices and adapted itself to fit them. I didn't find out the truth until I talked to Louis Castle, executive producer on the game, years later, when he also told me he'd been inspired by what we'd done with *Fate of Atlantis*. The recent title *Mass Effect* (BioWare, 2007) did much the same, and *BioShock* (2K, 2007) also gives the player a difficult dilemma with consequences based on the player's choice.

MULTIPLAYER AND VIRTUAL WORLDS

Thus far I've talked about how games can be crafted to adapt to players' preferences and skills by creating alternate paths that re-use game assets and add to play variation while minimizing the cost of additional game assets. But there are other alternatives available when the games in question are meant for multiple simultaneous players.

It is possible to allow players a wide range of choices of avatar and to have specific consequences based on those choices. This was done in the early text-based MUDs (as Richard describes in Step 4) when, with no graphics and with user-created descriptions of characters, you could be anyone you chose to be. And it is done now in the giant MMORPGs like *World of Warcraft* and *EverQuest* (Sony Online, 1999) and non-game virtual worlds like *Second Life* (Linden Research, 2003). By spending tens of millions of dollars, a studio can create games that feature dozens of character types with user-customizable looks, and have hundreds of individual quests that allow those different characters to interact in meaningfully different ways. If they do it well, they can make their money back—and much more. Unfortunately many do fail along the way, but it is possible, if not to please everyone all the time, at least to please millions of people simultaneously.

These virtual worlds also have the interesting quality of featuring other human beings as potential friends, partners, or adversaries. This in turn creates a very rich set of interactions, allowing many of the different player types, races, genders, and abilities to coexist in the same space. The social interactions that Katherine describes in Step 2 would not be possible without a game medium that supports multiple players. It is something of a brute force approach, making a game big enough and rich enough to be able to include a wide range of player types, but the design of these worlds and games is tremendously complex and subtle. All game designers need to take the actions of the players into account, and ask themselves not only "what if they do this?" but also, "what if they don't do this?"

With massively multiplayer games, the designers also have to ask what the players will do with—and to—each other. Others in this book have already spoken about some of how that is done. I will add the observation that design of multiplayer games can often take a subtle turn. Designers must create incentives and disincentives to reward each player for behavior that will please not only the players, but also others in the world. As Richard suggests in Step 4, it is not enough to know that some players like to kill others and to enable them to do it, but a designer must set up the rules of the world so those players can do so without driving everyone else away.

Finally, I cannot discuss adaptive design techniques without acknowledging one of the best examples of all time: *Diablo II* (Blizzard North, 2000).

Some of what I love about this game is present in other games by Blizzard Entertainment, notably *StarCraft* (1998) and *World of Warcraft*, but *Diablo II* represents for me at least a high water mark in ingenuity of design. It is adaptive to different play styles in many delightfully subtle ways, and although a fairly expensive game at the time, it is also a model of how to effectively use, re-use, and use yet again the same basic assets to craft very different play experiences.

For one thing, it has been very popular both as a single-player and multi-player game. That is a very tough thing to do, chiefly for reasons of balance—if a game is optimized for single-player experience it often feels repetitive, or worse, pointless with multiple players. For example, a story that drives the single-player experience cannot effectively be shared by other players if they go off in different directions and trigger story points out of sight of each other, and yet *Diablo II* manages to create a rich and interesting single-player narrative that can be effectively shared by a party of players working together. And, in what I at least believe is a clear nod to Richard Bartle's groundbreaking work, the game allows Killer-type gameplay as well. In fact, it does a good job at hitting every quadrant of Richard's player type diagram in its multiplayer incarnation.

It is some of the more subtle techniques for adapting to player skill levels that impress me the most about this title. In the single-player experience, the player progresses through the game, clearing out levels of monsters, and eventually fighting boss monsters that are gatekeepers to the next group of levels. This structure itself is a classic game structure that allows both some freedom of choice and some inflexible progression to provide the best of both of those features. What *Diablo II* does with great cleverness is to allow players to repeat levels that are regenerated each time they are cleared out. Bold, very competent players can progress through the game quite quickly in real time, doing so by using their skills to battle the boss monsters with finesse and subtle use of weapons, spells, and the many useful items players can accumulate and even craft themselves, and not repeating any levels.

So when an aggressive and skillful player defeats the first boss monster at the end of Act 1, she might be controlling a character that is, for example, a level 9 warrior and not particularly powerful, prevailing through skill. Now consider a timid novice player. He may barely get through level 1, having to restart several times before finishing it. Then he tries it again and again before tackling level 2, and so on. By replaying levels many times, this player accumulates many experience points, increases the abilities of his avatar, and accumulates lots of useful and powerful items and weapons to use. By the time he reaches the boss at the end of Act 1, he may be controlling an avatar that is a level 15 warrior, very powerful—but because of his relative inexperience as a player, that battle for him is just as challenging, and ultimately just as satisfying to win, as the first player who accomplished it with a much weaker character.

And it goes far beyond that. There are only five basic avatar types to choose from—two female and three male—but these can be endlessly customized with their armor, magic items, weapons, and other accoutrements. It lacks the wide range of character appearance customization present in later MMORPGs, but provides much of the same satisfaction.

Playing in the Sandbox

MMORPGs have another interesting adaptive design trait, including a tremendous variety of ways that players can enjoy the game. These games tend to include huge amounts of content, and allow players not only extensive customization of their avatar's looks, but also of their avatar's abilities. Players enjoying one of these games as a heavily armored warrior will have quite a different experience from players who have chosen to be healers. In fact, players in some of these games may spend hundreds of hours just socializing, or trading virtual real estate, or organizing guilds.

The concept of allowing players to choose their own way to play in a game that supplies a world rich in options is generally known as *sandbox play*. The *Grand Theft Auto* series of games in particular is well known for encouraging this style of play, but *SimCity* (Maxis, 1989)—and many of Will Wright's other games of the "software toys" style—has also popularized the idea of players choosing their own goals in a game. Many people credit the classic space-trading game *Elite* (David Braben and Ian Bell, 1984) as being the first widely popular game to feature a largely open-ended universe in which to play.

Designing a game that supports a wide variety of play styles and player-defined goals can be difficult, and often the biggest problem is simply that of expense. The more ways for players to interact that you build into a game, the more complex and costly the game tends to become, and I mentioned earlier how keeping production budgets down is a prime consideration in all games. Another challenge is that by inviting players to invent their own goals and roles in a game, the designer necessarily must cede more control to the players, and emergent behaviors can result that were not intended in the original design.

For example, virtual worlds have their own economies and people quickly learned that they could make real-world money with virtual world goods and services. This resulted in the phenomenon of *gold farmers*, who are people (often in third-world countries) playing online games merely to accumulate wealth or build valuable characters and accounts that can be sold online for real money—sometimes by victimizing the core paying customers of the game in the process.

One early example of this type of emergent behavior appeared in Lucasfilm's *Habitat* game, back in 1986. Players were given an avatar and a virtual room to live in, and that room could be furnished with items purchased online in the game's virtual currency. But the rooms were pre-furnished with a few items as well, and about 10% of the rooms were randomly assigned an aquarium with a couple of fish in it, an item that was not for sale in the rest of the virtual world.

The scarcity of this item and the vagaries of human nature created a huge demand for these fish tanks. Some unscrupulous players began befriending new *Habitat* citizens in order to procure an invitation to visit their room—at which point if they saw a tank, they grabbed it and ran, only to sell it later on the black market. This unexpected complication caused problems for the people running the virtual world, but the buzz and notoriety generated from this kind of incident also drives the popularity and glamour surrounding the worlds. It is probably (dare I say "virtually"?) impossible to exclude the darker aspects of human behavior from games and online worlds, and welcoming the full range of choices while providing checks and balances to check the worst transgressions is perhaps the best that designers can do. As Richard's description of the exploits of Dextrus in Step 4 illustrates, you can't fight human nature.

THAT'S ALL FOLKS

This final step—indeed this whole book—may not be sufficient to teach designers everything they need to know to make games that appeal to the wide range of players that the various authors have described. But it should provide a good start for the serious student of design, and study of the techniques and games mentioned and described here is a great first step towards that lofty and admirable goal.

GLOSSARY

AAA game (triple A): Any game that has been developed with sufficient budget and emphasis on quality to be considered to be of the highest quality in comparison to other games developed at the same time.

Achiever: One of the four *Bartle types* (q.v.), representing players focused upon acquiring concrete measures of success in the game world, such as experience points or money.

Agon: Games of competition. The class of games identified by Roger Caillois that are focused around competition and the desire to prove oneself in direct contest with others [Caillois58].

Alea: Games of chance. The class of games identified by Roger Caillois which, in their purest form, are focused around surrendering to chance or destiny such that one's own abilities are irrelevant to the outcome [Caillois58].

Alternate reality games (ARGs): Games in which the players are delivered or discover content in the real world, through websites, text messages, and other multimedia methods. The content may also develop dynamically, according to the actions of the players.

Amusement: The emotion associated with laughter.

Amygdala: A part of the *limbic system* (q.v.) associated with emotional memory, and in particular with fear.

Anger: An emotion that provokes action; the fight of the *fight or flight response* (q.v.).

Artisan: One of the four patterns of behavior in temperament theory. The Artisan temperament is associated with a desire for freedom to act, and the ability to make an impact.

Association area: An area in the brain involved in forming memory, a process apparently coordinated by the *hippocampus* (q.v.).

Audio center: An informal name for the *temporal lobe* (q.v.), focusing on its main sensory function.

Audio cues: A sound intended to signal information to the player, such as a noise that tells the players their avatars have been spotted, or that they have leveled up.

Auditory disabilities: Hearing problems of any kind, from mild hearing difficulty to total deafness.

Avatar: Another name for the player's character or game world representative.

Bartle type: An audience model developed by Richard Bartle for describing players in virtual worlds such as *MMORPGs* (q.v.) [Bartle96].

Blind testing: Examining how players who have never encountered a game before cope with the rules, the interface, and the nature of the play of such a game, in order to improve the game's accessibility and perhaps also to reduce the *learning curve* (q.v.).

Casual game: A game targeting *casual gamers* (q.v.), characterized by being based on few rules, and thus easy to learn, and having a more forgiving attitude towards play [Elrod08]. The three common genres are *match 3, time management,* and *hidden objects* (q.q.v.) [Irwin08].

Casual gamers: An audience segment that spends less money and time playing videogames than the *hardcore gamer* (q.v.) audience. However, many casual gamers still play games every day.

Cerebellum: A region of the brain, at the back and underneath, associated with motor control and the learning of motor skills.

Cerebral cortex: See *cortex* (q.v.).

Closed captioning: Text that delivers both subtitles for speech, and also text versions of relevant sound effects and other non-speech elements.

Cognitive disabilities: A wide range of disabilities including (but not restricted to) memory loss, attention deficit disorder, learning disabilities, and dyslexia.

Computer role-playing game: A game in which the player adopts the role of one or more characters, and which traditionally involves a number of progress mechanics through which the character or characters are developed. Compare with *tabletop role-playing game* (q.v.), from which the videogame form evolved. In this book, computer role-playing game is abbreviated cRPG.

Conqueror: The archetype of the Type 1 play style in *DGD1* (q.v.), focused on challenge and fiero.

Core gamer: Synonym for *hardcore gamer* (q.v.).

Cortex: The outer layer of the brain, often divided into the *frontal, parietal, temporal,* and *occipital lobes* (q.q.v.).

cRPG: Acronym for *computer role-playing game* (q.v.).

Cut scene: A short movie presented to the player at specific points in a game.

Decision center: An informal name for the *orbito-frontal cortex* (q.v.).

DGD1: An audience model developed by Chris Bateman and Richard Boon that examines relationships between certain psychological models and play.

Diplomatic: The skills associated with the *Idealist* temperament (q.v.), focused around empathy, the resolution of differences, and abstract thinking.

Dollplay: A form of *mimicry* (q.v.) in which one acts out stories with dolls or similar simulacrums.

Dopamine: A neurotransmitter, primarily produced by the *nucleus accumbens* (q.v.), that is involved in the formation of habits and the process of addiction.

Easy Fun: One of Nicole Lazzaro's *Four Fun Keys* (q.v.) concerned with games of curiosity, and associated especially with the emotion of *wonder* (q.v.).

Emotional Contagion: The tendency to express and feel emotional states that are similar to those people nearby. This is especially true of laughter, but can be observed with almost all emotions.

Engagement: A state of focus upon an activity, such as a videogame.

Epinephrine: Technical name of the neurotransmitter adrenalin, associated with *excitement* and *fear* (q.q.v.).

Excitement: An emotional response to novelty, challenge, or pressure.

Explorative learning style: A *learning style* (q.v.) in which a person prefers to experiment, and is willing to take risks to do so, rather than being explicitly taught. Compare with *modeling learning style* (q.v.).

Explorer: One of the four *Bartle types* (q.v.), representing players focused upon learning about the game world, and finding hidden places and things.

Fear: *Excitement* (q.v.) under the expectation of negative outcomes.

Fear center: An informal name for the *amygdala*.

Fiero: The emotional feeling of triumph over adversity. It is often expressed in body language by raising one's arms above one's head.

Fixed schedule: A type of *reinforcement schedule* (q.v.) in which reward comes after a predictable number of actions (fixed ratio schedule) or a predictable time duration (fixed interval schedule). These schedules produce a pause after the reward because from the player's perspective "you must do it all over again for your next reward".

Flow: The experience of devoting total concentration effortlessly upon a task; also known as "optimal experience" [Csikzentmihalyi90].

Flow channel: The state of optimal experience that occurs in *Flow* (q.v.) when the degree of challenge is proportionate to the individual's skills.

Four Fun Keys: A model of play developed by Nicole Lazzaro based on observations of the emotions observed when players engage with their favorite videogames.

FPS: Acronym for First Person Shooter.

Frontal lobe: An area at the front of the human cerebral *cortex* (q.v.) associated with cognitive function and decision making, especially in the *orbito-frontal cortex* (q.v.).

Fun factor: A generalized term for anything about an experience that is engaging, entertaining, or amusing to people.

Game literacy: Experience playing games. Players with considerable game literacy can be considered *hardcore* (q.v.), and those without this experience can be considered *casual* (q.v.).

Game mechanics: The rules of a game that determine how play will be structured.

Gamer hobbyists: Players who spend a lot of their time and money on playing games (including videogames); effectively a synonym for *hardcore gamers* (q.v.).

Ganking: A frowned-upon approach to *PvP* in *MMO* games (q.q.v.) involving attacking players when they are compromised in some way.

Goal-oriented: An approach to play or other activities in which achieving the stated outcome is paramount in the mental model of the person in question. Compare with *process-oriented* (q.v.).

Gold farmers: Repeatedly performing certain actions in an *MMO* (q.v.) in order to accumulate the ingame resource (often gold, hence the name).

Guardian: One of the four patterns of behavior in temperament theory. The Guardian temperament is associated with the need to belong, and a sense of duty.

Hard fun: One of Nicole Lazzaro's *Four Fun Keys* (q.v.) concerned with games of challenge, and associated with the emotions of *fiero* and *anger* (q.q.v.).

Hardcore gamers: An audience segment associated with buying and playing a considerable volume of games. Also known as *core gamers* or *gamer hobbyists* (q.q.v.).

Hidden objects: A genre of the *casual game* (q.v.) based around finding specific objects in a complex scene in a manner similar to the *Where's Wally?* books (*Where's Waldo?* in North America).

Hippocampus: A part of the *limbic system* (q.v.) that has a major role in coordinating associative memory.

Hobby games: Tabletop board games with relatively complex mechanics, which thus take some time to both learn and play.

Hotspot: A point in the game world where the avatar can interact with the world in a meaningful way.

Housekeeping: A type of play activity concerned with repeated actions that are either unconnected, or tangentially connected, to progress, such as collecting items in a platform game, or customizing the player's avatar.

Hyper-sexualized: The exaggeration of certain features that relate to being sexually receptive, such as a flushed face, half-closed eyes, erect nipples, or an arched back.

Hypothalamus: A part of the *limbic system* (q.v.) that regulates a number of bodily functions such as appetite, anger, and trust.

Idealist: One of the four patterns of behavior in temperament theory. The Idealist temperament is associated with a desire for unique identity, and a search for meaning and significance.

Ilinx: Games of vertigo. The class of games identified by Roger Caillois that are focused around temporary annihilation of consciousness by surrendering to acceleration, dizziness, or any other tendency that is contrary to self-awareness [Caillois58].

Imagined agency: The illusion of control over a situation that exists when a player uses dice to resolve a random outcome. Although technically they have no control over the dice (barring a validation of certain psi research), they still feel as if they are contributing to the outcome, and thus have a kind of illusion of agency.

Immersion: The process of experiencing deep *engagement* with a *virtual world* (q.q.v.).

Interval schedule: A type of *reinforcement schedule* (q.v.) in which reward comes after a certain amount of time. These produce pacing to the player's behavior because "your next reward will come later".

IP: Acronym for intellectual property, which in the context of games usually refers to the characters, setting, and other details associated with a particular brand.

Killer: One of the four *Bartle types* (q.v.), representing players primarily interested in competition with other players.

Landscape function: The use of random chance to create an entirely unique playfield in a game, such that the play of the game can be different every time.

Learning curve: A conceptual measure of how hard it is to learn to control or use a game.

Learning style: The manner in which a person prefers to learn new information, principally discussed in this volume as either an *explorative* or *modeling learning style* (q.q.v.).

Limbic system: A structure deep in the center of the human brain that is associated with basic emotional behavior, and consisting of several key structures, notably the *nucleus accumbens*, the *amygdala*, the *hippocampus*, and the *hypothalamus* (q.q.v.).

Logistical: The skills associated with the Logistical temperament, focused around optimization and standardization.

Ludus: Tending towards play regulated by rules. Roger Caillois considered games to vary between ludus at the most regulated extreme, and *paidia* (q.v.).

Manager: The archetype of the Type 2 play style in *DGD1* (q.v.), focused on mastery and problem solving.

Massively Multiplayer Online: A class of games that have as the center of their play the interaction of many players in a common *virtual world* (q.v.).

Mass market gamer: A synonym for *casual gamer* (q.v.), stressing the greater numbers of such players relative to the *gamer hobbyist* or *hardcore gamer* (q.q.v.)

Match 3: A genre of *casual game* (q.v.) involving switching the positions of elements in a grid to make patterns, exemplified by *Bejewelled* (PopCap, 2001).

Mere exposure effect: A psychological phenomenon whereby what is familiar is preferred to what is unfamiliar.

Micro expressions: Small facial movements that reveal the emotions being experienced.

Mimicry: Games of simulation. The class of games identified by Roger Caillois that are focused around emulation—a make-believe experience in which the participant steps outside of conventional reality in order to pretend to be something else [Caillois58].

Mirror neurons: Elements in the brain that respond whether one is carrying out an action, or watching someone carry out an action.

MMO: Acronym for *massively multiplayer online* (q.v.).

MMORPG: Acronym that combines *MMO* and *RPG* (q.q.v.), that is, a massively multiplayer online role-playing game.

Mobility disabilities: A wide range of disabilities including (but not restricted to) paralysis (via accident, disease, or a birth defect), neuro-logical disorders, repetitive stress injury, and age-related issues.

Modeling learning style: A *learning style* (q.v.) in which a person prefers to have skills demonstrated, and observe the consequences of actions, before attempting to do the same. Compare with *modeling learning style* (q.v.).

MUD: Acronym for multi-user dungeon, a form of text-based *MMO* (q.v.) that represents the original instances of these kinds of games.

Naches: The emotion of taking pleasure in the achievements of someone you have helped, such as a tutor feeling pride in the achievements of her student.

Nerf: A change to the parametric values or design of a game to reduce a perceived imbalance, usually by reducing the effectiveness of a particular option.

Noise function: The use of random chance to create a degree of uncer-tainty in the play of a game, for instance via random driving forces in artificial intelligence.

Norepinephrine: A neurotransmitter associated with *anger* (q.v.).

Nucleus accumbens: A part of the *limbic system* (q.v.) associated with the formation of habits.

Occipital lobe: An area at the middle of the human cerebral *cortex*, below the *parietal lobe* (q.q.v.) associated with the processing of visual information.

Orbito-frontal cortex: A part of the *frontal lobe* of the human *cortex* (q.q.v.) associated with cognitive processes and decision-making.

Paidia: Tending towards spontaneously creative play, unfettered by rules (as termed by Roger Caillois). Its polar opposite is *ludus* (q.v.). It is similar in some respects to *toyplay* (q.v.).

Parietal lobe: An area at the back of the human cerebral *cortex* (q.v.) associated with spatial sense, navigation, and the sense of touch.

Participant: The archetype of the Type 4 play style in *DGD1* (q.v.), focused on enjoyment in a social or emotional context.

Pathfinding: A type of *goal-oriented* (q.v.) play activity concerned with direct progress, especially finding the route to advance within the game.

People Fun: One of Nicole Lazzaro's *Four Fun Keys* (q.v.) concerned with games that derive their fun from people playing together, and associated especially with the emotion of *amusement* (q.v.).

Plate spinning: A synonym for *time-management* games (q.v.).

Play style: The manner in which a particular player approaches play. There are many models for play styles, including *DGD1* and *Temperament Theory* (q.q.v.).

Player experience: Internal sensations produced by the interplay between player actions, choices, and feedback when someone is playing a videogame; abbreviated PX.

Player versus environment: Play where the challenge is provided by the game itself, and not by other players; abbreviated PvE.

Player versus player: Competition between players within a videogame; abbreviated PvP.

Playground world: A game world in which players are given immediate access to a large environment containing many different elements which they can experiment with at their leisure.

Pleasure center: An informal name for the *nucleus accumbens* (q.v.).

Process-oriented: An approach to play or other activities in which focusing on the quality of the activity itself takes precedence over achieving the stated outcome in the mental model of the person in question. Compare with *goal-oriented* (q.v.).

PvE: Abbreviation for *player versus environment* (q.v.).

PvP: Abbreviation for *player versus player* (q.v.).

PX: Abbreviation for *player experience* (q.v.).

Ratio schedule: A type of *reinforcement schedule* (q.v.) in which reward comes after a certain number of actions. This kind of schedule produces a high rate of activity because "the more you do, the more you get".

Rational: One of the four patterns of behavior in temperament theory. The Rational temperament is associated with a desire for knowledge and competence.

Relief: A relaxing emotion that occurs after a strong emotion subsides.

Reward structure: The rules of a game that determine when players earn a reward, and how they progress (which is also an intrinsic reward), and thus the structure of the game.

RPG: Acronym for role-playing game. This can mean a *tabletop role-playing game*, or a *computer role-playing game* (q.q.v.).

Rushgames: An informal name for games that evoke *ilinx* (q.v.).

Sandbox play: A form of *toyplay* (q.v.), in which players are encouraged to experiment and try whatever they choose with little or no significant consequences.

Schadenfreude: The emotion of taking pleasure in another person's misfortune.

Schedule of reinforcement: A protocol that determines when a behavior is to be encouraged (reinforced). Common types of schedule include *ratio schedules, interval schedules, fixed schedules,* and *variable schedules* (q.q.v.).

Serious fun: One of Nicole Lazzaro's *Four Fun Keys* (q.v.) concerned with games of altered states, and associated with the emotions of *excitement* and *relief* (q.q.v.).

Serious games: Videogames used for a training or educational purpose. In general, any game created for a purpose other than entertainment can be considered a serious game.

Social center: An informal (and slightly misleading) name for the *hypothalamus* (q.v.).

Socializer: One of the four *Bartle types* (q.v.), representing players more interested in interacting with the other players than with the game world.

Social tokens: A word, phrase, or ingame object that is symbolic in nature, and that increases in value with use. The creation and exchange of social tokens enhances and deepens friendships.

Strategic: The skills associated with the *Rational* temperament (q.v.), focused around the capacity to anticipate problems, and to determine how to reach an imagined future state.

Structured play: A type of play that is regulated by rules, equivalent to Caillois' term *ludus* (q.v.).

Surprise: A brief emotional response, probably related to *fear* (q.v.).

Tabletop role-playing game: A type of game played with paper and dice by a group of players, in which dramatic situations are played out by virtue of a set of mechanics that support various interactions, often resolved by dice. The spiritual and mechanical forebear to *computer role-playing games* (q.v.).

Tactical: The skills associated with the *Artisan* temperament (q.v.); principally the ability to swiftly read context and react appropriately.

Temperament Theory: A psychological model, which can also be adapted into a *play style* model (q.v.).

Temporal lobes: Areas at the sides of the human cerebral *cortex*, below the *frontal lobe* (q.q.v.), associated with audio senses (speech and hearing). The *hippocampus* (q.v.) is situated in the temporal lobes.

Time management: A genre of *casual game* (q.v.) involving making quick decisions about which situations to attend to out of a collection of possible options, each of which increases in urgency if it remains unattended. The genre is exemplified by *Diner Dash* (Gamelab, 2005).

Touch center: An informal name for the *parietal lobe* (q.v.), focusing on its main function in processing sensory information.

Toyplay: Unstructured play within a game, that is, play that does not consist of set goals or objectives (except those that the players set for themselves). This book uses toyplay as a synonym for *paidia* (q.v.).

Unstructured play: A type of play that happens without rules, equivalent to Caillois' term *paidia* (q.v.).

Usability: The ease with which people can deploy a particular tool to achieve goals.

User experience: The experience of use, how accessible the interface for a particular piece of software might be, and how easily players can accomplish what they expect.

UX: Abbreviation for *user experience* (q.v.).

Value proposition: The sum of all benefits that a vendor is offering with its product.

Variable schedule: A type of *reinforcement schedule* (q.v.) in which reward comes after a variable number of actions (variable ratio schedule) or a variable time duration (variable interval schedule). This type of schedule produces constant activity because "everything has a chance of reward".

Vertigo: A synonym for *ilinx* (q.v.).

Virtual world: A digital environment that presents itself as a physical space to be explored and interacted with, such as is found in any 3D game (and many 2D and text-based games too).

Visual center: An informal name for the *occipital lobe* (q.v.), focusing on its function as the sensory center for vision.

Visual disabilities: Problems of sight, principally one of three kinds: blindness, low vision, and color blindness.

Wanderer: The archetype of the Type 3 play style in *DGD1* (q.v.), focused on seeking a unique experience and having fun without being hindered by difficulty.

REFERENCES

Step 3 is based upon six articles entitled "The Anarchy of Paidia," "The Complexity of Ludus," "The Challenge of Agon," "The Rituals of Alea," "The Joy of Ilinx," and "The Imagination of Mimicry" written in 2004, as well as some additional material from "Kinaesthetic Mimicry" and "Emotions of Play Revisited" (2007), as well as "Rushgames (Fight or Flight)," "Designing Luck," and "Malone on Curiosity" (2008), all of which appeared upon *Only a Game*, Chris Bateman's blog, which can be found at http://onlyagame.typepad.com.

Step 8 is based upon a series of articles entitled "Strategic Play," "Logistical Play," "Tactical Play," and "Other Play Styles" written from December 2006 through February 2007, also on *Only a Game*.

[AbleGamers] Available online at http://www.ablegamers.com/; accessed 27 November 2008.

[AFP05] "Hollywood and video game makers are 'very much in love'," *Taipei Times*, July 1 2005, quoting from AFP, available online at http://www.taipeitimes.com/News/feat/archives/2005/07/01/20032618 14; accessed 25 August 2008.

[Ahn04] Ahn, L. von and Dabbish, L. "Labeling images with a computer game," *Proceedings Association for Computing Machinery (ACM) Special Interest Group on Computer-Human Interaction Conference* (CHI 2004): 319–326. Vienna, Austria. Publisher: ACM Press New York, NY, USA, 2004.

[Alensina03] Alensina, Alberto and La Ferrara, Eliana. "Ethnic Diversity and Economic Performance," Harvard Institute of Economic Research Working Papers 2028, Harvard Institute of Economic Research, 2003.

[Amaya08] Amaya, G., Davis, J.P., Gunn, D.V., Harrison, C., Pagulayan, R.J., Phillips, B., and Wixon, D. "Games User Research (GUR): Our Experience with and Evaluation of Four Methods." In Isbister, K. and Schaffer, N. (Eds.) *Game Usability: Advice from the Experts for Advancing the Player Experience*. San Francisco, Morgan Kaufmann, 2008.

[Andreasen99] Andreasen, E., Downey, B., "Measuring Bartle-Quotient." (1999). Available online at *http://www.gamerdna.com/quizzes/bartle-test-of-gamer-psychology*; accessed November 2008.

[Arias07] Arias-Carrión, Ó. and Pöppel, E. "Dopamine, learning and reward-seeking behaviour." *Acta Neurobiologiae Experimentalis* (2007), 67 (4): 481–488.

[Ax53] Ax, A.F., "The physiological differentiation between fear and anger in humans." *Psychosomatic Medicine* 15: 433, 1953.

[Bandura77] Bandura, A. *Social Learning Theory*. Englewood Cliffs, NJ, Prentice Hall, 1977.

[Bartle03a] Bartle, R. "A self of sense," 2003. Available online at *http://www.mud.co.uk/richard/selfware.htm*; accessed 29 December 2005.

[Bartle03b] Bartle, R. *Designing Virtual Worlds*. New Riders Games. Berkeley, CA: Peach Pit Press, 2003.

[Bartle05] Bartle, R., Alexander, T (ed.), "Virtual Worlds: Why People Play" (pp 3–18) *Massively Multiplayer Game Development 2*. Charles River Media, Hingham MA, 2005.

[Bartle08] Bartle, R., Novak, J., "On Player Types" (pp 39–40): Game Development Essentials 2nd ed. Delmar Cengage Learning, Clifton Park NY, 2008.

[Bartle96] Bartle, R. "Hearts, clubs, diamonds, spades: Players who suit MUDs," 1996. Available online at http://www.brandeis.edu/pubs/jove/HTML/v1/bartle.html; accessed 29 December 2005.

[Bateman04] Bateman, Chris, Boon, Richard, "Demographic Game Design: How to make game design as important as marketing," brochure published by International Hobo in 2004.

[Bateman05] Bateman, Chris, Boon, Richard, *21st Century Game Design*. Charles River Media, 2005.

[Bateman08] Bateman, Chris, Boon, Richard, Lowenhaupt, Rebecca, "Player Diversity: The DGD2 Survey Results," unpublished paper by International Hobo based upon research conducted in 2008.

[BBC02] "The gambling habits of Britons," BBC website, July 24 2002. Available online at http://news.bbc.co.uk/2/hi/uk_news/2148568.stm; accessed 25 August 2008.

[BBC08] British Broadcasting Corporation, "Stepping into a World of Hurt," September 18, 2008. Available online at http://news.bbc.co.uk/1/hi/technology/7618626.stm; accessed November 2008.

[Berens00] Berens, Linda V., *Understanding Yourself and Others: An Introduction to Temperament*. Telos Publications, 2000.

[Berens01] Berens, Linda V., *Understanding Yourself and Others: An Introduction to Interaction Styles*. Telos Publications, 2001.

[Berlinger08] Berlinger, Yehuda, "The press won't shut up about the world Monopoly vote," February 1, 2008. Available online at http://jergames.blogspot.com/2008/02/press-wont-shut-up-about-world-monopoly.html; accessed 29 August 2008.

[Bethke07] Bethke, E., "MMO Goal Structures as a Panacea." Proc. Austin Game Developers Conference 2007, Austin TX (2007). Available online at http://gopedia.gopetslive.com/twiki/pub/GoPedia/ConferenceMaterials/MMOGoalStructuresasaPanacea.ppt; accessed November 2008.

[Biederman06] Biederman, I., Vessel, E. A., "Perceptual Pleasure and the Brain." *American Scientist* (May-June 2006) 94, 249–255.

[Bierre05] Bierre, K., Chetwynd, J., Hinn, D. M., Ludi, S., and Westin T., "Game not over: Accessibility issues in video games." Paper presented at the Annual Human-Computer Interaction International Conference, 2005, Las Vegas, NV. Available online at http://www.igda.org/accessibility/ HCII2005_GAC.pdf; accessed 25 November 2008.

[Boorstin90] Boorstin, J., *Making Movies Work*. Beverly Hills, CA, Silman-James Press, 1990.

[Brandon08] Shefield, Brandon, "Interview: Hirokazu Yasuhara," *Game Developer Magazine* (August 2008): p 17–22, available online at http://www.gamasutra.com/view/feature/3769/game_design_ psychology_the_full_.php; accessed 8 September 2008.

[Bruce95] Bruce, L.L. and Neary T.J., *"The limbic system of tetrapods: a comparative analysis of cortical and amygdalar populations." Brain Behaviour & Evolution*, 1995, 46 (4–5).

[Bryant07] Bryant, J.A., Akerman, A., and Drell, J. 2007. "Wee Wii: Preschoolers and Motion-based Game Play." Presented at the International Communication Association Conference, Montreal, Canada, 2008.

[Bull51] Bull, Nina, *The Attitude Theory of Emotion, Nervous, and Mental Diseases (Monographs No. 81)*, New York, Coolidge Foundation, 1951.

[Burnett05] Leo Burnett Ltd, *Revels* Russian Roulette commercial, 2005. Available online at *http://www.visit4info.com/details.cfm?adid=23652*; accessed 29 August 2008.

[Caillois58] Caillois, Roger, *Les Jeux et Les Hommes*. Gallimard, 1958.

[Cannon15] Cannon, W.B., *Bodily Changes in Pain, Hunger, Fear and Rage: An Account of Recent Researches into the Function of Emotional Excitement*. New York, Appleton, 1915.

[Canossa08] Gamasutra. "Hitman Designer: Metrics Plus Personas Equal Fun" (3 July 2008). Available online at http://www.gamasutra.com/ php-bin/news_index.php?story=19129; accessed September 2008.

[Capella96] Capella, J.N. "Dynamic coordination of vocal and kinesic behavior in dyadic interaction: Methods, problems, and interpersonal out-comes," pp 353–386 in Watt, J.H. and VanLear, C.A. (Eds.) *Dynamic Patterns in Communication Processes*. Thousand Oaks, CA, Sage Publications, 1996.

[Costa07] Costa, Dan, "Turn It Off, Kids!" *PCMag.com* (April 2007). Available online at http://www.pcmag.com/article2/0,2817,2109568,00.asp; accessed 6 August 2008.

[Cottrell72] Cottrell, N.B. "Social facilitation." In C.G. McClintock (Ed.) *Experimental Social Psychology*. New York, Holt, Rinehart & Winston, 1972.

[Creekmur08] Creekmur, Jamilah Barnes, "All Hip Hop Week," Production Report from Allhiphop.com, 2008.

[Csíkszentmihályi75] Csíkszentmihályi, M., *Beyond Boredom and Anxiety*. Jossey-Bass Publishers, 1975.

[Csíkszentmihályi90] Csíkszentmihályi, M., *Flow: The Psychology of Optimal Experience*. HarperPerennial, 1990.

[Del Vechio03] Del Vechio, Gene, *The Blockbuster Toy*. Louisiana, Pelican, 2003.

[Ditton95] Ditton, Elaine, Game Developers Conference presentation, circa 1995.

[Ekman03] Ekman, P., *Emotions Revealed*. Times Books Henry Hold and Company, 2003.

[Elrod08] Elrod, Corvus, "Forgiving Casual Games" (January 30 2008). Available online at http://blog.pjsattic.com/corvus/2008/01/forgiving-casual-games/; accessed 30 August 2008.

[ESA08] Entertainment Software Association. Essential Facts About the Computer and Video Game Industry. Available online at http://www.theesa.com/facts/pdfs/ESA_EF_2008.pdf; accessed 17 July 2008.

[ESPgame] Available online at http://www.gwap.com/gwap/gamesPreview/espgame/; accessed November 2008.

[Everitt01] Everitt, B.J., Dickinson, A., and Robbins, T.W., "The neuropsychological basis of addictive behavior." *Brain research: Brain research reviews* (Oct 2001), 36 (2–3),129–38.

[Faure05] Faure, A., Haberland, U., Condé, F., and El Massioui, N., "Lesion to the Nigrostriatal Dopamine System Disrupts Stimulus-Response Habit Formation." *The Journal of Neuroscience* (March 2005), 25(11):2771–2780.

[Ferster57] Ferster, C.B. and Skinner, B.F., *Schedules of Reinforcement*. New York, Appleton-Century-Crofts, 1957.

[FreeRice] Available online at http://www.freerice.com/; accessed 9 November 2008.

[GameDeveloper08] "2008 State of Game Development Survey," *Game Developer Research* (Available (for a fee) online at http://www.gamedev-research.com/); accessed August 2008. Think Services, 2008.

[Gamespot07] "Nerjyzed Entertainment Announces Black College Football Videogame: BCFx," September 2008. Available online at http://www.gamespot.com/pc/sports/blackcollegefootballexperience/news.html?sid=6178197&om_act=convert&om_clk=gsupdates&tag=updates;title;3; accessed 13 January 2009.

[Gottfried86] Gottfried, A. and Brown, C., Play Interactions: The Contribution of Play Materials and Parental Involvement to Children's Development, Lexington Books Mississippi, 1986.

[Hassenzahl00] Hassenzahl, M., Platz, A., Burmester, M., and Lehner K. "Hedonic and ergonomic quality aspects determine a software's appeal." *Proceedings Association for Computing Machinery (ACM) Special Interest Group on Computer-Human Interaction Conference (CHI)*, (2000): 201–208, The Hague, The Netherlands.

[Hatfield94] Hatfield, E., Cacioppo, J.T. and Rapson, R.L. *Emotional Contagion*. Paris, Cambridge University Press, 1994.

[Hight08] Hight, J. and Novak, J., *Game development essentials: Game project management*. Thomson Delmar Learning, Clifton Park, NY, 2008.

[Hill65] Hill, Greg and Thornley, Kerry, *Principia Discordia, or How I Found Goddess And What I Did To Her When I Found Her*. Rip-off Press, 1965/Loompanics 1970.

[Hillis07] Hillis, Scott, "'Hidden object' series hit for holidays," *Reuters*, 20 December 2007. Available online at http://www.reuters.com/article/sphereNews/idUSN1851179620071220?sp=true&view=sphere; accessed 30 August 2008.

[Hopson04] Hopson, John, *Behavioural Game Design*. Presented at the Game Developer's Conference, San Jose CA, March 2004.

[Huizinga55] Huizinga, Johan, *Homo Ludens: A Study Of The Play Element In Culture*. Beacon Press, Boston, 1955.

[Iacoboni99] Iacoboni, M., Woods, R.P., Brass, M., Bekkering, H., Mazziotta, J.C., and Rizzolatti, G. "Cortical Mechanisms of Human Imitation." *Science* (December 1999) Vol. 286, No. 5449, 2526–2528.

[IGDA04a] "IGDA Quality of Life White Paper," Available online at http://www.igda.org/qol/whitepaper.php#dl; accessed 12 November 2008.

[IGDA04b] International Game Developers Association. "Accessibility in games: Motivations and approaches," Game Accessibility Special Interest Group Whitepaper No. 1. San Francisco, CA, June 2004. Available online at http://www.igda.org/accessibility/IGDA_Accessibility_WhitePaper.pdf; accessed 25 November 2008.

[IGDA05] "Game Developer Demographics: An Exploration of Workforce Diversity," October 2005. Available online at http://www.igda.org/diversity/IGDA_DeveloperDemographics_Oct05.pdf; accessed 12 November 2008.

[IGDA06] International Game Developers Association. "Top 10 ways to improve game accessibility," Game Accessibility Special Interest Group Brochure No. 1, 2006. San Francisco, CA. Available online at http://www.igda.org/wiki/Top_Ten; accessed 25 November 2008.

[Irwin08] Irwin, Mary Jane, "Casual Gold Bust." *Forbes*, 1 August 2008. Available online at http://www.forbes.com/2008/08/01/casual-games-money-tech-ebiz-cx_mji_0801games.html; accessed 30 August 2008.

[Jordan00] Jordan, P.W. *Designing Pleasurable Products: An Introduction to the New Human Factors*. London, Taylor & Francis, 2000.

[Karlsen04] Karlsen, F., "Media Complexity and Diversity of Use: Thoughts on a Taxonomy of Users of Multiuser Online Games," Proc. Other Players Conference ITU, Copenhagen (2004). Available online at http://jonas-smith.dk/otherplayers/papers/karlsen.pdf; accessed November 2008.

[Keirsey78] Bates, M. and Keirsey, D., *Please Understand Me: Character & Temperament Types*. Prometheus Nemesis, 1978.

[Khoo08] Khoo, E.T., Cheok, A.D., Nguyen, T.H.D., and Pan, Z. "Age Invaders: Social and Physical Inter-generational Mixed Reality Family Entertainment." *Virtual Reality*, March 2008, Vol. 12, No. 1, 3–16.

[Kim00] Kim, A. J. *Community Building on the Web*. Berkeley, CA, Peach Pit Press, 2000.

[Kim98] Kim, J., "The Threefold Model FAQ," Usenet: rec.games.frp.advocacy, September 1998. Available online at http://www.darkshire.net/jhkim/rpg/theory/threefold/faq_v1.html; accessed November 2008.

[Kisilevsky03] Kisilevsky, B.S., Hains, Lee, K., Xie, X., Huang, H., Hueye, H., Zhang, K., and Wang, Z. "Effects of Experience on Fetal Voice Recognition." *Psychological Science*, May 2003, Vol. 14, No. 3, 220–224.

[Klov93] Originally by Mike Hughey with contributions by Jeff Hansen, revised 1993 by Jonathon Deitch, revised 1998–1999 by Brian L. Johnson, *The Killer List of Videogames*. 1993, 1998–1999, 2000. Available online at www.klov.com.

[Knapp02] Knapp, M.L. and Hall, J.A. *Nonverbal Communication in Human Interaction*. Australia, Wadsworth Thomson Learning, 2002.

[Koepp98] Koepp, M. J., Gunn, R. N., Lawrence, R. N., Cunningham, V. J., Dagher, A., Jones, T., Brooks, D. J., Bench, C. J., and Grasby, P. M., "Evidence for striatal dopamine release during a video game." *Nature*, May 1998, 393, 266–268.

[Kohler07] Kohler, C. "A Glimpse into Harmonix's Punk-Rock Design Process." *Wired Magazine*, 15(10), available online at http://www.wired.com/gaming/gamingreviews/magazine/15-10/mf_harmonix_sb; accessed September 2008.

[Kolko00] Eds. Kolko, B.E., Nakamura, L., and Rodman, G. B. *Race in Cyberspace*. Routledge, New York, 2000.

[Koster05] Koster, R., *A Theory of Fun for Game Design*. Paraglyph Press, Scottsdale AZ, 2005.

[Lazzaro04] Lazzaro, Nicole, "Why We Play Games: 4 Keys to Emotion without Story." Presented at the Game Developer's Conference, 2004.

[Lazzaro04a] Lazzaro, N. and Keeker, K. "What's My Method? A game show on games." *Proceedings Association for Computing Machinery (ACM) Special Interest Group on Computer-Human Interaction Conference (CHI)*, Vienna, Austria, 2004, 1093–1094.

[Lazzaro04b] Lazzaro, N. "Why we play games" *User Experience Magazine*, 2004, 8: 6–8.

[Lazzaro04c] Lazzaro, N. "Why we Play Games: Four Keys to More Emotion in Player Experiences." Proceedings of the Game Developers Conference, San Jose, California, 2004. Available online at www.xeodesign.com/whyweplaygames.html; accessed 28 December 2005.

[Lazzaro05] Lazzaro, N. "Diner Dash and the People Factor," 2005. Available online at www.xeodesign.com/whyweplaygames.html; accessed 2 March 2005.

[Lazzaro07] Lazzaro, N. Editors Jako, J. and Sears, A. "Why We Play: Affect and the Fun of Games: Designing Emotions for Games, Entertainment Interfaces and Interactive Products." *The Human-Computer Interaction Handbook: Fundamentals, Evolving Technologies and Emerging Applications*, 2007, 679–700 Lawrence Erlbaum Associates, Inc., Mahwah, NJ.

[Lazzaro08a] Lazzaro, N. Editors Kafai, Y., Heeter, C., Denner, J., and Sun, J., *Beyond Barbie and Mortal Kombat: New Perspectives on Gender and Gaming*, MIT Press, 2008.

[Lazzaro08b] Lazzaro, N. Editors Isbister K. and Schaffer, N. *Game Usability: Advancing the Player Experience*, pp 315–344. Morgan Kaufmann, 2008.

[Lazzaro08c] Lazzaro, N. (2008c). "Halo vs. Facebook: Emotions that Drive Play," Proceedings of the Game Developers Conference, San Jose, California. Available online at www.xeodesign.com/whyweplaygames.html; accessed 13 April 2008.

[Maguire00] Maguire, E. A., Gadian, D. G., Johnsrude, I. S., Good, C. D. Ashburner, J., Frackowiak, R.S., and Frith, C. D. "Navigation-related structural change in the hippocampi of taxi drivers." Proceedings of the National Academy of Sciences, Vol. 97(8): 4398–403, 2000.

[Malone80] Malone, Thomas W., "What makes things fun to learn? Heuristics for designing instructional computer games," ACM, 1980.

[Malone81] Malone, T., "Heuristics for Designing Enjoyable User Interfaces: Lessons from Computer Games." Proceedings Association for Computing Machinery (ACM) Special Interest Group on Computer-Human Interaction Conference, CHI 1981, 63–68.

[Mandryk07] Mandryk, R.L. and Atkins, M.S. "A Fuzzy Physiological Approach for Continuously Modeling Emotion During Interaction with Play Technologies." *International Journal of Human Computer Studies*, 2007, Vol. 65, Issue 4, 329–347.

[McGonigal06] McGonigal, J., "This Might Be a Game: Ubiquitous Play and Performance at the Turn of the Twenty-First Century," (PhD Dissertation) University of California, Berkeley, 2006. Available online at http://avantgame.com/McGonigal_THIS_MIGHT_BE_A_GAME_sm.pdf; accessed November 2008.

[Mollman07] Mollman, S., "Video games' new frontier: The visually impaired." CNN.com International/World Business: Digitalbiz, 6 September 2007. Available online at http://edition.cnn.com/2007/BUSINESS/09/02/video.blind/; accessed 25 November 2008.

[Mulligan03] Mulligan, J. and Patrovsky, B., *Developing Online Games*. New Riders, Indianapolis, 2003.

[Nass96] Nass, C., Fogg, B.J., and Moon, Y. "Can Computers be Teammates?" *International Journal of Human Computer Studies*, December 1996, Vol. 45, No. 6, 669–678.

[Nintendo08] Nintendo, "Financial Results Briefing for the Fiscal Year Ended March 2008: Supplementary Information," 25 April 2008. Available online at http://www.nintendo.co.jp/ir/pdf/2008/080425e.pdf#page=6; accessed 29 August 2008.

[Norman04] Norman, D. A., *Emotional Design: Why We Love (or Hate) Everyday Things*. New York, Basic Books, 2004.

[Novak08] Novak, J., *Game development essentials [Second edition]*. Thomson Delmar Learning, Clifton Park, NY, 2008.

[NPD05] NPD FunWorld, "Top 60 Selling PC, Console, and Hand Held Games 2005."

[Olds54] Olds, J. and Milner, P. *"Positive reinforcement produced by electrical stimulation of septal area and other regions of rat brain."* Journal of Comparative and Physiological Psychology, 1954, 47 (6), 419–27.

[PackagedFacts08] "The Young Urban Consumer: How Hip-Hop Culture Affects the Lifestyle and Buying Decisions of 12- to 34-Year Olds," *Packaged Facts report*, 1 May 2008. Available online at http://www.packagedfacts.com/Urban-Youth-Trendsetters-1692747/; accessed 8 September 2008.

[Perls69] Perls, Fritz. *Ego, Hunger and Aggression: The beginning of Gestalt Therapy*. Random House, New York, 1969.

[Piaget62] Piaget, J. *Play, Dreams, and Imitation in Childhood*. New York, Norton, 1962.

[QuadControl] Available online at http://www.quadcontrol.com/; accessed 25 November 2008.

[Reeves96] Reeves, B. and Nass, C. *The Media Equation: How People Treat Computers, Television and New Media Like Real People and Places*. Stanford, CA, CSLI Press, 1996.

[Rickenberg00] Rickenberg, R. and Reeves, B. "The Effects of Animated Characters on Anxiety, Task Performance, and Evaluations of User Interfaces." Proceedings of CHI Conference on Human Factors in Computing Systems (held at the Hague, Netherlands, 2000), pp 49–56.

[Rizzolatti96] Rizzolatti, G., Fadiga, L., Fogassi, L., and Gallese, V., "Premotor cortex and the recognition of motor actions," *Cognitive Brain Research*, 1996, 3 131–141.

[Rizzolatti04] Rizzolatti G. and Craighero L., "The mirror-neuron system," *Annual Review of Neuroscience* (2004), 27, 169–92.

[Rolls00] Rolls, E.T., "The Orbitofrontal Cortex and Reward." *Cerebral Cortex*, March 2000, Vol. 10, No. 3, 284–294.

[Romero05] Romero, R., *Befuddlement in Action: Classic Usability Problems in Games and How to Avoid Them*. Presented at the Game Developer's Conference, San Jose, CA, March 2005.

[Salen05] Salen, K. and Zimmerman, E., *The Game Design Reader*. MIT Press, 2005.

[Sanchanta07] Sanchanta, Mariko, "Nintendo's Wii takes console lead." *Financial Times*, 12 September 2007. Available online at http://www.ft.com/cms/s/0/51df0c84-6154-11dc-bf25-0000779fd2ac.html; accessed 29 August 2008.

[Saunders07] Saunders, K. and Novak, J., *Game development essentials: Game interface design*. Thomson Delmar Learning, Clifton Park, NY, 2007.

[Schubert07] Schubert, D., "Is the Bartle Four Important? Zen of Design," 13 September 2007. Available online at http://www.zenofdesign.com/2007/09/13/is-bartle-important/; accessed November 2008.

[Shaw81] Shaw, M.W. *Group Dynamics: The Psychology of Small Group Behavior*. New York, McGraw-Hill Book Company, 1981.

[Sinha06] P. Sinha, B. Balas, Y. Ostrovsky, and R. Russell, "Face Recognition by Humans: 19 Results All Computer Vision Researchers Should Know About," Proceedings of the IEEE, November 2006, Vol. 94 No. 11, 1948–1962.

[Skinner38] Skinner, B. F., *The Behavior of Organisms: An Experimental Analysis*. New York, D. Appleton-Century Company, Inc, 1938.

[Smith85] Smith, C.A. and Ellsworth, P.C., "Patterns of cognitive appraisal in emotion." *Journal of Personality and Social Psychology*, 1985, 48, 813–838.

[Take-Two07] Take-Two Interactive, presentation at Piper Jaffray Second Annual London Consumer Conference (Webcast), Thomson Financial (2007-09-26). Available online at http://www.corporate-ir.net/ireye/confLobby.zhtml?ticker=TTWO&item_id=1642557; accessed 29 August 2008.

[Taylor06] Taylor, T.L. *Play Between Worlds: Exploring Online Game Culture*. Cambridge, MA, The MIT Press, 2006.

[Thach96] Thach, W. T., "On the specific role of the cerebellum in motor learning and cognition: Clues from PET activation and lesion studies in man." *Behavioral and Brain Sciences*, 1996, 19(3): 411–431.

[Thompson95] Thompson, D. (editor). *The Concise Oxford Dictionary of Current English*. Oxford, Clarendon Press, 1995.

[Tiger92] Tiger, L. *The Pursuit of Pleasure*, pp 52–60. Boston, Little, Brown & Company, 1992.

[Tschannen-Moran00] Tschannen-Moran, M. and Hoy, W.K. "A Multi-disciplinary Analysis of the Nature, Meaning, and Measure of Trust." *Review of Educational Research*, 2000, Vol. 70 No. 4, 547–593.

[Turkle95] Turkle, S. *Life on the Screen: Identity in the Age of the Internet*. New York, Simon and Schuster, 1995.

[USAToday05] Hill, Michael. "More colleges offering videogame courses." Available online at http://www.usatoday.com/tech/products/games/2005-09-25-video-game-colleges_x.htm; accessed 12 November 2008.

[USCensus06a] U.S. Census Bureau, "2006 American Community Survey." Available online from American FactFinder, http://factfinder.census.gov; accessed November 2008.

[USCensus06b] U.S. Census Bureau, "2006 American Community Survey Definitions." Available online at http://www.census.gov/acs/www/Downloads/2006/usedata/Subject_Definitions.pdf; accessed 25 November 2008.

[VanTol06] Van Tol, R. and Huiberts, S., "What blind gamers want the video game industry to know" (unpublished raw data). Available online at http://www.game-accessibility.com/index.php?pagefile=papers; accessed 25 November 2008.

[Volkow00] Volkow, N.D. and Fowler, J.S., "Addiction, a disease of compulsion and drive: involvement of the orbitofrontal cortex." *Cerebral Cortex*, March 2000, 10 (3): 318–25.

[Watts57] Watts, Alan, *The Way of Zen*. New York, Vintage Books, 1985 (First published 1957).

[WikiEO] "Endless Ocean," Wikipedia.org. Available online at http://en.wikipedia.org/wiki/Endless_Ocean; accessed 30 August 2008.

[Woodard08] Woodard, C., "WIM Summit: GoPets' Bethke on MMO Goal Structures as a Panacea" *Gamasutra*, 18 February 2008. Available online at http://www.gamasutra.com/php-bin/news_index.php?story=17452; accessed November 2008.

[Wright03] Wright, P., McCarthy, J., and Meekison, L. "Making Sense of Experience" M. A. Blythe, K. Overbeeke, A. F. Monk, and P. C. Wright (Eds.), *Funology: From usability to enjoyment* (2003), 43–53. Dordrecht, The Netherlands: Kluwer Academic Publishers.

[Yee02] Yee, Nicholas, "Facets: 5 Motivation Factors for Why People Play MMORPGs," 2002. Available online at http://www.nickyee.com/facets/home.html; accessed 5 September 2008.

[Yee04] Yee, N. "Daedalus Gateway," 2004. Available online at http://www.nickyee.com/daedalus/gateway_identity.html; accessed 11 September 2008.

[Yee07] Yee, N., "Motivations of Play in Online Games." *Journal of Cyber-Psychology and Behavior*, 2007 Vol. 9, pp 772–775. Available online at http://www.nickyee.com/pubs/Yee%20-%20Motivations%20(2007).pdf; accessed November 2008.

[Yoon05] Yoon, U., "A Quest for the Legal Identity of MMORPGs—From a Computer Game, Back to a Play Association." *Journal of Game Industry and Culture*, 2005, Vol. 10. Available online at http://papers.ssrn.com/sol3/papers.cfm?abstract_id=905748; accessed November 2008.

[Yue07] Yue, X., Vessel, E.A., and Biederman, I., "The neural basis of scene preferences." *NeuroReport*, April 2007, 18, 525–529.

[Zajonc68] Zajonc, R. B., "Attitudinal Effects of Mere Exposure." *Journal of Personality and Social Psychology*, 1968, 9, 2, 1–27.

INDEX